BEGINNING
PRE-CALCULUS
FOR GAME
DEVELOPERS

JOHN P. FLYNT
BORIS MELTREGER

THOMSON

COURSE TECHNOLOGY

Professional ■ Technical ■ Reference

ISBN-10: 1-59863-291-4
ISBN-13: 978-1-59863-291-0
Library of Congress Catalog Card Number: 2006923484
Printed in the United States of America
07 08 09 10 11 PH 10 9 8 7 6 5 4 3 2 1

Publisher and General Manager, Thomson Course Technology PTR:
Stacy L. Hiquet

Associate Director of Marketing:
Sarah O'Donnell

Manager of Editorial Services:
Heather Talbot

Marketing Manager:
Heather Hurley

Senior Acquisitions Editor:
Emi Smith

Project Editor:
Jenny Davidson

Technical Reviewer:
Marcia Flynt

PTR Editorial Services Coordinator:
Erin Johnson

Interior Layout Tech:
Interactive Composition Corporation

Cover Designer:
Mike Tanamachi

CD-ROM Producer:
Brandon Penticuff

Indexer:
Larry Sweazy

Proofreader:
Kim Benbow

Thomson Course Technology PTR,
a division of Thomson Learning Inc.
25 Thomson Place
Boston, MA 02210
http://www.courseptr.com

This book is dedicated to its readers.

ACKNOWLEDGMENTS

John: To Emi Smith and Stacy Hiquet for arranging for the publication. To Jenny Davidson, for watching over the schedule and making it happen. Thanks to Marcia for the tremendous technical editing effort. You have made this book possible. To Boris for creating Visual Formula and working on a tight schedule. And to Janet for being an inspiration. Amy, thank you for working problems.

Boris: Thanks to my wife Janet and son Leonid for creative advice about how to present math and for testing Visual Formula. Also, to John and Marcia for involving me in this exciting project.

ABOUT THE AUTHORS

John P. Flynt, Ph.D., has taught at colleges and universities, and has authored courses and curricula for several college-level game development programs. His academic background includes work in information technology, the social sciences, and the humanities. Among his works are *In the Mind of a Game, Perl Power!, Java Programming for the Absolute Beginner, UnrealScript Game Programming All in One, Software Engineering for Game Developers,* and *Simulation and Event Modeling for Game Developers* (with co-author Ben Vinson). John lives in the foothills near Boulder, Colorado.

Boris Meltreger received an advanced degree (Candidate of Technical Science) while still a citizen of Russia. He has extensive experience in R&D for sonar, optical computing, and laser therapy equipment. He has authored 18 inventions and many technical articles, research reports, and manuals. Now a citizen of the U.S., for the past few years, Boris has been with Rogue Wave Software, specializing in the development of products and software libraries for Visual C++ and C#. His dedication to the study of mathematics goes back to high school, where he specialized in physics and math as a student in the renowned School 239 in St. Petersburg. He is the creator of Visual Formula. Boris lives in Aurora, Colorado.

Contents

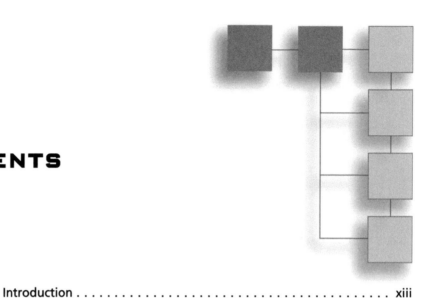

INTRODUCTION

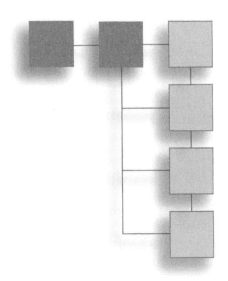

About This Book

You can benefit from reading this book if you are interested in supplementing pre-calculus math studies with a secondary book or seeking a non-traditional approach to introductory studies of mathematics. This book is suitable for game developers because it provides a playful approach to learning math. Its use of Visual Formula provides a ready way for anyone to explore pre-calculus math in a ready, creative way.

Who Should Read This Book

This book is suitable for anyone who is seeking fundamental knowledge of algebra and trigonometry. It is also ideal if you are seeking friendly software to help you along with your studies of math. While it does not provide a comprehensive examination of either subject, it focuses on those areas that prove essential to success in pre-calculus studies. This book also provides you with software that allows you to explore its topics in a way that is engaging and easy to manage.

The Chapters

Chapter 1 provides you with an introduction to the philosophy of this book. It also provides you with a first glimpse of Visual Formula.

Chapter 2 dwells on number systems and the properties you can apply to them. In addition, you explore notions concerning sets and ways to work with sets. You also experience your first user session with Visual Formula.

Chapter 3 takes you into a review of exponential and radical numbers.

Chapter 4 allows you to explore the essentials of such notions as domains and ranges, factoring, and functions.

Chapter 5 provides a deeper view of working with functions and extends the discussion into inequalities.

Chapter 6 furnishes you with discussion of the lines, slopes, and intercepts.

Chapter 7 includes the distance formula, translation, and shifting. The topics also include uses of inverse and absolute values.

Chapter 8 ventures into polynomial equations, the FOIL method, and long division involving polynomials.

Chapter 9 centers on solving quadratic equations. Among the topics are completing the square and working with the discriminant.

Chapter 10 showcases the use of Visual Formula. Although you explore Visual Formula in almost every chapter in the book, Chapter 10 provides you with a multitude of examples that allow you to deepen and broaden your knowledge of how to use Visual Formula.

Chapter 11 involves you in a discussion of systems of equations and matrices. You explore equations with two, three, and more variables.

Chapter 12 finishes off your study by introducing several topics of trigonometry. Among these are the six basic ratios of trigonometry and their associated functions.

Appendix A provides you with solutions to the problems the book provides.

Appendix B shows you how to install Visual Formula and obtain support packages from Microsoft.

The CD

You can find Visual Formula on the CD that accompanies this book. Instructions for installing Visual Formula appear in Appendix B, which is also on the CD. In addition, you can find an additional software package called Visual Code on the CD. While Visual Code allows you to explore programming pre-calculus problems using C#, no reference is made to it in the book.

Answers to the Exercises

You'll find the solutions to almost all of the problems in this text in Appendix A, which is available as a PDF file on the CD. The solutions are worked out. Most math books do not provide worked out problems, so the appendix that contains them is fairly long and must be presented electronically.

Worked-out means precisely that: rather than just an answer, you find the solution to each problem presented in steps, much as you might expect to find them in an instructor's guide.

In addition to the CD, you can find the solutions on the book's Internet site (www.courseptr.com). If additions or corrections are added to the versions you find on the CD, then notice of these will be posted on the Internet site. Otherwise, you can assume that the Internet and CD versions are the same.

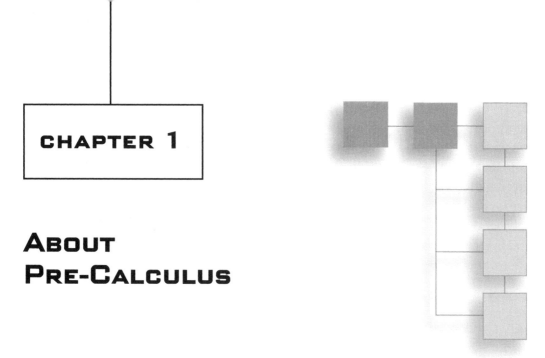

CHAPTER 1

ABOUT PRE-CALCULUS

It is shocking to find how many people do not believe they can learn, and how many more believe learning to be difficult.

—Frank Herbert, *Dune* (from "The Humanity of Maud'Dib"
by the Princess Irulan)

This book attempts, among other things, to present math in a fairly open-ended way. It offers what you might view as a conversational approach to math, which is an older way of teaching math. If you survey the history of math books, you see that a hundred or more years ago authors often tended to teach math using dialogues. In other words, as a reader you would follow a conversation among two or more characters in a dialogue, much along the lines of reading a play. That is not precisely the way this book unfolds, but it is in the background. This book draws from experiences of teaching in computer game development and play settings. When you learn to develop or play a computer game, you seldom stand back and spend a long while learning formal rules. Instead, you follow a path that involves immediately immersing yourself in playing or developing the game. This book tries to follow the same path. It attempts to make learning about math more an activity of conversation than of applying rules. Your study of math then becomes a relaxed form of conversation. To explore this notion in a bit more detail, this chapter offers the following topics:

- Language and conversation
- Visual Formula as a way to play games with math
- Starting the conversation with algebra and trigonometry

Talk of Math

In a short book about his life, friends, colleagues, and thoughts called *A Mathematician's Apology,* the renowned mathematician G. H. Hardy wrote, "It is quite true that most people can do nothing well." The value of such a reflection in an autobiographical work by one of the great mathematicians of the twentieth century is that it proves to be one of the most helpful of all beginnings for someone trying to learn math. Professor Hardy's contention was not an attempt to disgrace or criticize anyone. In fact, more than anything else, it was an observation about his own discovery of his love of math.

One of the world's greatest mathematicians, he did not regard math as something he did particularly well. In fact, he did not really care whether he did it particularly well. He just did it. That he could just do it, without consideration of what others thought or whether what he did he did particularly well allowed him to become a preeminent mathematician.

Most people do not have this perspective when they attempt to advance their study of math. Further, math teaching often promotes the notion that if you are going to do math, then you must do it well. If you do not do it well, then you are advised to find something else to do. The consequences of this approach are somewhat enormous. Consider, for example, that in places like the United States, some experts say that around 90 percent of the population is math illiterate. Granted, that figure might be exaggerated, but even if you lower the figure, the fact is that most people go through their lives and spend almost no time at all doing or learning math.

It is easy to get the impression that being able to do math is something along the lines of a genetically established capability. If you are genetically endowed, it is worth your while to involve yourself in it. Otherwise, you need to find something else to do.

Imagine what it would be like if participating in conversations with friends, relatives, and others was based on such an assumption. You might find your cell phone privileges revoked. You might find yourself barred from cafes, political meetings, school lunchrooms, and churches. You might have to take a test before being allowed to order a sandwich or tell your neighbor good morning.

Such notions are extreme and absurd, but it remains that if you speak with people who have given up on math, you often find such reasoning at work.

Why don't people allow themselves to just do it, even badly, in the same way that they talk or ride a bicycle? Why isn't it open for exploration and enjoyment in the same way that conversation is open for exploration and enjoyment? Why is it that it has to be presented in a context in which G. H. Hardy's observation is completely forgotten?

These are not intended as criticisms. Many math teachers do, indeed, seem to agree with Professor Hardy. On the other hand, many clearly do not. As one student reported after failing introductory calculus, "The teacher told us that the purpose of first-year calculus is to determine who cannot do math."

Most People

To pursue Professor Hardy's notion a step further, consider that many people cannot tell you the difference between a participle and an infinitive. Still, they carry on endless conversations. Such conversations go in many directions and ultimately end up leading to beneficial results.

The student who contended that college calculus is a way that college professors determine who cannot do math lacked the perspective afforded by a trade school teacher who once remarked, "Not everyone can do all the math that there is to do, but almost everyone can do some."

This perspective could probably cause something on the order of a revolution if extended to encompass college classrooms and other arenas in which people set about trying to learn math. This perspective ultimately leads to the idea that math can become a medium of conversation.

When something is a medium of conversation, it becomes a language itself rather than a topic you address using a language. You just do it. You do not question whether you can do it, have the genetic capacity to do it, or have earned the right to do it.

Professor Hardy's notion was that math is a medium of conversation, something you just do. When you do it, you do not need to make the first question one of whether you do it well. You do not need to judge yourself or be judged.

Places for Games

Some games are matters of play. Others are matters of rules. Most are mixtures of both. A game that is wholly defined by play might not have goals or ways of winning. It might be something akin to an ongoing conversation in which the objective is one of just continuing to converse.

Rules strictly regulate other games, to the point that there seems to be almost no play at all. The focus of such games is on winning. The play is often reduced to the exercise of meticulously planned strategies.

Figure 1.1 provides a simple rendition of these notions. A game is a context in which you can explore play or rules. It can work in any number of ways. Games are endless. Some people play games to figure out rules. Others play games to apply rules. Still others play to defy rules.

When you deal with math as a conversation, it becomes a game that you can play in many ways. The rules can become secondary. The play can become secondary. Carrying on the conversation becomes an activity of making things up as you go along.

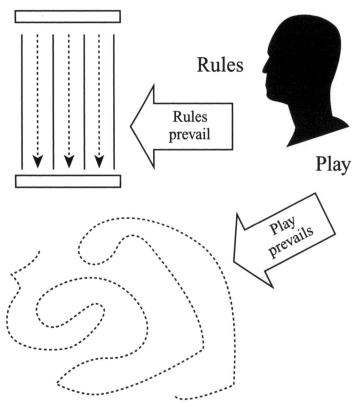

Figure 1.1
Games involve rules and play.

How is this possible? It is possible in the same way that a coffee shop or a shaded spot on a sidewalk becomes a place in which people carry on conversations. Such conversations emerge from the daily activity of life. They emerge because they do not require you to do anything other than what you are doing.

The notion that conversation can simply spring to life in any given setting is in part one of the reasons that this book presents its topics in an essential, randomized way. The essential presentation eschews "word problems." While word problems are tremendously important and are hardly ever left out of standard math textbooks, in this context they are left out so that when you decide to flick to a page and begin a conversation, you can do so immediately.

This is a book of beginnings. It seeks no end other than providing the most direct possible inroad to a few starting points in your exploration of math. It leaves out much more than it includes. It avoids systematic learning. It strives instead to be analogous to a shaded place on a sidewalk or a table in a cafe.

Computer Games and Classrooms

When it comes to the conversation math provides, many people know only silence or something near silence. It is not even a conversation in a foreign language for these people. It is not a conversation at all. They have abandoned it because they have learned that they do not do it well and therefore should not do it at all.

In many classrooms, math is taught in a non-conversational, exclusionary way. People who do well with such studies find such settings perfectly comfortable. They do not learn what they cannot do. Others find the case the complete opposite. They learn only what they cannot do.

An alternative approach to the classroom would be to make it so that each day the goal is to find something everyone can do. Each day becomes an occasion of confirmation.

This book endeavors to be such a classroom. Professor Hardy, it is hoped, would approve. You are here because you want to carry on a conversation. The conversation has no solid end or aim beyond continuing the conversation.

This book is about mathematics for computer game development in the sense that it provides an approach to math that draws from classrooms in which computer game development and play have been the central activities. Such activities have shaped the understanding and teaching practices of the author. In such classrooms, the notion has prevailed that each day of class can offer something to everyone.

What characterizes a classroom extends to the games played and developed in classrooms. A computer program that allows you to converse mathematically or otherwise on an open basis often ends up being a computer game. What distinguishes a computer game from a computer application, a calculator, or a program is its extensibility—its open-endedness. A computer game that brings an open-ended, conversational experience to you becomes something similar to a shaded place on a sidewalk or a coffee shop.

Visual Formula

This book makes use of a computer game that provides you with a way to experience math as an ongoing conversation. This program is called Visual Formula. The inventor of Visual Formula is an engineer who decided one day to see if it might be possible to create a simple, straightforward way that people seeking to learn math could approach creating an equation in the same way that they might paint colors on a canvas.

A successful conversation involves continuation and extension of the conversation. As mentioned previously, if you speak with people who have told you that they decided to discontinue the study of math, they often recount an episode in which they say they encountered a problem they could not solve.

Their account of encountering this problem is usually accompanied by a story about how they took a test. After encountering the problem, they felt wholly convinced that they could not or should not go on. The test told them what they could not do. Officially halted in this way, their conversation with math ended.

Extending a conversation involves finding topics at hand that you feel inclined to explore. You do not fear them. If you do fear them, your fear does not prove overwhelming. The topics might prove challenging, but you always have a way back to what you have already explored. You can try again and again, viewing the new topic in different ways.

In contrast, you can also listen to people recall how they became lost. They ventured one day into a new area, found everything strange, and panicked. Inevitably, a few days later a teacher administered a test. The test took them back into the strange place that provoked the panic. Trauma resulted. The conversation ended.

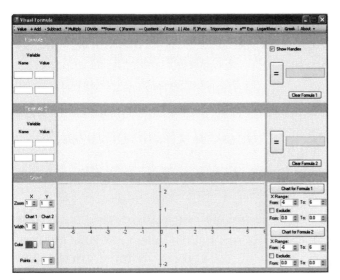

Figure 1.2
Everyone can do something.

Visual Formula is something like a friend who can enter the picture at important junctures. It allows you to place the problem in a controlled context. It allows you to explore. If you go into a strange place, it all but provides a panic button. You can start over. You can see where you have been. The problem is no longer an event meant to teach you what you cannot do. The problem is an occasion for confirming what you can do. If a problem is strange, you have at hand a tool with which to make it familiar.

A Part of Life

Millions of people learn each year that they should feel bad about doing math because, alas, they do not do it well. This is very strange. It would be such a different thing if you could dispense with the "doing it well" stipulation. If it could be taught some other way, then it would become a real conversation, one that anyone might participate in. It would become a common way that most people could communicate. People could make it a part of their lives. That proves a novel notion, of course.

Disorganized Territory

In this book, you find math presented in a fairly unorganized manner, as though it might be regarded as a conversation that you join whenever you feel like it. Visual Formula complements this disorganization. It provides a context in which you can play a game that addresses conversational mathematics. It is designed to draw you into an activity that forces you to set aside notions that you can do only what you do well. There is none of that here. You just do what you do and leave it at that.

To gain the most from such an experience, play with Visual Formula and learn how to set up equations and view the values and graphs that result from them. Then change the equations. Each time you change an equation, you extend your explorations. Each time you change an equation, you make something familiar strange but at the same time something strange familiar.

Likewise, from the first realize that it is not necessary to be systematic. The chapters in this book may convey a sense of disorganization. View your study of math along the lines of a novel by Joseph Conrad. You can venture from island to island, finding new adventures on each one. Just because one proves a little strange just now does not mean that you cannot go on to another and return later. Chance can prevail.

One way to understand this approach to the topic at hand is to consider that in the vast majority of instances, people study grammar and composition only after they have learned the language. Along the same lines, if you have a way of visualizing and playing with math before you pursue a systematic knowledge of it, your adventure becomes one of recognizing familiar features in new and more intricate ways.

This provides a way that you can increase the chance that you can acquire knowledge and feel confident about the knowledge you acquire. It also allows you to review what you have learned with greater confidence. Along with these benefits, Visual Formula can serve as a special sort of map that allows you to explore a new territory in a way you find more comfortable.

Algebra and Trigonometry

Algebra allows you to converse using variables. It allows you to set up equations. It allows you to explore the properties of numbers. It also allows you to explore how to graph equations using the Cartesian coordinate system. When you can graph the relations you explore using algebra, you find that you begin examining the behavior of numbers as specific types of patterns.

Math might be viewed as a way of formally expressing patterns. Likewise, everything can be viewed as a pattern. Some patterns are found. Others are created. The serrations of a leaf or the path of a ball when you toss it are patterns that you find. On the other hand, at times you fidget with math and find a pattern, and then go looking for something in nature you can use to illustrate the pattern.

Algebra in part deals with patterns you can explore using linear and nonlinear relations between sets of numbers. You find one set of numbers, for example, and then map this set of numbers to another set. The map is an equation.

Trigonometry extends the ways that you can map one set of numbers to another. It begins with explorations of triangles. A triangle allows you to bring three values into different relations with each other. These relations constitute the trigonometric ratios.

The ratios of trigonometry allow you to extend the notion of patterns to encompass the different ways that patterns can behave. Among other things, patterns can be periodic. One period pattern is known as the *sine* wave. Another is known as a *cosine* wave. From cosines and sines you can continue on to tangents, cotangents, secants, and cosecants.

Algebra and trigonometry together provide a foundation for the study of calculus. They allow you to explore relationships between sets of numbers and to generate graphical representations of these relationships in a multitude of ways.

They are usually viewed as fundamental mathematics, although there are disciplines of mathematics in which trigonometry and algebra are studied on advanced levels. As it is, in the context provided here, the objective remains one of inviting you to explore math in a conversational way. Everyone can learn something. Each act of learning is an act of confirmation. Each act of learning becomes a way to make what is strange familiar. Each act of learning is a way to extend what you know into new places.

Additional Reading

Hardy, G. H. *A Mathematician's Apology*. Forward by C. P. Snow. New York: Cambridge University Press, 1993.

Herbert, Frank. *Dune*. Radnor, PA: Chilton Book Company, 1990.

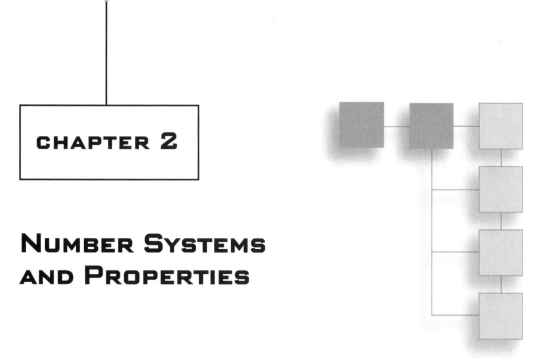

CHAPTER 2

NUMBER SYSTEMS AND PROPERTIES

This chapter introduces you to concepts relating to how you identify and talk about numbers. Not all numbers are the same. Even when they are the same, you can organize and represent them in different ways. The primary number systems consist of counting numbers, whole numbers, integers, rational numbers, irrational numbers, and real numbers. In addition to systems of numbers, you investigate the commutative, associative, and distributive properties of numbers. Further, you explore how combinations of positive and negative numbers affect the outcomes of your calculations. With this prospect in view, this chapter offers the following topics, among others:

- Natural or counting numbers

- Whole numbers

- Integers

- Rational and irrational numbers

- Real numbers

- Number properties

- Inverses and identities of numbers

- Multiplication and division involving negative and positive numbers

Number Systems

When you solve math problems, you work with different systems of numbers. The systems of numbers often allow you to express the same numbers differently. In your earlier studies of math, it is likely that you became familiar with some of the numbering systems. As you study more math, you work extensively with several systems of numbers. The next few sections discuss the different systems.

Natural or Counting Numbers

The natural or counting numbers start at 1 and proceed in increments of 1 indefinitely. You work with situations in which your activities may lead to an object or objects that you might point to, or count. For this reason, it is fairly easy to recognize that the natural numbers system probably constitutes the oldest way of counting things. You might imagine, for example, a potter working in a situation in which he or she makes a series of pots. To count the pots, it's necessary only to line them up or draw lines in the earth. Consider Figure 2.1.

The mathematical symbol for natural numbers is **N**. Here is one way to mathematically describe natural numbers:

$$\mathbf{N} = \{1, 2, 3 \ldots\}$$

The **N** preceding the equals sign indicates that all the numbers belong to the set of natural or counting numbers. The three periods trailing the 3 indicate that the

Figure 2.1
Natural or counting numbers allow to you readily account for things you can point to.

numbers continue indefinitely. The curly braces that enclose the numbers indicate that they constitute a *set* of numbers. We read this as the natural numbers are the set of numbers 1, 2, 3, and so on. A set is a group or collection. In this light, then, all number systems consist of sets of numbers.

Whole Numbers Offer You Zero

The marks and pots you see in Figure 2.1 provide you with a way to depict things that you can point to. What happens when you encounter situations in which you want to explain that you do not have an item of a given type? Suppose that the potter makes five pots and then sells them all? Enter the concept of zero, which is a way of saying that you recognize the possibility of having something even though you do not, in fact, have something at hand to point to. In other words, you have none of the objects.

Figure 2.2 illustrates how the use of 0 in the whole numbers system proves to be a useful way of dealing with a complex notion. The whole numbers allow you to both point to something and point to the absence of something. As with the counting numbers, historians generally recognize the whole number system as being fairly old.

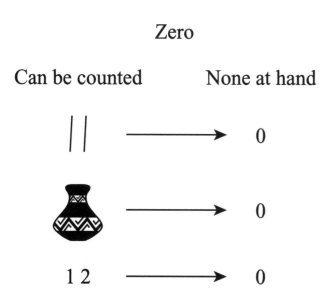

Figure 2.2
Whole numbers allow you to acknowledge something that can be counted and also indicate that you have nothing at hand to count.

The mathematical symbol for whole numbers is **W**. As with the natural numbers, you can mathematically describe whole numbers as a set:

$$\mathbf{W} = \{0, 1, 2, 3\ldots\}$$

The **W** preceding the equals sign indicates that all the numbers belong to the set of whole numbers. The only difference between the natural numbers system and the whole numbers system is that the whole numbers system adds the use of 0. As before, the three periods trailing the 3 indicate that the numbers continue indefinitely. The curly braces that enclose the numbers indicate that they constitute a set of numbers. The natural numbers (**N**) are a subset of the whole numbers (**W**). That is, every natural number is also a whole number.

Integers Provide Negative Numbers

Given the notion that you can have items at hand or that you can think about items of a given type without having any at hand, it seems almost inevitable that you run into another situation. This situation is one in which you need an item of a given type that is not at hand. Consider, for example, a situation in which you have no pots at hand but five people approach you and ask for pots. You now need to make five pots. You express this situation using negative numbers, as Figure 2.3 illustrates.

Integers include the positive numbers, zero, and the negative numbers. While the whole numbers start at 0 and proceed indefinitely in a positive way, the set of integers includes the whole numbers and proceed indefinitely in a negative way. You can think of 0 as a starting point between the positive and negative groups of numbers. The mathematical symbol for integers is **Z**. Here is how to mathematically

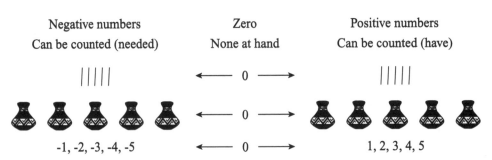

Figure 2.3
Negative numbers allow you to account for needed items not at hand.

represent the set of integers:

$$Z = \{0, \pm1, \pm2, \pm3, \pm4, \pm5 \ldots\}$$

As with counting numbers and whole numbers, you see the curly braces, which represent a set. You also see a *plus-or-minus* sign preceding each of the numbers in the set. Use of the plus-or-minus sign serves as a way to shorten the mathematical expression from its longer form:

$$Z = \{\ldots -5, -4, -3, -2, -1, 0, +1, +2, +3, +4, +5 \ldots\}$$

The second expression conveys the same information as the first, but in this case, a minus sign ($-$) precedes each negative number and a positive sign ($+$) precedes each positive number. Likewise, you see that ellipses precede and follow the numbers. Notice the zero possesses no sign. You can certainly apply a sign to a zero without doing any harm, but the fact remains that the sign has no effect on zero. Zero is neither negative nor positive.

When you use integers, you never need to indicate a positive value using a plus sign. As a matter of common practice, if you see a number standing alone without a sign, it is positive. Here is another way to show the longer form of the set of integers:

$$Z = \{\ldots -5, -4, -3, -2, -1, 0, 1, 2, 3, 4, 5 \ldots\}$$

So far you have looked at natural numbers, whole numbers, and integers. The relationship between these number systems is as follows: Every natural number and every whole number is a number in the set of integers. In other words, **W** is a subset of **Z** and **N** is a subset of **Z**. Also, recall that **N** is a subset of **W**.

Rational Numbers

Even if you can count things at hand, recognize things when they are entirely absent, or count them in a negative or absent form, you still face situations in which you need to account for things that are not quite whole. To deal with this situation, one approach involves working with the concept that you can establish a ratio between two numbers.

As Figure 2.4 illustrates, picture the situation of a potter whom customers have asked to make five pots. The potter has made three pots. A customer arrives and requests to know how much of the work of making the pots has been completed. The potter can reply by asking the customer to imagine the whole set of five pots

Show a ratio

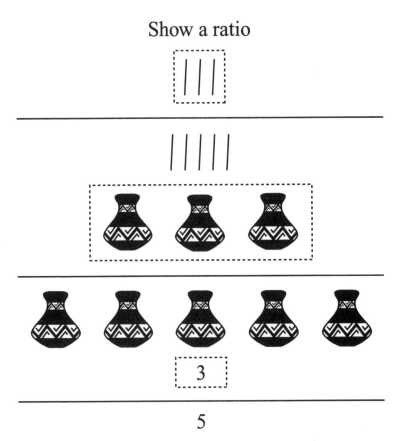

Figure 2.4
Rational numbers allow you to create ratios between integers.

and then another set of three pots. Of the five needed pots, the potter has finished three. So the reply of the question can be, "The number is 3 of 5." This expresses a ratio.

A rational number is a number you use to express a ratio or relationship between two other numbers. You can communicate a ratio by creating a quotient. A quotient is a result you obtain when you perform a division.

Consider the ratio of 3 to 5. In simple terms, you divide 3 by 5. Here are a couple of common ways to express this activity mathematically:

$$\frac{3}{5} \qquad 3:5$$

The mathematical symbol for rational numbers is **Q**. Here is how to mathematically represent the set of rational numbers:

$$Q = \left\{ \frac{p}{q} \,\middle|\, p, q \in Z \; q \neq 0 \right\}$$

The vertical bar means "such that," and the $\in$ means "is a member of." The hashed equal sign means "not equal to." The definition reads, "A rational number (**Q**) is any number p/q, such that p and q are elements of the set of integers (**Z**) and q is not equal to 0."

Here is a set of rational numbers:

$$\{-1/5, -3/4, -2/3, -1/2, -1/6, 0, 6/7, 4/2, 21\}$$

Notice that the elements in this set are negative, include zero, and positive. Also note that 0 and 21 can be expressed as ratios: 0/0 and 21/1.

No Division by Zero

When you formally define a rational number, the two numbers you include in the quotient, p and q, are both integers. The lower number, q, cannot be equal to 0. You cannot divide by 0.

We know that $\frac{6}{2} = 3$ because $2 \times 3 = 6$. If we consider $\frac{6}{0}$, the answer must be a number that, when multiplied by zero, results in 6 (i.e., $\frac{6}{0} = x$ where $x \times 0 = 6$), but $x \times 0 = 0$ for all x's. Therefore, $\frac{6}{0}$ has no value. Mathematicians say that such a relation where any number is divided by zero is *undefined*.

Staying Clear on Your Numbers

Just because you can represent a number as a quotient does not mean that it is only a rational number. The fact is that you can represent counting numbers, whole numbers, integers, and rational numbers as quotients. Consider the following representations of numbers:

- $2 = \frac{2}{1} = \frac{4}{2}$ All of the representations denote 2, which is a counting number, a whole number, an integer, and a rational number. When the quotient provides a "rational" way to represent the number, whether in its quotient or non-quotient form, the number remains a rational number.

- $-2 = \frac{-2}{1} = \frac{-6}{3}$ The representations of -2 on each side of the equal sign designate integers. The number -2 can be represented as $\frac{-6}{3}, \frac{-4}{2}, \frac{-8}{4},$ or $\frac{-12}{6}$. Therefore, it is a rational number as well as an integer.

Variations on Rational Numbers

When you carry out division, you end up with different types of quotients. To repeat, a rational number is a number that you can express as a ratio. You can express an integer as a ratio, as you can a whole number. In some cases, you can reduce the quotient form of the number to a whole number. In other cases, the quotient form of the number cannot be reduced to a whole number, and therefore has a decimal representation. A number is rational if its decimal representation is terminating or repeating.

Terminating Rational Numbers

If the decimal representation of the quotient can be expressed by an exact number of digits, then it is a terminating rational number. Consider the following numbers and their decimal representations:

$$\frac{1}{2} = 0.5, \qquad \frac{1}{4} = 0.25, \qquad \frac{3}{4} = 0.75, \qquad \frac{3}{6} = 0.5$$

In each case, the result of the division is exact. A melon can be divided into two equal parts. It can also be divided into equal fourths. Likewise, you can have exactly three fourths of a melon, as you can have five sixths of a melon.

Repeating Rational Numbers

In some cases, when you establish a ratio between two numbers, the quotient is not terminating. You do not end up with exact pieces or proportions (i.e., the decimal representation does not have an exact number of digits). The most you can do is approximate the piece or proportion. Consider, for example, what happens when you divide 1 by 3 or 2 by 3. The result is a repeating rational number:

$$1/3 = 0.3333333333\ldots \quad \text{and} \quad 2/3 = 0.6666666666\ldots$$

Mathematicians indicate the repeating part of the fraction by placing a bar above the number that repeats:

$$1/3 = 0.\overline{3} \quad \text{or} \quad 2/3 = 0.\overline{6}$$

When a single number repeats, you need only one number bearing a bar. In other cases, the pattern of repetition involves several numbers. In that case, you use the bar to designate the sequence of numbers that repeat. Consider the pattern that results when you divide 1 by 7 and 1 by 17:

$$1/7 = 0.142857142857\overline{142857142857}$$

$$1/17 = 0.0588235294117647\overline{0588235294117647}$$

Whether you encounter a single repeating number or, as in the case of 1/17, groups of 16 repeating numbers, you are still working with a number that you can represent explicitly. You can show that at a given point, the number begins to repeat itself. You need not show the repeating decimals more than once. For example, you can also represent the numbers this way:

$$1/7 = 0.\overline{142857142857}$$

$$1/17 = 0.\overline{0588235294117647}$$

Irrational Numbers

When you perform some divisions, the number you end up with is neither exact nor repeating. Consider, for example, the ratio of the length of the circumference of a circle to the length of its diameter. The ancient Greek letter mathematicians use to designate this ratio is π (pi). When you try to find a terminating or repeating rational number to designate π, you fail. The quotient you generate is not exact, and it does not repeat itself at periodic intervals. Here is a sampling of the number that results:

3.14159265358979323846264338327950288419716939937...

At this point in history, π has been calculated to billions of digits. No repeating set of numbers has turned up. Such a number is known as an irrational number. The mathematical symbol for an irrational number is **H**. Here is how to mathematically represent the set of rational numbers:

$$H = \{x \mid x \in R \; x \notin Q\}$$

Again, the vertical bar means "such that" and the $\in$ means "is a member of." The **R** designates the set of real numbers (discussed below), and the $\notin$ means "is not a member of." The definition reads, "An irrational number (**H**) is any number x, such that x is an element in the set of real numbers and is not in the set of rational numbers."

Some other numbers that fall into the irrational category are the square root of 3 ($\sqrt{3}$), the cube root of 5 ($\sqrt[3]{5}$), and the base of the natural logarithm, e ($\log_e x$). A number is irrational if its decimal representation is non-terminating and non-repeating.

Real Numbers

All of the numbers you have investigated so far are considered real numbers. The mathematical symbol that represents real numbers is **R**. Figure 2.5 reveals the relationship between the various number systems. Accordingly, both rational and irrational numbers are real numbers.

It remains important to emphasize that a number may be represented in many number systems. For example, a rational number may also be a counting number, a whole number, or an integer.

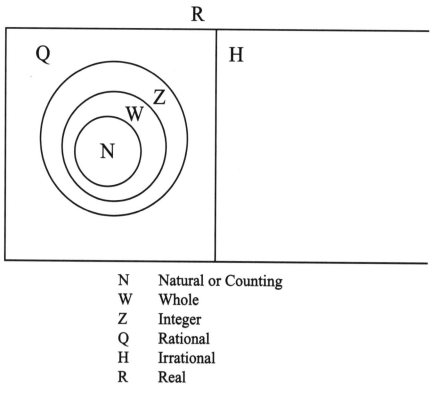

N	Natural or Counting
W	Whole
Z	Integer
Q	Rational
H	Irrational
R	Real

Figure 2.5
Real numbers encompass all rational and irrational numbers.

Exercise Set 2.1

To test your understanding of the systems of numbers, please identify the number set the following numbers belong in. Identify the innermost set for each number.

Example: $4/2 \in N$

a. π

b. -2

c. $-6/3$

d. $-5/2$

e. $-2/3$

f. $4/5$

g. $2/1$

h. $1/8$

i. $1/5$

j. $\sqrt{7}$

Properties

When you work with real numbers, you do so according to a set of rules that mathematicians often describe as *properties*. The properties of a number system pertain to how the numbers behave when you carry out operations using them. Figure 2.6 illustrates the basic properties of the real numbers. These properties apply to all the number systems you have dealt with so far. However, not all properties are applicable to all number systems. The next few sections review these properties in detail.

Commutative Property

When you work with two numbers, a and b, the order in which you add or multiply them is commutative. The commutative property pertains to addition and multiplication. Consider these equations:

$$a + b = c \quad 3 + 5 = 8 \quad a \times b = c \quad 3 \times 4 = 12$$
$$b + a = c \quad 5 + 3 = 8 \quad b \times a = c \quad 4 \times 3 = 12$$

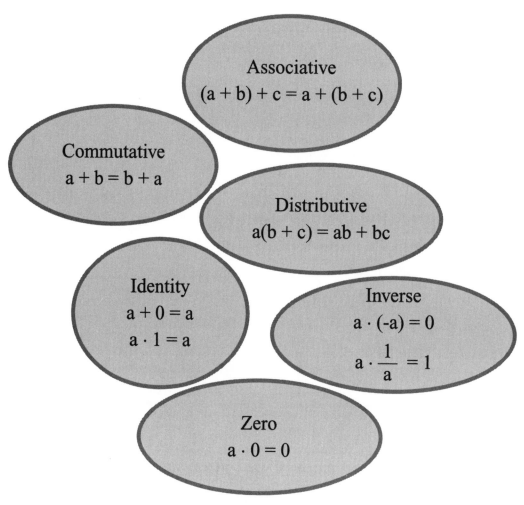

Figure 2.6
Six groups of properties allow you to work with the real and other number systems.

If you start with 3 and then add 5 to it, you obtain the same result as when you start with 5 and add 3. If you multiply 3 by 4, you obtain the same result as when you multiply 4 by 3. The commutative property allows you to change the order in which you carry out an addition or multiplication operation without changing the outcome of the operation.

Associative Property

When you work with three or more numbers, *a*, *b*, and *c*, you can group them in different ways as you perform the addition or multiplication operations that join them together. How you associate them depends on the type of operations you perform with them. The associative property applies to addition and multiplication. Consider these equations:

$$a + (b + c) = (a + b) + c$$

$$3 + (5 + 7) = (3 + 5) + 7$$

$$3 + (12) = (8) + 7$$

$$15 = 15$$

When you add 3 to the sum of 5 and 7, you obtain the same result as when you add the sum of 3 and 5 to 7. The difference is in the order of operations. The associative property allows you to alter the way that you group items in an expression as you reduce or solve the expression.

Distributive Property

Distribution allows you to reorganize the terms of an expression so that you can more easily work with them. This property applies to addition and multiplication. Consider the following equations:

$$b(a - c) = b(a) - b(c)$$

$$5(8 - 3) = 5(8) - 5(3)$$

$$5(5) = 40 - 15$$

$$25 = 25$$

In this instance, you can solve the problem in two different ways. What the distributive property enables is for you to distribute the multiplication activity so that you multiply 8 by 5 and then 3 by 5. Alternatively, you could just as easily subtract 3 from 8 and multiply the result by 5.

Now consider the following expression:

$$3(x + 2)$$

In this expression, note that you may not just add 2 to x because you do not know the value of x. However, you may distribute the 3. Here is how you would apply the distributive property:

$$3(x + 2)$$
$$= 3x + 3(2)$$
$$= 3x + 6$$

Exercise Set 2.2

Here are a few equations that relate to commutative, associative, and distributive properties. For each equation, identify the property or properties that best explain the operations.

a. $(6 + 3) + 7 = (3 + 6) + 7$

b. $2(6 + 5) = (2 \times 6) + (2 \times 5)$

c. $(8 + 6) + 3 = 8 + (6 + 3)$

d. $4 + 6 + 3 = 3 + 4 + 6$

Use the associative property to write an expression equivalent to each of the following:

e. $y + (z + 3)$

f. $(3x)y$

Use the commutative property to write an expression equivalent to each of the following:

g. $a + 7$

h. $9(b + 2)$

Use the distributive property to factor each of the following. Check by multiplying.

i. $4a + 4b$

j. $15 + 15x$

Identity and Inverse Properties

When working with real numbers, there are properties that pertain specifically to the addition and multiplication of 0 and 1. These properties are called identity and inverse properties.

Additive Identity

When you add zero to a number, the outcome is the number itself. Zero in this case is called the additive identity, such that:

$$a + 0 = 0 + a = a$$

Multiplicative Identity

When you multiply a number by 1, you get the number itself. 1 in this case is called the multiplicative identity, such that:

$$a \times 1 = 1 \times a = a$$

Consider the following equations:

$$1 \times a = a \quad -1 \times a = -a$$

If you multiply a by 1, you get a. If you multiply a by -1, you still get a, but the *sign* of a is now changed to match the *sign* of 1.

Additive Inverse

For a given number a, if you add a value to a that is equal to and opposite in value to a, then the result is zero. The number you add to a is called the additive inverse, or negative, of a such that:

$$a + (-a) = (-a) + a = 0$$

The additive inverse of a is $-a$. The additive inverse of $-a$ is a.

Multiplicative Inverse

A number multiplied by its inverse is 1. The inverse of a number is the fraction (or ratio) by which you can multiply the number to create the value of 1. For a given number a, as long as $a \neq 0$, there is a number $\frac{1}{a}$, called the multiplicative inverse, or reciprocal of a, such that:

$$a \cdot (1/a) = (1/a) \cdot a = 1$$

Consider the following equations:

$$a \cdot \frac{1}{a} = 1, \quad 5 \cdot \frac{1}{5} = 1, \quad 4000000 \cdot \frac{1}{4000000} = 1, \quad \frac{3}{4} \cdot \frac{4}{3} = 1$$

The multiplicative inverse of a is $\frac{1}{a}$. The multiplicative inverse of 5 is $\frac{1}{5}$. The multiplicative inverse of 4000000 is $\frac{1}{4000000}$. The last example proves a little more involved than the first three. Consider that you can rewrite the equation as $\frac{3}{1} \times \frac{1}{4} \times \frac{4}{1} \times \frac{1}{3} = 1$. Inverses prove useful as ways to reduce the complexity of problems.

Multiplicative Property of Zero

When you multiply a number by zero, the result is zero.

$$a \times 0 = 0 \times a = 0$$

Division Involving Zero

While division by zero is undefined, if you divide zero by any number, the result is zero. The rules for division involving zero are

$$\frac{a}{0} = undefined \qquad \frac{0}{a} = 0$$

Exercise Set 2.3

Here are a few problems that involve working with additive and multiplicative identities, inverses, and the zero properties. Solve each problem.

a. $\frac{1}{5} \times 5$

b. $\frac{2}{3} \times \frac{3}{2}$

c. $-10 + 10$

d. $\frac{0}{9}$

Change the sign (find the opposite or additive inverse) of each number:

e. -2

f. 45

g. -7.14

h. $\frac{9}{5}$

Find $-(-x)$ when x is each of the following:

i. $-\frac{3}{4}$

j. 0.12

Multiplication and Division

When you combine positive and negative numbers through division, results vary according to the signs of the numbers. There are two general ways to view the results of multiplication and division operations involving numbers with different signs. First, consider multiplication and division problems involving only two numbers. Then consider multiplication and division problems involving more than two numbers.

Multiplication and Division with Two Numbers

When you carry out multiplication and division operations that involve two numbers, you deal with a few basic possibilities:

- **Both numbers are positive.** If both numbers are positive, then the result of the multiplication or division is positive. Here are a few examples:

$$2 \times 2 = 4, \quad 2 \div 2 = 1, \quad \frac{2}{2} \times \frac{1}{2} = \frac{2}{4} = \frac{1}{2}, \quad 5 \times \frac{2}{5} = \frac{10}{5} = 2$$

- **Both numbers are negative.** If the two numbers are negative, then the result is positive. Here are a few examples:

$$(-4) \times (-4) = 16, \quad \frac{-4}{-2} = 2, \quad -\frac{4}{3} \times -\frac{3}{4} = 1,$$

$$\frac{-4}{-2} \times \frac{-4}{-2} = \frac{16}{4} = 4$$

In the last example, when you multiply the numerators, −4 and −4, you arrive at a positive value of 16. Along the same lines, multiplying the denominators, −2 and −2, results in a positive number. Alternatively, you can first carry out the divisions. In both cases, −4 ÷ −2, the quotient is positive 2.

- **One number is negative and the other is positive.** If you multiply a negative number by a positive number, then the result is negative.

$$(-4) \times (4) = -16, \quad \frac{4}{-2} = -2, \quad -\frac{4}{3} \times \frac{3}{4} = -1,$$

$$\frac{4}{-3} \times \frac{-3}{-4} = -\frac{-12}{12} - 1$$

In the last example, when you carry out the multiplication of the denominator, you arrive at a positive number. When you multiply the numerators, you end up with a negative number. Alternatively, you can first carry out the divisions. In the first case, you divide a positive number by a negative number, resulting in a negative number. In the second case, you divide a negative number by a negative number resulting in a positive number. The final multiplication then is a negative number multiplied by a positive number, resulting in a negative number.

Multiplication and Division with More Than Two Numbers

When you deal with a sequence of divisions or multiplications, the outcome differs according to the last operation you carry out. Consider the following operations:

$$(-4) \times (-4) \times (-4) = -64$$

$$-2 \times 3 \times -3 = 18$$

$$\frac{-1}{2} \times \frac{3}{8} \times \frac{-3}{2} = \frac{9}{32}$$

$$(-2) \times (-2) \times (-2) \times (-2) = 16$$

In the first example, three negative numbers multiplied together result in a number that is negative (-64). One way to examine this activity involves considering that the first two numbers when multiplied result in a positive number (16). When you multiply 16 by -4, however, you end up with a negative number.

To trace how a negative number results from multiplication of an odd sequence of negative numbers, consider that when you multiply the first two negative numbers, the result is positive. However, when you then multiply this number by a negative number, the result is negative. When you multiply by yet another negative number, then the result becomes positive. Consider a set of multiplications that proceed in this way:

$(-2) \times (-2) = 4$	Two numbers are even.
$(-2) \times (-2) \times (-2) = -8$	Three numbers are odd.
$(-2) \times (-2) \times (-2) \times (-2) = 16$	Four numbers are even.
$(-2) \times (-2) \times (-2) \times (-2) \times (-2) = -32$	Five numbers are odd.

With respect to division, the same relationship applies:

$(-32) \div (-2) = 16$	Two numbers are even.
$(-32) \div (-2) \div (-2) = -8$	Three numbers are odd.
$(-32) \div (-2) \div (-2) \div (-2) = 4$	Four numbers are even.
$(-32) \div (-2) \div (-2) \div (-2) \div (-2) = -2$	Five numbers are odd.

If you are dealing with a sequence of divisions, and if the sequence contains an odd number of negative numbers, the result is negative. If it contains an even number of negative numbers, then the result is positive.

Exercise Set 2.4

Determine whether the result for each problem is negative or positive and then solve the problem.

a. $\dfrac{(8+7)(-1)}{2+1}$

b. $\dfrac{-3}{4} \times -2 \times \dfrac{-2}{-4}$

c. $\dfrac{-3}{2} \times \left(\dfrac{1}{2} \div \dfrac{-3}{-2} \right)$

d. $7 \times \dfrac{1}{-5}$

e. $\dfrac{-2}{3} \times \dfrac{3}{-2}$

f. $-10 \div (-1) + 10$

g. $-3(-2)(-5)$

h. $16 \div (-8)$

i. $\dfrac{-21}{0}$

j. $-5 \times \dfrac{1}{-5}$

Using Visual Formula

To become acquainted with the appearance of rational and irrational numbers, use Visual Formula to perform a few divisions that result in different types of numbers. Here are a few divisions to perform:

a. 1/2

b. 1/3

c. 2/4

d. 4/3

e. 1/17

f. 21/1

g. 0/6

h. 7/3

i. 1/7

j. 5/5

When you use Visual Formula to perform these divisions, one way to proceed involves creating a ratio with fields you program to receive variable values equivalent to the two numbers making up the ratio. Figure 2.7 illustrates how

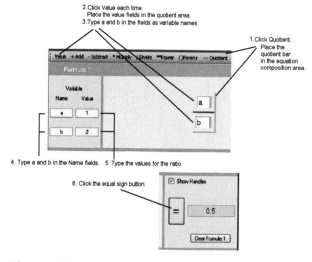

Figure 2.7
How Visual Formula appears after you set up the ratio.

Visual Formula appears after you set up the ratio. Here are the steps you take to create it:

1. Click the Quotient menu item in the top menu list Visual Formula provides. Then click in the upper equation composition area to position the quotient bar.

2. Click the Value field menu item. To position the Value field, click just above the quotient bar in the upper equation composition area. Once again, click the Value field menu item, and this time when you position the field, click just below the quotient bar.

3. Now name the two fields. Working in the equation composition area, in the upper (numerator) field of your ratio, type *a*. In the lower (denominator) field, type *b*.

4. Now move to the panel to the left of the equation composition area. Beneath the Variable label, you see the names of sets of fields. In the top Name field, type *a*. In the bottom Name field, type *b*.

5. To perform the divisions, begin by typing the numerator and denominator values in the Value fields you have set up in the right panel.

6. After you type the numbers, move to the other side of Visual Formula and click the button with the equal sign. You see the result of the division in the field to the right of the button.

Given this beginning, you can now enter new numbers in the Value fields you have set up. Each time you do so, click the button with the equal sign. If the value you enter is a repeating decimal, you see the set of repeating numbers. When you type 1 and 17, for example, you see the following result:

$$0.0588235294117647$$

Conclusion

In this chapter, you have reviewed basic number systems and some of the properties relating to them. In addition to the commutative, associative, and distributive properties of numbers, you have explored the additive and multiplicative identities and inverses of numbers. Also, you have investigated how use of different combinations of positive and negative values influences the outcome of operations. Such activities have immediate applications when you work with exponents, scientific notation, and root and radical expressions, which are topics of the next chapter.

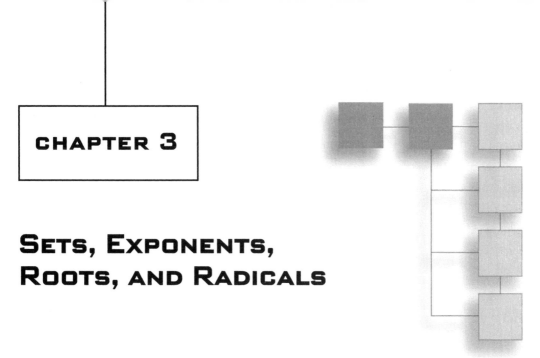

CHAPTER 3

SETS, EXPONENTS, ROOTS, AND RADICALS

This chapter explores the concept of sets and how you can use them to help organize groups of numbers. Among key concepts in this respect are unions, intersections, and subsets. Additionally, you can have disjunctions. One approach to illustrating sets involves Venn diagrams, which allow you to visualize relationships between sets. After investigating sets, you then move on to exponents. When you work with exponents, you can perform multiplication operations that involve the same base values by adding the exponents. Likewise, you can perform division operations by subtracting the exponents. After exploring the preliminaries of exponents, you investigate scientific notation, which provides a convenient way to represent microcosmic and macrocosmic values. After exploring scientific notation, you turn to absolute values, which provide a brief introduction to using the number line to represent numbers. As a final measure, you return to exponents, this time to explore how to use radical and root notations in conjunction with exponents. The discussion pursues the following topics, among others:

- How sets and subsets allow you to more easily group numbers

- Basic operations with exponents, including negative values

- How to work with large and small numbers using scientific notation

- Absolute values

- Radical and root notation as an extension of basic exponents

Sets

A set is a collection of items. Mathematicians usually refer to the items as *elements*. A set is said to *contain* elements. The order of the elements makes no difference. A set emerges from the *elements* that it contains. When you define a set, such as the set of integers or counting numbers, you define the set of all elements it can contain. You might not name all the elements, however, because a set can consist of a finite or infinite number of elements. You still define the condition by which you can determine whether a given item is or is not an element of the set.

Elements

For example, you might picture a set of prime numbers. A prime number is a positive integer that you can generate by multiplication using only the number itself and 1. The other number must be distinct from the prime number. For this reason, 1 is not a prime number.

Using such a definition, you can describe an infinite set of numbers. At the same time, you can create sets of prime numbers using definitions that are more restricted. Here is the set of prime numbers less than or equal to 47:

$$\{2, 3, 5, 7, 11, 13, 17, 19, 23, 29, 31, 37, 41, 43, 47\}$$

You identify a set using opening and closing curly braces, and you separate the elements in a set using commas. To denote that a number is a member of a set, you provide your set with a name. Although no strict rule applies, mathematicians commonly represent the names of sets with italicized capital letters. You might see the following, for example:

$$A = \{2, 3, 5, 7, 11, 13, 17, 19, 23, 29, 31, 37, 41, 43, 47\}$$

You can employ a small italic letter to represent the element symbolically. You use $\in$ to designate that an element "is a member of" a set. If a equals 3, then

$$a \in A \quad \text{and} \quad 3 \in A$$

The number 1 is not a prime number, nor is 4. Assume that the value of a equals 1. To designate that 1 and 4 are not members of set A, you use the following notation:

$$a \notin A \qquad 4 \notin A$$

If it so happens that you have a set that has no elements, then the set is said to be empty. To designate an empty set, you can use the symbol $\emptyset : A = \emptyset$.

Subsets and Supersets

Any collection of items can be a set. At the same time, if you have a set, you can also create a *subset*. One set is a subset of another if the elements it contains are also contained by the superset. Consider the set of prime numbers less than or equal to 17. Designate that as set B:

$$B = \{2, 3, 5, 7, 11, 13, 17\}$$

Set B is a subset of set A (defined in the previous section as prime numbers less than or equal to 47), because each element that is in set B is also in set A. The notation you employ to denote that set B is a subset of set A is as follows:

$$B \subseteq A$$

You can also designate that A is a *superset* of B:

$$A \supseteq B$$

Expressions to Define Sets

When you define a set, you can create a list of the elements of a set, separate them using commas, and enclose the result in opening and closing curly braces. Such an approach to set creation suffices in many practical situations. For other situations, you can use a form of notation that allows you to describe the conditions of membership. In such situations, you make use of a vertical bar and a few other symbols.

Consider a situation in which you want to designate any number that is an element of set A. To accomplish this task, you use the following expression:

$$\{a \mid a \in A\}$$

The previous expression reads, "a such that a is an element of set A." If you want to designate numbers less than 17, you can write:

$$\{a \mid a < 17\}$$

If you want to designate that a number a is less than 17 and is also an element of set A, then you can use a logical "and" symbol ($\wedge$):

$$\{a \,|\, a < 17 \wedge a \,|\, a \in A\}$$

This expression reads, "a such that a is less than 17 *and* a such that a is an element of set A."

Unions and Intersections

Consider sets A and C:

$$A = \{2, 3, 5, 7, 11, 13, 17, 19, 23, 29, 31, 37, 41, 43, 47\}$$
$$C = \{1, 2, 3, 5, 7, 10, 11, 12, 14, 17\}$$

You can find some of the elements of set C in set A and some of the elements of set A in set C. In other words, between sets A and C exists a group of elements that are common to both sets. When you have a set of elements that are common to both sets, you find the *intersection* of the two sets. To indicate the intersection of two sets, you employ the $\cap$ symbol:

$$A \cap C$$

More explicitly, you indicate the members of the set using an equation:

$$A \cap C = \{2, 3, 5, 7, 11, 17\}$$

Not all of the elements in set C are in set A, and not all of the elements in set A are in set C. When you combine the elements of the two sets so that you have the elements of both sets without duplicates, you create the union of the two sets. To indicate the union of two sets, you employ the $\cup$ symbol:

$$A \cup C$$

To show the union explicitly, you use the same approach you use when showing an intersection explicitly:

$$A \cup C = \{1, 2, 3, 5, 7, 10, 11, 12, 13, 14, 17, 19, 23, 29, 31, 37, 41, 43, 47\}$$

Disjunctions

Unions and intersections allow you to explore how different sets share elements. Situations also arise in which you find sets that share no common elements, but you still want to show that they constitute a set. The logical term that you apply to such situations is *or*. Consider, for example, the set of all elements contained in sets *D* and *E*:

$$D = \{1, 2, 3, 4\}$$
$$E = \{6, 7, 8, 9\}$$

Set *D* contains numbers that are less than 5 and greater than 0, whereas set *E* contains numbers that are greater than 5 and less than 10. If you want to create a set in which you can account for both of these sets, you can start with a logical expression that employs the *or* symbol ($\vee$). For example, if *a* expresses any number of the two sets, then

$$\{a \mid a < 5 \wedge a \mid a > 0\} \quad \vee \quad \{a \mid a > 5 \wedge a \mid a < 10\}$$

This expression allows you to say that the set includes numbers less than 5 and greater than 0 *or* numbers greater than 5 and less than 10. It so happens, however, you can create a set *F* that consists of a union of these two sets:

$$F = \{a \mid a < 5 \wedge a \mid a > 0\} \quad \cup \quad \{a \mid a > 5 \wedge a \mid a < 10\}$$

Venn Diagrams

A Venn diagram allows you to easily show subsets, intersections, unions, and disjunctions. To create a Venn diagram, you employ rounded figures that you overlap and shade to show relationships between them. Figure 3.1 illustrates Venn diagrams that represent different types of relationships between sets. Table 3.1 provides a discussion of each of the diagrams.

Exponents

When you multiply a number by itself, you raise it to a power. A power is a product in which all of the factors are the same. To indicate that you are raising a number to a given power, you employ an exponent. An exponent tells you the

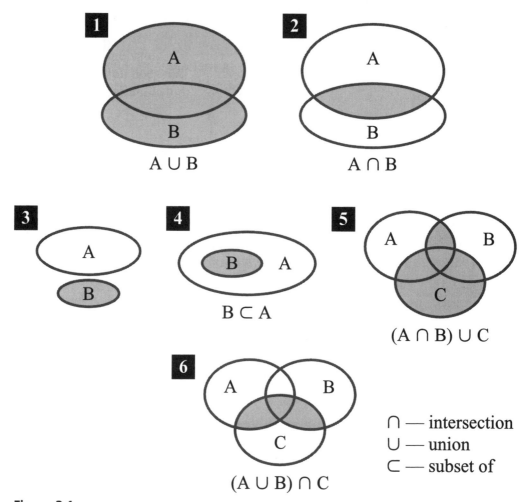

Figure 3.1
Venn diagrams allow you to visualize relationships between sets.

number of times by which you multiply a number by itself to arrive at the value you seek. Consider the following expressions:

$$a \times a = a^2 \qquad 2 \times 2 = 2^2 = 4$$

$$a \times a \times a = a^3 \qquad 2 \times 2 \times 2 = 2^3 = 8$$

$$a \times a \times a \times a = a^4 \qquad 2 \times 2 \times 2 \times 2 = 2^4 = 16$$

In the expression a^2, the a is the base of the expression, and the 2 is the exponent. The base provides the number you use in the multiplication. The exponent tells you how many times to multiply the number by itself.

Table 3.1 Venn Diagram Descriptions

Item	Discussion
Diagram 1	Set A forms a union with set B. In this relationship, the two sets share common elements, but at the same time, the resulting set consists of all elements that the two sets contain.
Diagram 2	Set A forms an intersection with set B. The two sets contain common elements, and the common elements constitute the intersection of the two sets.
Diagram 3	The disjunction of the two sets, A and B, creates a situation in which you must form an "or" statement to account for the elements of the two sets.
Diagram 4	Set B is a subset of set A. In this case, each element of set B is also an element of set A.
Diagram 5	This is a compound relationship. First, you create an intersection between sets A and B. Given this intersection, you then find the union of the intersected elements and set C.
Diagram 6	This is a compound relationship. First, you find a union of sets A and B. Such a union takes the form of Diagram 1. However, the second part of the statement defining Diagram 6 calls for set C to form an intersection with the union of A and B. The intersection then excludes elements that are not common to A, B, and C.

Negative Numbers with Powers

When you use a negative number as an exponent, you create the inverse of the power. Consider the following expressions:

$$a^{-2} = \frac{1}{a^2} \qquad 2^{-2} = \frac{1}{2^2} = \frac{1}{4}$$

$$a^{-3} = \frac{1}{a^3} \qquad 2^{-3} = \frac{1}{2^3} = \frac{1}{8}$$

$$a^{-4} = \frac{1}{a^4} \qquad 2^{-4} = \frac{1}{2^4} = \frac{1}{16}$$

In each instance, the negative exponent signals that you are dealing with the inverse of the number. This holds true for all numbers not equal to zero and all exponents greater than zero. A number multiplied by its inverse equals 1.

Multiplication

If you are working with base numbers that are the same, then you can add the exponents of the numbers to multiply the numbers. Consider the following expression with relation to multiplication:

$$a^m \times a^n = a^{m+n}$$

$$2^2 \times 2^4 = 2^{2+4} = 2^6 = 64$$

Both of the terms provide 2 as a base. Given this situation, as long as you express the numbers you are working with using the same base terms, you can add the exponents to carry out the multiplication.

What if the bases are not the same? If you start with numbers that differ, you can in many cases change them so that they represent the same base. Consider this example:

$$2^2 \times 4^2 = 2^2 \times 2^4 = 2^{2+4} = 2^6 = 64$$

In the first expression, the bases 2 and 4 are not the same. However, $4 = 2^2$ and $4^2 = 2^2 \times 2^2 = 2^{2+2} = 2^4$. By manipulating the base, you can create an expression that allows you to add the exponents to carry out the multiplication.

Division

If you are working with the same base number and you divide one base number by the other, then you can subtract one exponent from the other. Consider the following:

$$a^m \div a^n = a^{m-n}$$

$$2^4 \div 2^2 = 2^{4-2} = 2^2 = 4$$

Alternatively, to test the relationship, do the multiplication for each term:

$$2^4 \div 2^2 = 16 \div 4 = 4$$

When you multiply a number that has a positive exponent by a number that has a negative exponent, you create a situation characterized by division. Here is such a situation:

$$a^n \times b^{-n} = a^n \times \frac{1}{b^n} = \frac{a^n}{b^n}$$

$$2^2 \times 3^{-2} = 2^2 \times \frac{1}{3^2} = 4 \times \frac{1}{3^2} = \frac{4}{9}$$

In this instance, in the lower example, the negative exponent turns 3 into $\frac{1}{3}$. At the same time, 3 is still raised to the power of 2, so you see $\frac{1}{3^2}$ or $\frac{1}{9}$. The first term, 2, possesses a positive exponent, and $2^2 = 4$.

Division with a Negative Exponent

Consider likewise the effect of dividing a number by a number that possesses a negative exponent:

$$\frac{4^3}{4^{-4}} = 4^3 \times 4^4 = 4^{3+4} = 4^7$$

Dividing 4^3 by 4^{-4} is the same as multiplying 4^3 by 4^4.

Negative Numbers and Exponents

When you raise a negative number to a given power, whether you raise it an even or odd number of times makes a difference. If you raise a negative number by an even power, then you multiply it by itself an even number of times, so the result is positive. If you raise a negative number by an odd power, then you multiply the number by itself an odd number of times, so the result is negative. Consider the following expressions:

$(-3)^2 = (-3) \times (-3) = 9$ Even number power is positive.

$(-3)^3 = (-3) \times (-3) \times (-3) = -27$ Odd number power is negative.

$(-3)^4 = (-3) \times (-3) \times (-3) \times (-3) = 81$ Even number power is positive.

Powers of Powers

You can raise a power by a power. In this case, you multiply one exponent by another. Here is an example:

$$(2^2)^3 = 2^{2\times3} = 2^6 = 64$$

$$(5^2)^2 = 5^{2\times2} = 5^4 = 625$$

Powers of Zero and One

A number that possesses an exponent of 1 is equal to itself:

$$a^1 = a \qquad 3^1 = 3$$

A number raised to the power of zero is equal to 1:

$$a^0 = 1 \qquad 3^0 = 1$$

Worked Problems with Exponents

Here are a few worked problems. Study them to prepare yourself for the next section.

$$\frac{x^6 \cdot x^5}{x^{-3}} = \frac{x^{11}}{x^{-3}} = x^{11+3} = x^{14}$$

In this example, you face the problem of first adding the exponents on the top of the fraction. Then, on the bottom, you have a negative exponent, so you divide by $\frac{1}{x^3}$, which is the same as multiplying by x^3.

$$\frac{x^2 y^3 z^{-4}}{x^7 y\, z^{-8}} = \frac{x^2 y^3 \frac{1}{z^4}}{x^7 y \frac{1}{z^8}} = \frac{\frac{x^2 y^3}{z^4}}{\frac{x^7 y^1}{z^8}} = \frac{x^2 y^3}{z^4} \times \frac{z^8}{x^7 y^1} = \frac{x^2 y^3 z^8}{x^7 y^1 z^4} = x^{-5} y^2 z^4 = \frac{y^2 z^4}{x^5}$$

The key here lies in recognizing the need to deal with the two negative exponents. After you have created fractions that remove the negative signs, you can then carry out the divisions. You invert the bottom fraction, placing z^8 on the top of the fraction. In the end, to remove the negative exponent from the top (x^{-5}), you end up with a fraction.

$$\frac{(x^2 + y^2)^7}{(x^2 + y^2)^{-3}} = (x^2 + y^2)^7 \times (x^2 + y^2)^3 = (x^2 + y^2)^{7+3} = (x^2 + y^2)^{10}$$

This problem presents difficulties because it anticipates work with polynomials, which receives attention in the next chapter. You cannot reduce an expression like $(x^2 + y^2)$ without factoring it, so to work with it in this context, you treat it as a single term.

Exercise Set 3.1

Simplify these problems involving exponents:

a. $7^2 \times (6 + 3)$

b. $2(-5^2) + 2^2$

c. $6^{-2} - \times(-1^2) \times (-1)$

d. $\dfrac{(8^2 + 7)(-1)}{2 + 1}$

e. $(2^2)^2 \times 4^0$

f. $\dfrac{-2}{3} \times \dfrac{3^{-2}}{-2}$

g. $-90 \div (-3)^2 + 10$

h. $n^2 \cdot n^{30}$

i. $\dfrac{(a+b)^9}{(a+b)^9}$

j. $\dfrac{r^9 s^8}{r^0 s^4}$

Things That Go Wrong

Simple uses of exponents sometimes create situations in which it is easy to make mistakes. To investigate how this happens, begin by considering the following situation, in which you are dealing with a sum enclosed in parentheses and then raised by the power of 3:

$$(2+3)^3 = 5^3 = 125$$

This solution for the problem is correct. You carry it out by first resolving the addition enclosed in the parentheses. The result of the addition is 5. You then raise 5 to the power of 3, which results in 125.

Here are a couple of other such problems, each solved correctly:

$$(2+5)^2 + (2+4)^2 = 49 + 36 = 85$$

$$(2^2+4)^2 + (4+2)^2 = (4+4)^2 + (6)^2 = 8^2 + 6^2 = 64 + 36 = 100$$

With both of these problems, you first attend to the operations enclosed in the parentheses before dealing with the exponents that apply to the value within the parentheses.

Things go wrong, however, if you inappropriately apply the distributive property to such operations. Here is the **wrong** approach to solving a problem:

$$(2+3)^3 = 2^3 + 3^3 = 8 + 27 = 35 \qquad \text{Not correct}$$

This is not the correct approach to solving problems because you cannot distribute the operation of the exponent across the two values in the parentheses. The parentheses make (2 + 3) into one expression. You must add these values before you move on to working with the power of 3.

Here is another way you can represent the problem:

$$(2+3)^3 = (2+3)(2+3)(2+3) = 5 \times 5 \times 5 = 125$$

In this representation of the problem, the expression in the parentheses is multiplied by itself three times. This is what the power 3 instructs you to do. It applies to the whole expression, not to the values in the parentheses separately.

Scientific Notation

The large numbers that characterize many scientific problems become much easier to manage if you employ scientific notation. Scientific notation involves taking a large, bulky number and replacing it with an expression that involves two numbers that express the value of the large, bulky number but do so in a more compact way. Of the two numbers, the first usually consists of a rational number less than 10. For example, you might see 3.4, 4.5, or 9.2. The second consists of 10 with an exponent. For example, you might see 10^2, 102^2, or 10^{22}. The exponent can be negative or positive, depending on whether you are addressing a number less than 1 or a number greater than 1. An example of a number less than one is 0.0003.

The first part of an expression given in scientific notation is usually called the coefficient of the number. The second part offers 10 raised exponentially. Consider, for example, the distance to the sun in miles. Expressed without scientific notation, this number is usually rounded to 92.9 million miles, which you express in this way:

$$92,900,000$$

Expressed in terms of scientific notation, this number becomes

$$9.29 \times 10^7$$

Table 3.2 provides a few other representative values expressed in scientific notation.

To represent the mass of the earth, you shift the decimal point to the right. The figure of 6.6×10^{21} becomes

$$6,600,000,000,000,000,000,000$$

Table 3.2 Numbers Rendered in Scientific Notation

Item	Scientific Notation	As a Number
Distance from sun to farthest galaxy	1.49×10^{10} light years	14,900,000,000
Distance from sun to Andromeda	2.14×10^6 light years	2,140,000
Distance to farthest object yet seen	1.57×10^{10} light years	15,700,000,000
Age of the solar system	4.6×10^9 years	4,600,000,000
Age of the universe	1.65×10^{10} years	16,500,000,000
Mass of the earth	6.6×10^{21} tons	
Speed of light in miles per second	1.86×10^5	186,000
100	1.0×10^2	100
1/10,000	1.0×10^{-4}	0.0001
Mass of an electron	9.1×10^{-31} kilograms	
Wavelength of a gamma ray	3.0×10^{-13} centimeter	
Planck's Constant	6.626×10^{-34} joules	

Very small numbers, such as Planck's Constant, are represented with a negative exponent, and the effect is to shift the decimal point 34 places to the left. Represented literally, 6.626×10^{-34} becomes

$$0.0000000000000000000000000000000006626$$

Carrying out calculations using scientific notation involves performing the usual mathematical operations with the coefficients, and then using the practices that pertain to exponents to deal with the powers of 10. Consider, for example, the problem of how far light travels in a year. If you begin with the speed of light as shown in Table 3.2, it is 1.86×10^5. On the other hand, there are (generally speaking) 365 days per year. To calculate the number of seconds in a year, you can use the relationship of days to hours, hours to minutes, and minutes to seconds: $365 \times 24 \times 60 \times 60 = 31,536,000$ seconds per year.

Expressed scientifically, you have 3.1536×10^7 seconds. To calculate the distance light travels in years you can set up the following expression:

$$(1.86 \times 10^5)(3.1536 \times 10^7) =$$

$$(1.86 \times 3.1536) \times 10^{5+7} = 5.865696 \times 10^{12} \text{ miles per year}$$

A Few Worked Problems

Here are a few worked problems that involve various uses of scientific notation.

- This problem calls for you to convert a number in scientific notation to an integer value.

$$6.3 \times 10^4 = 6.3 \times 10,000 = 63,000$$

To convert a number from its scientific form to an integer, you begin with the rational form of the number, and then multiply it by a number consisting of 1 and a number of zeros corresponding to the number of the exponent of 10.

- When you deal with values that are a fraction of 1, you can determine how to shift the number by converting the exponential form of 10 into a fraction.

$$6.3 \times 10^{-2} = \frac{6.3}{10^2} = \frac{6.3}{100} = 6.3 \times \frac{1}{100} = 0.063$$

10 raised to the power of 2 is 100, and when you multiply 6.3 by 1/100, you shift the decimal point two digits to the left.

▪ In this situation, to represent the rational number in scientific notation, you begin by converting the denominator to a power of ten.

$$\frac{5.2}{1000} = \frac{5.2}{10^3} = 5.2 \times 10^{-3}$$

You then use a negative exponent to convert the number into scientific notation.

▪ Here are a couple of examples of converting back and forth. In the first example, you shift the decimal point to the right two places to reflect the exponent of 10. In the lower example, you begin with an integer value. To make it clearer how to convert the number from scientific notation to a rational number, you can convert the integer to a rational number, and then shift the decimal point three digits to the left.

$$2.908 \times 10^2 = 290.8$$

$$4 \times 10^{-3} = 4.0 \times 10^{-3} = .004$$

▪ If you can find ways to reduce the complexity of fractions, then it becomes easier to deal with scientific notation. In this case, you begin with a numerator that requires you to multiply two numbers given in scientific notation.

$$\frac{2 \times 10^5 (4 \times 10^{-3})}{8 \times 10^{-7}} = \frac{8 \times 10^2}{8 \times 10^{-7}} = 1 \times \frac{10^2}{10^{-7}} = 10^{2-(-7)} = 10^{2+7} = 10^9$$

You multiply 2 by 4 to arrive at 8 in the numerator. When you rewrite the expression so that 8/8 equals 1, then you are in a position to work with only the exponents of 10. To carry out the division, you subtract the negative exponent of the denominator from the positive exponent of the numerator, resulting in 10 to the power of 9.

Exercise Set 3.2

Solve the following problems. Express the answer in scientific notation.

a. $(3.45 \times 10^6) \times (5.0765 \times 10^3)$

b. $(5.43 \times 10^{-3})^2$

c. $\dfrac{2.56 \times 10^3}{3.45 \times 10^4}$

d. From Table 3.2, what is the ratio of the age of the solar system to the age of the universe?

Convert these numbers to scientific notation.

   e. 73,400

   f. 0.04764

   g. 0.0000000000000000000002

   h. 1,354,050,000,000,000

Answer the following questions.

   i. Without performing actual computations, explain why 4×10^{-14} is smaller than 3×10^{-14}.

   j. Why is scientific notation so useful?

Absolute Values

Consider what happens when you provide someone with directions to a given destination. You might receive instructions that indicate distances without necessarily providing you with the direction in which you are traveling. Consider, for example, an instruction that reads,

"After you turn onto Highway 36, proceed 7 miles."

Given this instruction, Figure 3.2 illustrates two scenarios. Starting at a given point, you can then proceed in one of two directions. The distance you travel involves real movement regardless of whether it takes you nearer to or farther from your destination. The distance you travel, then, has an *absolute* value.

Absolute value is the value of a number without respect to whether it is positive or negative. A number line provides a convenient way to illustrate an absolute value. Figure 3.3 illustrates a number line. You can use a number line to represent the arrows depicted in Figure 3.2 in numerical terms. Given this vision, the number line translates the absolute values of the two directions Figure 3.2 depicts. The number line depicts the distances from 0 to 7 and from 0 to −7. In both cases, the absolute value is 7.

To express mathematically the absolute values of positive and negative numbers, you enclose the number in vertical bars.

$$|-7| = 7$$
$$|7| = 7$$

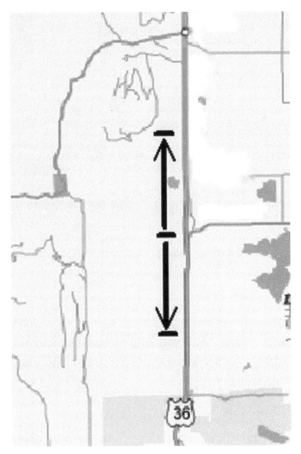

Figure 3.2
Distance without direction involves absolute values.

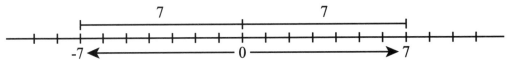

Figure 3.3
The number line depicts the absolute value.

The absolute value of a positive number is the number itself. The absolute value of a negative number is the additive inverse of the number. Consider the following operations with respect to absolute values:

$$|-7 \times 3| = |-7| \times |3| = 7 \times 3 = 21$$

Radicals and Roots

In a previous section, you examined the fundamentals of using exponents. You can also express exponents as fractions, and when you do so you enter the realm of roots and radicals. To explore a root, begin with the notion that to discover the power of a number, you begin by multiplying the number by itself, as the discussion in Chapter 2 detailed:

$$a \times a = a^2 \qquad 3 \times 3 = 9 \qquad \text{The square of 3 is 9.}$$
$$a \times a \times a = a^3 \qquad 3 \times 3 \times 3 = 27 \qquad \text{The cube of 3 is 27.}$$

If you raise 3 by the power of 2, you obtain its square. If you raise 3 by the power of 3, you obtain its cube. Suppose now that you begin with 9 and 27. You ask the following questions:

- Given 9, what number can you multiply by itself to arrive at 9? What is the square root of 9?

- Given 27, what number can you raise by a power of 3, or multiply by itself three times to arrive at 27? What is the cube root of 27?

To represent a root, you use one of two options. First, you can employ a fractional exponent. The denominator indicates the degree or value of the root. The numerator indicates the power to which you are raising the number. A numerator of 1 allows you to indicate any simple root you choose. As a second option, you can translate the exponent using a radical sign ($\sqrt{\ }$). If you use the radical sign alone, by convention it indicates the square root of the number it designates. Here are examples of exponential and radical approaches to expressing roots:

$$9^{\frac{1}{2}} = \sqrt{9} = 3$$
$$8^{\frac{1}{3}} = \sqrt[3]{8} = 2$$

You can work with any number of fractional forms of exponents, and these allow you to express powers and roots simultaneously. Consider the following expression:

$$3^{\frac{5}{2}} = \sqrt[2]{3^5}$$

As Figure 3.4 illustrates, positive exponents render radical expressions in which the numerator designates the power and the denominator then serves as the root.

Figure 3.5 illustrates a further extension of such activity. When you work with a negative exponent, the result, as with other exponents, renders the multiplicative inverse of the entire radical expression.

Positive Exponent

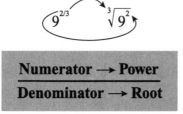

$$\frac{\text{Numerator} \rightarrow \text{Power}}{\text{Denominator} \rightarrow \text{Root}}$$

Figure 3.4
With positive fractional exponents, you convert the numerator to the power.

Negative Exponent

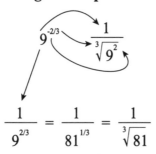

$$\frac{1}{9^{2/3}} = \frac{1}{81^{1/3}} = \frac{1}{\sqrt[3]{81}}$$

The radical expression becomes the denominator of the inverse expression.

Figure 3.5
Fractional exponents translate into radicals, and negatives behave in the same way as exponents.

Generally, you can manipulate fractional exponential expressions in the same way that you manipulate other fractions. Consider the following expression:

$$a^{\frac{5}{6}} \times a^{\frac{2}{3}} = a^{\frac{5}{6}} \times a^{\frac{4}{6}} = a^{\frac{9}{6}} = a^{\frac{3}{2}} = \sqrt{a^3}$$

In this case, the common denominator of $\frac{5}{6}$ and $\frac{2}{3}$ allows you to perform the multiplication operation by adding the two exponents. This gives you $\frac{9}{6}$, which you can then reduce and convert to a radical form.

A Few Worked Problems

Here are a few more worked problems. Study them to acquaint yourself with the use of different operations you can perform with exponents.

■ This problem combines a cube root with the multiplicative inverse of a value:

$$8^{\frac{-1}{3}} = \frac{1}{8^{\frac{1}{3}}} = \frac{1}{\sqrt[3]{8}} = \frac{1}{2}$$

In this instance, the negative exponent $(-1/3)$ calls for the multiplicative inverse of the cube root of 8. Having expressed the problem in this form, you can then extract the root and arrive at 1/2.

■ This problem involves working with both a negative exponent and the need to simplify an expression that involves a root and a power:

$$4^{\frac{-3}{2}} = \frac{1}{4^{\frac{3}{2}}} = \frac{1}{(\sqrt{4})^3} = \frac{1}{2^3} = \frac{1}{8}$$

With this problem, you begin by dealing with the negative exponent. You change the exponent into radical notation and then work on simplifying the radical. There are a few approaches to this. One involves emphasizing that $\sqrt{4} = 2$. You can then raise 2 to the third power, which results in 8. An alternative approach is to write the denominator as

$$\sqrt{(4)^3} = \sqrt{4 \times 4 \times 4} = \sqrt{64} = 8$$

■ This problem involves a situation in which you must carry out a multiplication operation in the denominator of the fraction.

$$\frac{4^{\frac{7}{3}}}{4^{\frac{2}{3}} \times 4^{\frac{5}{3}}} = \frac{4^{\frac{7}{3}}}{4^{\frac{7}{3}}} = 4^{\frac{7}{3} - \frac{7}{3}} = 4^0 = 1$$

To carry out the multiplication, since you are working with the same base (4), you can add the exponents $(2/3 + 5/3)$ of the two numbers in the denominators. Then, to carry out the division, you can subtract the exponent of the denominator from the exponent of the numerator. The result is 0, and any number raised to the power of 0 is equal to 1.

■ This problem has a denominator that includes several radical expressions:

$$\frac{25^{\frac{-2}{3}}}{25^{\frac{1}{3}} \times 8^{\frac{1}{3}}} = \frac{1}{25^{\frac{1}{3}} \times 25^{\frac{2}{3}} \times 8^{\frac{1}{3}}} = \frac{1}{25^{\frac{1}{3} + \frac{2}{3}} \times 8^{\frac{1}{3}}} = \frac{1}{25^1 \times 8^{\frac{1}{3}}} = \frac{1}{25 \times \sqrt[3]{8}} = \frac{1}{25 \times 2} = \frac{1}{50}$$

Resolution of the problem involves first moving the numerator to the denominator, and then adding the two exponents of 25. When you add 1/3 and 2/3, the result is 1, and any number raised to the power of 1 is the number itself. When you express the fractional exponent of 8 in a radical form, you see clearly that you are looking for the cube root of 8, which is 2.

Exercise Set 3.3

Write the equivalent expression using radical notation.

   a. $a^{\frac{4}{5}}$

   b. $a^{\frac{3}{2}}b^{\frac{-1}{3}}$

   c. $14^{\frac{3}{4}}$

   d. $64^{\frac{2}{3}}$

Write the equivalent expression using exponential notation.

   e. $\sqrt[5]{a^4}$

   f. $\dfrac{\sqrt{a^3}}{\sqrt[3]{b}}$

   g. $\sqrt[4]{14^3}$

   h. $\sqrt[3]{64^2}$

Write the equivalent expression with positive exponents and simplify.

   i. $8^{\frac{-1}{3}}$

   j. $\left(\frac{3a}{8a}\right)^{\frac{-5}{2}}$

Using Visual Formula

Visual Formula allows you to work with problems involving exponents. You can use Visual Formula to check your work. You can also extend the work you have started in new directions. Here are a few problems to get you started with expressions involving exponents:

   a. $9^2 \times (6+5)^2$

   b. $3(-7^2) + 2^3$

   c. $6^{-3} - \times(-1^2) \times (-1)$

   d. $\dfrac{(2^4 + 4)(-1)}{3 + 1}$

e. $(2^2)^2 \times 6^0$

f. $\dfrac{-2}{3} \times \dfrac{3^{-2}}{-2}$

Note

To delete a sign, field, or other item as you are implementing a problem in Visual Formula, position the cursor on the item, press the Shift key, and click the left mouse button.

When you use Visual Formula to solve these problems, you make frequent use of the Power menu option. You also use the quotient bar. To demonstrate the use of Visual Formula for these operations, consider the following problem:

$$\frac{3^2}{6} + \frac{2^3}{5}$$

To implement this problem so that you can generate its solution, refer to Figure 3.6 and perform these steps:

1. Click the Quotient menu item. Then click in the upper equation composition area to position the quotient bar. Resize the quotient area by clicking on the bottom edge and pulling it down.

2. Click the Value field menu item. In the upper (numerator) part of the quotient area, click to position the Value field. Then click in the field and type 3.

3. Click the Power menu item. To the upper right of the numerator Value field, click to place the exponent field. When you click to position the exponent, note that 2 is the default value. Leave this value.

4. Click the Value menu item and position the corresponding (denominator) field below the quotient bar. Click in the field and type 6.

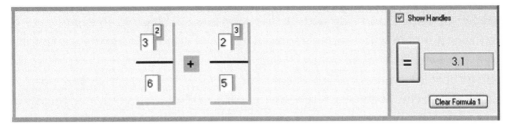

Figure 3.6
Use Visual Formula to generate numbers with decimals.

5. Click the Add menu item and to the right of the quotient you just created, click to position the plus sign.

6. Click the Quotient menu item and position it after the plus sign. Resize it so that it is the same size as the first quotient area.

7. Click the Value menu and position the field in the numerator area of the second quotient. Click in the field and type 2.

8. Click the Power menu item and position it to the upper right of the Numerator field. Click in the field and type 3 for the exponent.

9. Click the Value menu and position the field in the denominator area of the second quotient. Click in the field and type 5 as the value.

10. To calculate the value, click on the button with the equal sign. You see the answer in the field to the right of the button.

Note

As you go, it is not necessary to start from scratch. If you press the Shift key and click on the left mouse button, you can delete items. You can then insert new items. To change a value in the field, just activate the field and use the Backspace key to delete the number in the field.

Conclusion

In this chapter, you have explored how to use sets to help you conceptualize the relationships between groups of numbers. Among the key concepts in this respect are unions and intersections. You also made use of subsets and disjunctions. While sets prove endlessly engaging, other equally engaging topics also prove useful when working with relationships between numbers. In this respect, you explored exponents. Exponents allow you to represent how numbers can be raised to powers. Through negative values, they also allow you to create the inverses of values. Working with basic exponents enables you to use powers of ten in conjunction with rational representations of numbers to express extremely large and extremely small values. Along with this discussion, you explored the uses of absolute values, which enable you to view both negative and positive distances in terms of absolutes relative to zero. Finally, you investigated the use of roots and radicals to complement and extend the use of exponents.

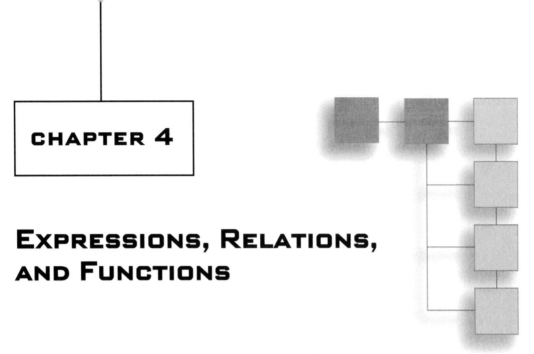

CHAPTER 4

EXPRESSIONS, RELATIONS, AND FUNCTIONS

In this chapter, you learn the fundamentals of factoring. Factoring allows you to reverse the work of the distributive property. When you factor an expression, you end up with a product. In other words, you end up with an expression that allows you to carry out a multiplication. If you carry out this multiplication, it allows you to check your work because it restores the expression to the form you started with. In addition to factoring, you investigate the notion of relations among numbers. You arrange numbers into sets based on the relationship the elements in the set have with each other. You can also use the notion of a relationship to see that numbers in a given set correspond to numbers in another set. One of the most primary relationships of this type is between the numbers in an ordered pair. An ordered pair consists of two values, one that constitutes a domain value, and the other that constitutes a range value. You can readily illustrate ordered pairs using the Cartesian coordinate system. When you generate ordered pairs in which the domain value corresponds to only one range value, then you create a function. You can test functions by using the vertical line test. Given this overview, this chapter includes the following topics of discussion:

- Factoring and the largest common factor

- The order of operations

- Cartesian coordinates and quadrants

- Expressions for functions

Basic Factoring

In an earlier chapter, you explored the distributive property of numbers. As a refresher, here is an example of the applications of the principle of distribution to a multiplication problem:

$$4(5 + 3) = 4(5) + 4(3) = 20 + 12 = 32$$
$$4(5 - 3) = 4(5) - 4(3) = 20 - 12 = 8$$

To perform the distributions, you begin by evaluating the terms in parentheses in relation to the numbers that are applied to them. You can then rearrange the terms so that you preserve the operators that characterize the relations between them. You can rearrange the terms because 4 constitutes a number that is common to each term. You distribute the multiplication activities of 4 so that you apply them separately to the numbers within the parentheses.

When you factor the terms of an expression, you reverse this activity. You begin with a situation in which a common number is applied to a set of terms. You then rewrite the expression so that you combine the common terms into groups. Here is how you factor the expressions shown previously:

$$4(5) + 4(3) = 4(5 + 3)$$
$$4(5) - 4(3) = 4(5 - 3)$$

These expressions both have 4 distributed across multiplication operations involving 3 and 5. To factor the expressions 4(5) and 4(3), you observe that 4 constitutes a common term. You can then factor this common term so that you apply it to the other terms in a collective way.

When you factor out a term, you usually try to factor out the largest common factor. The largest common factor represents other factors combined. Consider this equation:

$$14a - 56$$

You can rewrite this expression so that each expression consists of the lowest common factors:

$$(1)(2)(7)a - (1)(2)(2)(2)(7)$$

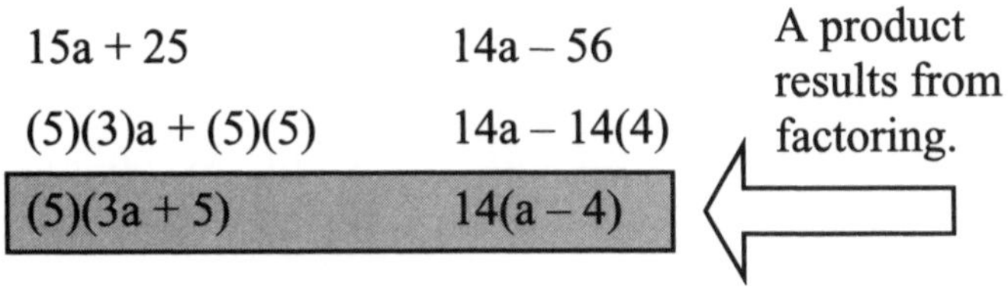

$$15a + 25 \qquad\qquad 14a - 56$$

$$(5)(3)a + (5)(5) \qquad 14a - 14(4)$$

$$\boxed{(5)(3a + 5)} \qquad \boxed{14(a - 4)}$$

A product results from factoring.

Figure 4.1
Factoring results in a product.

You are then in a position to group the common factors so that they reveal the largest common factor:

$$[(1)(2)(7)]a - [(1)(2)](2)(2)[(7)]$$

If you carry out the implied multiplication, you arrive at the largest common factor for the two terms:

$$(14)a - (14)(2)(2) = 14a - 14(4) = 14(a - 4)$$

One of the key notions in factoring is that when you factor an expression, you end up with a product. As Figure 4.1 illustrates, factoring two expressions results in a new expression that implies that a multiplication can take place. Generally, then, you have successfully factored an expression when you rewrite it as a product.

Given that you factor a term, you can then check the correctness of your activities if you carry out the implied multiplication:

$$14(a - 4) = 14a - 56$$

A further extension of factoring involves collecting like terms. If an expression contains terms that are exactly alike, then you can rewrite the expression so that you use one instead of several instances of the like term in the expression. As in previous examples, when you collect like terms, you create a product. As examples of expressions possessing collectable terms, consider the following:

$$8c + 6c = (8 + 6)c = 14c$$

$$7a^2 + 5a^2 + 6a^3 - 3a^3 = (7 + 5)a^2 + (6 - 3)a^3 = 12a^2 + 3a^3 = 3(4a^2 + a^3)$$

In the first example, c is common to both terms, so you can use the distributive property to factor the sum of 8 and 6 into a single expression that you can multiply by c. After you regroup the integers, you can carry out the addition and arrive at a single term, $14c$.

In the second expression, you perform slightly more involved activities. The expression contains two like terms, a^2 and a^3. You can group the coefficients of these terms into expressions that involve addition and subtraction. When you carry out these operations, you end up with 12 and 3 as coefficients. You then carry the process a step further by factoring 3 out of the expression.

Exercise Set 4.1

Here are a few problems for factoring. Find the largest common factor or the like terms.

a. $20a + 4b + 15c$

b. $7a + 42$

c. $ab + a$

d. $2a - 2b - 2b$

e. $\frac{2}{4}a - \frac{3}{4}b - \frac{1}{4}$

f. $9a + 5a + 7 + 3b - 2b - 3$

g. $2\sqrt{4c} + \sqrt{16c} - 4$

h. $15x^5 - 12x^4 + 27x^3 - 3x^2$

i. $30x^3 + 24x^2$

j. $7a^6 - 10a^4 - 14a^2$

Order of Operations

When you work with equations to simplify them, you work in specific ways. Generally, you perform multiplication and division first, working from left to right. Then you perform addition and subtraction, working from left to right. Consider these expressions.

$$3 \times 3 - 2 = 9 - 2 = 7$$

$$3 \times 3 - 2 - 2 \times 2 = 9 - 2 - 4 = 7 - 4 = 3$$

$$3 \times 3 - 2 - 2 \div 2 = 9 - 2 - 1 = 7 - 1 = 6$$

If you find the multiplication and division operations and perform those first, you are usually on safe ground. Still, to make it so that the order of operations is easier to understand, you can employ parentheses:

$$(3 \times 3) - 2 = 9 - 2 = 7$$
$$(3 \times 3) - 2 - (2 \times 2) = 9 - 2 - 4 = 7 - 4 = 3$$
$$(3 \times 3) - 2 - (2 \div 2) = 9 - 2 - 1 = 7 - 1 = 6$$

Parentheses override the standard order of operations. When you work with parentheses, you perform the operations in the innermost parentheses first and then proceed outward. After calculating the innermost grouping symbols, you then simplify the exponential expressions. After that, you carry out operations according to the usual order. Here is an example:

$$2^3 + 33 \times (3 + 4(2 + 2)) - (3 \times 3)(3)$$
$$= 2^3 + 33 \times (3 + 4(4)) - (9)(3)$$
$$= 2^3 + 33 \times (3 + 16) - (27)$$
$$= 2^3 + 33 \times (19) - (27)$$
$$= 8 + 33 \times (19) - (27)$$
$$= 8 + (33 \times 19) - 27$$
$$= 8 + 627 - 27$$
$$= 635 - 27$$
$$= 608$$

Exercise Set 4.2

Here are a few problems involving orders of operation. Reduce the expressions.

a. $4a - (2a + 6)$

b. $16b - c - 5(33a - 2b - +5b)$

c. $(3a + 12b) - 3(4a - 16b)$

d. $(6 \times 2)^2$

e. $(-r)^2$

f. $-r^2$

g. $16 \div 8 + 5[4 + 3(2 - 4)^3]$

h. $5s - 9 + 2(4s + 5)$

i. $98 \div 32 - 98 \div 32$

j. $(8 - 2 \cdot 3) - 9$

More on Sets

In Chapter 3, you investigated some of the activities that involve sets. To extend the previously developed notions, consider that when you define a set, you can define it so that its elements bear relationships with each other. If you investigate a set that consists of numbers that are less than 10 and greater than zero, for example, then you can create a definition along the following lines:

$$\{a \mid a < 10 \wedge a \mid a > 0\}$$

This expression reads along the lines of "*a* such that *a* is less than 10 *and a* such that *a* is greater than 0." While the numbers 0 and 10 are not part of the set, all the numbers in the set are defined by two common features: They must be greater than 0 *and* they must be less than 10. As Figure 4.2 illustrates, the features of the numbers are based on relations.

As shown in Figure 4.2, you can illustrate the numbers greater than 0 and less than 10 just by listing them within curly braces:

$$\{1, 2, 3, 4, 5, 6, 7, 8, 9\}$$

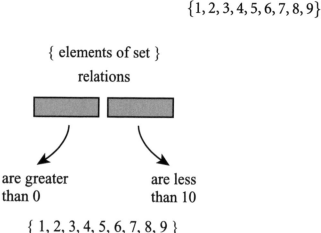

Figure 4.2
A set can be characterized by a set of numbers possessing common relations with numbers outside the set.

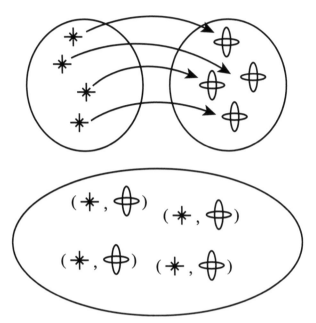

Figure 4.3
Correspondence can pertain between elements in the same set or elements in different sets.

As the discussion in Chapter 3 emphasized, you can relate any set to any other set through such operations as union, intersection, or disjunction. In this respect, then, it becomes evident that you can view some sets as collections of pairs. As Figure 4.3 illustrates, the relations between elements in the two sets allow you to see domain-range relations in the bottom set.

When you begin examining how sets of elements can be defined through relations, you can extend the discussion to include the notion of ordered pairs. A pair is a set of two items. These items can be elements you take from different sets. Likewise, when you can use one element in the pair to define the other element in the pair through a relationship that you can explicitly state, then the two elements exist as an ordered pair.

Consider a relationship in which the first element in the ordered pair is 1 less than the second element. You might state this formally using this expression: $(a, b) \mid a = b - 1$. Figure 4.4 illustrates the ordered pairs that follow from this relationship.

Formally defining a relationship and then generating values is one way to create ordered pairs. Another approach is to begin with a collection of ordered pairs that you somehow discover, and then search for a way to formally describe how

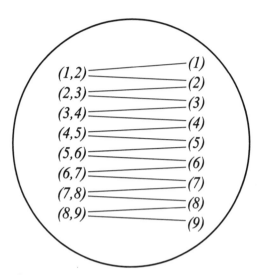

Figure 4.4
A relation establishes a way to discern ordered pairs.

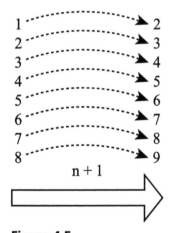

Figure 4.5
A set relation provides a standard way to generate ordered pairs of numbers.

the paired numbers relate to each other. Dealing with the ordered pairs Figure 4.4 illustrates, for example, you can observe that as you go from 1 to 8, you can detect a pattern. The pattern is that if you begin with the first number and add 1, then you get the second number. As Figure 4.5 illustrates, you can proceed to mathematically express the relationship.

As shown in Figure 4.6, when you are dealing with ordered pairs, a number line becomes an effective starting place for making mathematical translations of the relationships you observe.

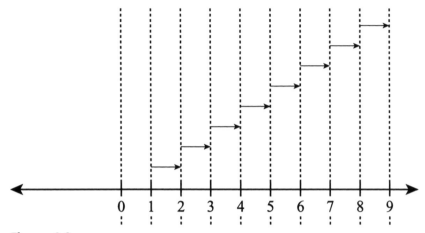

Figure 4.6
Use a number line to explore a relation that allows you to define ordered pairs.

Correspondence Between Sets

To take the examination of ordered pairs into slightly more detail, suppose that you create two sets, A and B, and you assign them elements as follows:

$$A = \{1, 2, 3, 4\} \qquad B = \{w, x, y, z\}$$

You then examine the correspondence between the two sets and create the following ordered pairs:

$$
\begin{array}{llll}
(1, w) & (1, x) & (1, y) & (1, z) \\
(2, w) & (2, x) & (2, y) & (2, z) \\
(3, w) & (3, x) & (3, y) & (3, z) \\
(4, w) & (4, x) & (4, y) & (4, z)
\end{array}
$$

To create these pairs, you begin with the first element from set A and pair it with the first element of set B. You then again draw on the first element of set A and go to the second element of set B. You continue this way until you have paired the first element of set A with all the elements of set B. You then use the second element of set A and proceed as before, pairing it with each element of set B. You continue this activity until you have created all possible ordered pairs that can pertain between sets A and B.

This correspondence of elements in the two sets is known as the Cartesian product of the two sets. You represent a Cartesian product as $A \times B$. The $\times$ in

(1,w)	(1,x)	(1,y)	(1,z)
(2,w)	(2,x)	(2,y)	(2,z)
(3,w)	(3,x)	(3,y)	(3,z)
(4,w)	(4,x)	(4,y)	(4,z)

Figure 4.7
If you examine the pairs in a Cartesian product, you can discern subsets.

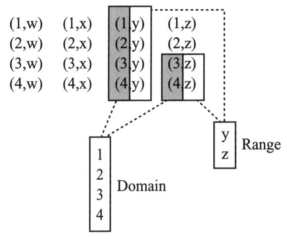

Figure 4.8
The domain is the set of the first elements, the range is the set of the second elements.

this case represents the exploration of the way the elements of the two sets relate to each other. The result of the exploration is called the product of the two sets.

When you proceed in this manner, you begin with a specific pattern of creating a correspondence—or product. At the same time, after you have created the Cartesian product, you can continue on to discover certain subsets. For example, consider the subset of all ordered pairs that contain 1 as a first element. On the other hand, as Figure 4.7 illustrates, you might also describe a subset that consists of the pairs with *y* as a second element.

Domain and Range

When you generate a set of ordered pairs, the set of all elements occurring first in the pairs is the *domain* of the relation. The set of all elements occurring second is the *range* of the relation. With respect to the subset of ordered pairs Figure 4.8

depicts, you can establish a domain that consists of the set {1, 2, 3, 4}. You can establish a range that consists of the set {y, z}.

Cartesian Coordinates

When Rene Descartes (1596–1650) invented the system of mapping coordinates that bears his name, he was lying ill in bed, watching a fly negotiate the space above him. To be able to determine the location of the fly as it buzzed above him, Descartes imagined a flattened world in which the fly moved around on a plane that roughly corresponded in dimensions to the ceiling.

To make it so he could trace the path of the fly on the plane, the mathematician drew axes that divided the ceiling area into four quadrants. He labeled the quadrants using Roman numerals, as shown in Figure 4.9. At the intersection he placed the origin of his mapping. The axes he divided into equal segments identified with positive and negative values. The vertical axis he labeled as the y axis. The horizontal axis he labeled as the x axis.

The horizontal axis of the Cartesian plane represents domain values. The x axis of the Cartesian plane represents range values. Each point on the Cartesian plane is a coordinate, and each coordinate consists of an ordered pair of values. The x value always occurs first in an ordered pair. The y value always occurs second.

Mathematicians sometimes refer to the first number in an ordered pair as the *abscissa*. They sometimes refer to the second number as the *ordinate*. Each number is a coordinate. The ordered pair designates a point within the quadrants of the coordinate system. At the center of the system, where the two axes intersect, you find the *origin* of the system.

If you picture the system upright, the quadrants of the Cartesian plane are set up so that quadrant I is in the upper right. You then move counter-clockwise through the quadrants. Quadrant II is on the top left. Quadrant III is on the bottom on the left. Quadrant IV lies on the bottom on the right. If you trace the flight of the fly, you can discern that the positive and negative values of the ordered pairs take on a specific pattern. Table 4.1 provides a summary of this pattern.

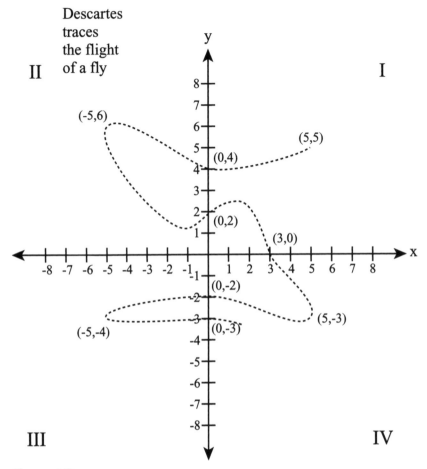

Figure 4.9
The Cartesian coordinate system makes it possible to map a domain to a range.

Table 4.1 Quadrant Characteristics

Quadrant	Values	Discussion
I	(+ , +)	Both x and y are positive. In other words, both the domain and range values are positive.
II	(− , +)	The value of y is positive, but the value of x becomes negative. In other words, the domain values become negative while the range values remain positive.
III	(− , −)	The value of x is negative, as is the value of y. In this instance, both the domain and the range become negative.
IV	(+ , −)	The value of x is positive, but the value of y becomes negative. In this instance, the domain is positive, and the range is negative.

Exercise Set 4.3

Here is a Cartesian coordinate system with a grid to help you position ordered pairs. Use the system to determine the quadrant in which the ordered pairs belong.

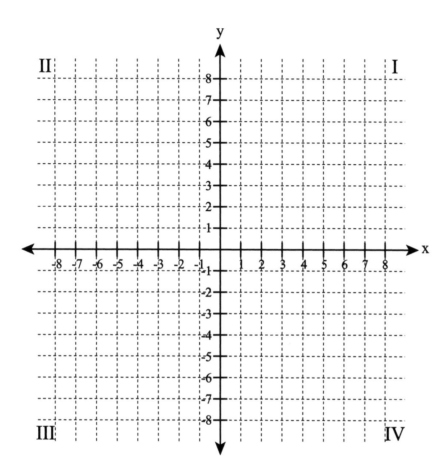

a. (3, 5)

b. (−4, 3)

c. (5, −1)

d. (−4, −4)

e. (7, −5)

f. (−8, −1)

g. (−6, 7)

h. (1, −6)

i. (2, 2)

j. (−2, −2)

Functions

A function results when you discover a relationship between the values in a domain and the values in a range. Certain limitations apply to this relationship, however. First, each domain value must be unique. Second, each range value must correspond to only one domain value. Expressed differently, if you designate a number in the domain, then you find only one number in the range that corresponds to it. In this respect, since a one-to-one correspondence pertains between the values in the domain and the values in the range, the value of the number in the domain *determines* the value of the number in the range.

In Figure 4.10, a Cartesian system allows you to illustrate the functional relationship. This function establishes a pattern that relates the values of the domain with those of the range. The domain and range constitute sets. While the numbers in the domain form a union with the numbers in the range, it remains that the domain-range pairs that result are all unique. The equation that generates these pairs is $y = x + 1$.

Given this equation, then, each value you designate for the domain generates a unique value. The equation, then, is a proper function. It is an equation or relationship that allows you to generate unique range values by using a set of domain values that are themselves unique. No two domain values generate the same range value.

Non-Functional Relationship

Not every pair of sets designating a domain and a range represent a functional relationship. One test you can use to determine whether the graphical depiction of a set of coordinates represents a function involves using a vertical line. Accordingly, if you apply the vertical line test to a graph, the graph cannot pass over the line more than once.

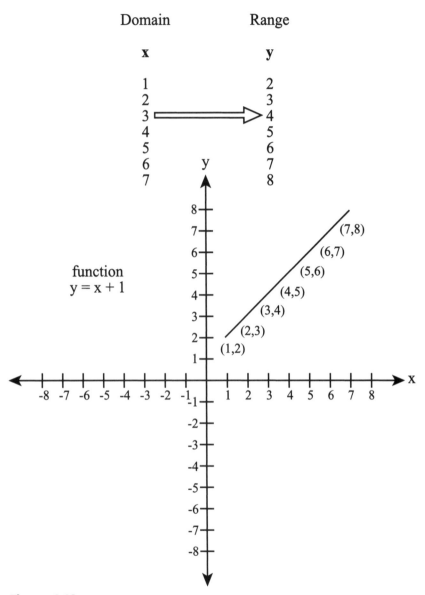

Figure 4.10
A function describes the relation between the domain and the range in which a value in the domain determines a value in the range.

Figure 4.11 illustrates, once again, the path of a fly. The fly's path does not constitute a function. In quadrants II and IV, you see that two of the pairs feature 5 as the domain (*x*) value. In quadrants II and III, you see that again, the domain value repeats itself, this time as −5. Given these redundancies, while it is clear that relations exist between the values of the domain and the range, the mapping of the domain to the range does not represent a function.

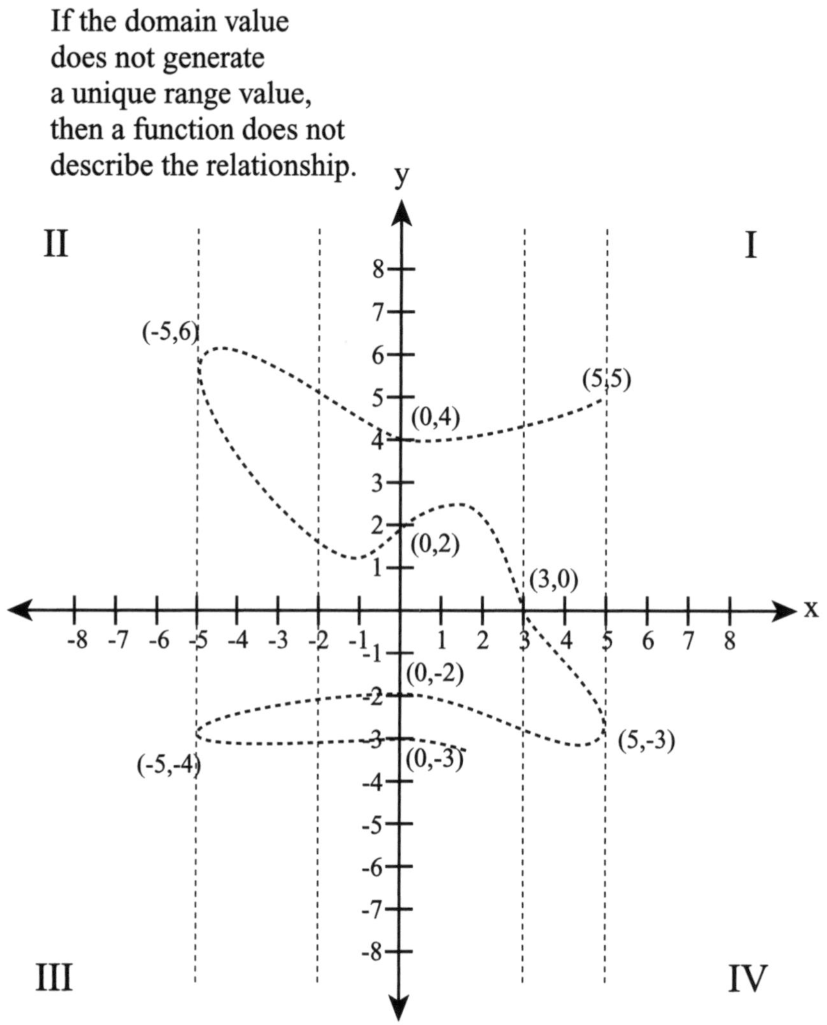
If the domain value
does not generate
a unique range value,
then a function does not
describe the relationship.
y
x
II
I
III
IV
(-5,6)
(5,5)
(0,4)
(0,2)
(3,0)
(0,-2)
(5,-3)
(-5,-4)
(0,-3)
-8 -7 -6 -5 -4 -3 -2 -1 1 2 3 4 5 6 7 8
8 7 6 5 4 3 2 1 -1 -2 -3 -4 -5 -6 -7 -8

Figure 4.11
The path of a fly does not unfold as a function.

Figure 4.12 illustrates three instances in which the vertical line test reveals that the graphs of lines do not represent functions. Graph A fails the test because any pair you identify above the *x* axis has a corresponding pair below the *x* axis. Graph B fails in the same way. For Graph C, the situation is a bit more complex, but the problem remains the same. Consider, for example, that the line crosses the *y* axis four times.

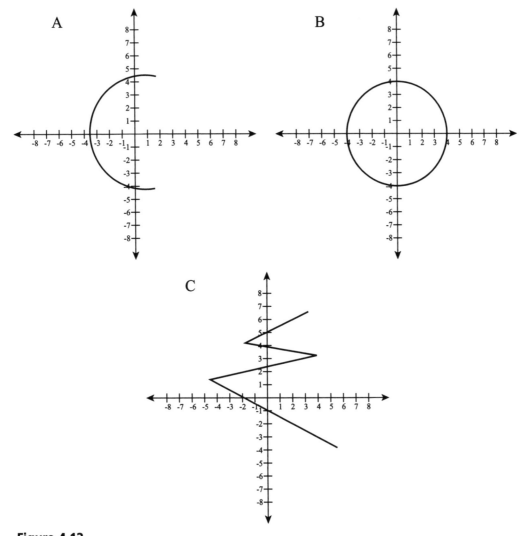

Figure 4.12
The vertical line test reveals that the graphical representations of different sets of coordinates do not represent functions.

Discontinuous Lines

Graphs that represent functions do not have to be continuous. Figure 4.13 illustrates a graph of a discontinuous line. The graph passes the vertical line test because all domain values generate unique range values. The fact that no values can be found along the x axis that are less than 5 and greater than -5 does not change things. The y, or range values, are all the same for the ordered pairs you

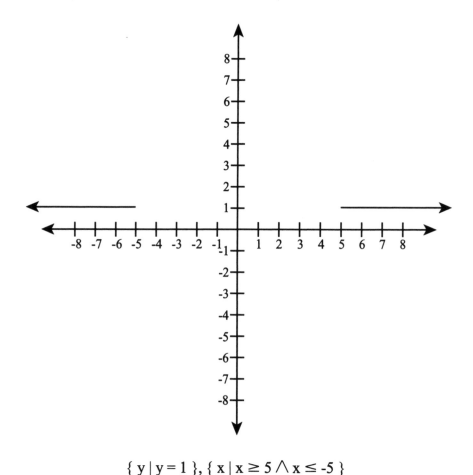

$$\{\, y \mid y = 1\,\},\, \{\, x \mid x \geq 5 \wedge x \leq \text{-}5\,\}$$

Figure 4.13
Lines can be discontinuous, but the outcome corresponds to a function.

might name for the function. You can formally represent the function in this way:

$$y = 1, \quad \text{where } \{x \leq -5 \cup x \geq 5\}$$

In this expression, you define the values of x as a union of all the values greater than or equal to 5 and less than or equal to -5.

Designating Functions

The notation you employ to designate functions allows you to substitute a short statement for the full expression of an equation. The substitution typically involves using a letter, such as f or g, to designate the equation. You then employ opening and closing parentheses to identify the value to use with the equation. You read the expression $f(x)$ as "f of x." To indicate that you are expressing a given equation as a function, you can use the equal sign to associate the function notation with the equation. Here's an example:

$$f(x) = 3x + 2$$

In this case, $f(x)$ becomes a way of saying $3(x) + 2$. You then employ the function notation to designate that you are generating a y (or range) value using the function. A table of values proves convenient as a way to organize your operations. Given a table of generated values, you can then create a graphical representation of the line, as Figure 4.14 illustrates.

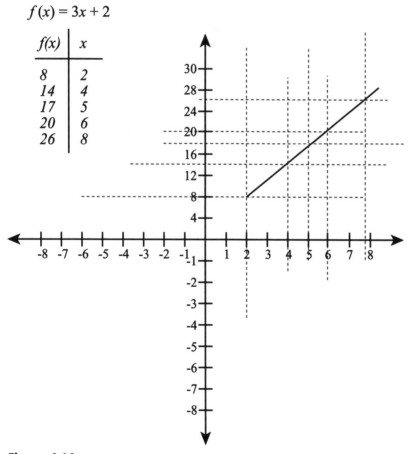

Figure 4.14
Function notation allows you to conveniently display work and generate tables of values to use in creating graphs.

Exercise Set 4.4

Carry out the operations indicated.

a. $f(5)$, for $f(x) = 3x + 7$

b. $f(2)$, for $f(x) = 3x + 5$

c. $f(x + 1)$, for $f(x) = 4x + 5 - 2x$

d. $f(x - 3)$, for $f(x) = 4x + 5 - 2x$

e. $f(2x)$, for $f(x) = 4x + 5 - 2x$

f. $g(-1)$, for $g(n) = 3n^2 - 2n$

g. $s(0)$, for $s(x) = 5x^2 + 4n$

h. $s(2a)$, for $s(x) = 5x^2 + 4n$

i. $g(-4)$, for $g(x) = x - 2$

j. $g(a - 1)$, for $g(x) = x - 2$

Using Visual Formula

Visual Formula allows you to explore relations between domain and range values. The equations you work with as you conduct these explorations can be characterized as functional relations. In subsequent chapters you explore such relations in greater detail. For now, you can use Visual Formula to program variables for fields so that you can explore how equations create domain-range relations.

To set up functions using Visual Formula, you use the f()Func menu item, which generates the $f()$ operator. This operator captures the expression you place between its open and closing parentheses. The output of the operation is stored in a special Visual Formula variable, z. As Figure 4.15 illustrates, the $f()$ operator allows you to operate on values you assign to x. You then access the value of the z variable in the lower equation composition area. When you click the equal sign button in the solution panel of the upper equation composition area, you retrieve the value of z.

Here are a few functions you can set up in the upper equation composition area. Refer to Figure 4.16 as you work. Detailed instructions for setting up the basic function follow.

You can use the variable fields to set values for x.

Add to the complexity of f( ) as you go.

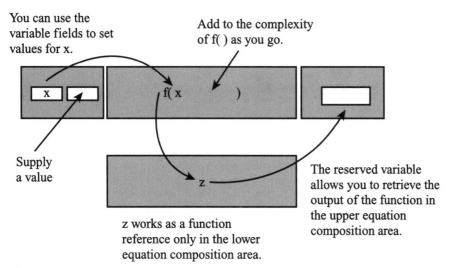

Supply a value

z works as a function reference only in the lower equation composition area.

The reserved variable allows you to retrieve the output of the function in the upper equation composition area.

Figure 4.15
The *z* variable allows you to access the output of a function.

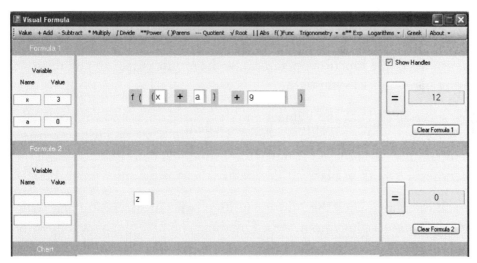

Figure 4.16
Set up a formula you can alter to accommodate different expressions.

1. $f(x) = x + 9$
   a. $f(2 + 1)$
   b. $f(5)$
   c. $f(9)$
   d. $f(x + 1)$

2. $f(x) = 3x + 5$
   a. $f(4)$
   b. $f(2)$
   c. $f(5 - 4)$
3. $f(x) = 4x + 5 - 2x$
   a. $f(1)$
   b. $f(8 - 3)$
   c. $f(23)$

To delete individual operators or fields, hold down the Shift key and click on the operator or field using the left mouse button.

To set up the function in the upper equation composition area illustrated in Figure 4.16, use these steps:

1. Click the f()Func menu item and position the f() operator in the upper equation composition area. Use the mouse cursor to pull the closing parenthesis to the right.

2. Click the ()Parens menu item and place a set of parentheses between the parentheses of the function operator. Use the mouse cursor to pull the inner closing parenthesis to the right.

3. Now successively click the Value menu item three times and with each click place a Value field, as shown in Figure 4.16. You place one just after the opening inner parenthesis. You place a second just before the closing inner parenthesis. You then place a third before the closing outer parenthesis.

4. To add operators, click the Add menu item twice in succession and with each click place a plus sign in your function. The first plus sign follows the first Value field. The second plus sign follows the closing inner parenthesis.

5. Having set up the shell of a function, you can now proceed to add constants and variables to it. Toward this end, type *x*, *a*, and 9, as shown in Figure 4.16.

6. To identify and assign values to the variables, in the top Name field of the Variable panel, type *x*. In the Value field to the right of this field, type 3. Follow up by typing an *a* in the lower Name field. Type 0 for the value you associate with this field.

7. Now proceed to the lower equation composition area. Click the Value menu item and place the corresponding field in the lower composition area. Type *z* in this field. The *z* variable allows you to capture the output of the function you have created in the upper equation composition area.

8. Given this work, you can now click the equal sign button in the upper solution panel and see the output of your function. It appears in the upper solution panel answer field. When you add 3 to 0 and then add this sum to 9, the outcome is 12.

Using your work in the preceding steps as a starting point, alter the function so that it accommodates the example functions given in items *1* through *3* preceding the detailed instructions. Change variable values, fields, and operators to accomplish these tasks.

Conclusion

In this chapter, you began with an exploration of basic factoring. A review of factoring at this point is worthwhile because it anticipates work to come in the next chapter and also serves as an occasion for reviewing the basic properties of numbers. In this respect, it also proves worthwhile to briefly review the order of operations as you solve problems. Given this start, the discussion then turned to an extension of the previous explorations of sets. In this context, the focus of attention lay on showing that you can define relations between numbers by using sets.

A central notion in this respect is that of the domain and range of an ordered pair of numbers. Given a relation that generates ordered pairs, you can identify the first element of each ordered pair as belonging to a set you can designate as the domain. You can identify the second element as belonging to another set, the range. Relations lead to functions, which formalize the expression of the correspondence of the values you find in the domain and range of a relation. You can plot functions using a Cartesian coordinate system. After plotting the domain and range values of ordered pairs, you can apply the vertical line rule to it to determine whether the relation constitutes a valid function.

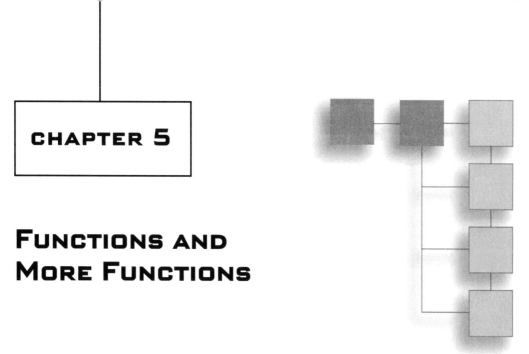

CHAPTER 5

FUNCTIONS AND MORE FUNCTIONS

In Chapter 4 you examined fundamental notions related to presenting numerical data in graphical form. The discussion ended with a review of approaches to representing and working with functions. In this chapter, you take up the theme of working with equations, which allows you to solve the problems that functions embody. When you solve an equation, you work with addition and multiplication to "undo" operations so that you can solve the equation for a specific value. You also make use of least common denominators to clear equations of fractions. When you solve equations, you can end up with a single solution or a set of solutions. Among the equations that generate sets of solutions are those involving absolute values and inequalities. A review of these concepts at this point helps focus the activities of previous chapters so that you can begin using Cartesian graphical representations to work with linear equations. Among topics this chapter covers are the following:

- Rethinking the fundamentals of equations

- Uses of addition and subtraction

- Dealing with fractions

- Absolute values and the number line

- Inequalities and the number line

Thinking About Equations

When you equate one thing to another, you usually proceed such that you examine two things in succession and then conclude they represent the same thing. When you look at a picture of a bird in flight and think about being free to sing, dance, or write a poem, you deal with an analogical form of equality. As Figure 5.1 illustrates, you can analogically equate an oval and a circle. The two forms are rounded, for example, or of the same shade. To the idea of analogy, you can also add that of balance. You can balance a single block on a scale with three smaller blocks if the combined weights of the three smaller blocks equal that of the larger block. With both analogy and balance, you establish equality by using a given quality or attribute to relate two or more items to each other.

When you equate two things to each other, you can do so because they possess a quality or qualities in common. Mathematicians assert generally that everything in the universe can be related to everything else using numbers. Numbers provide a universal medium of relation.

When you study math, it sometimes becomes easy to forget that numbers are abstractions of things. For example, you see an expression along the following lines:

$$7 = 2 + 4 + 1$$

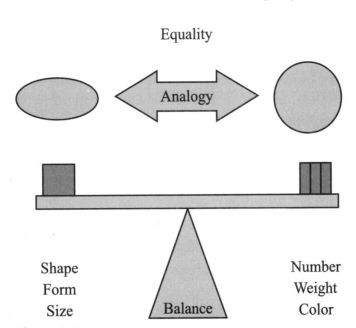

Figure 5.1
Analogy and balance provide two ways to examine equality.

This is a relationship of equality between numbers that might stand for other things, such as the weights of blocks or days of the week. Reasserting that numbers represent such things becomes important at times.

As Figure 5.2 illustrates, when you deal with equations, you deal with both analogy and balance, but in many ways the notion of a balance proves most

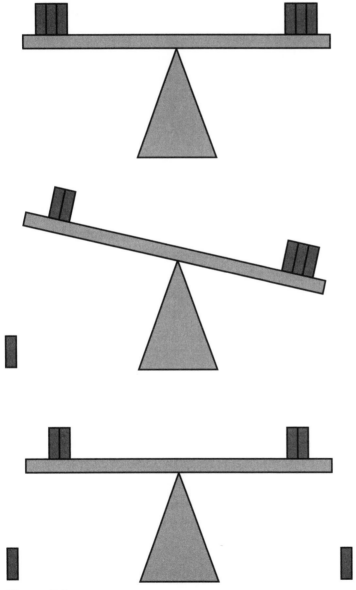

Figure 5.2
Working with an equation involves maintaining a balance.

effective as a way of understanding how equations work. Working with an equation is a process of balancing. When you relate numbers to each other using an equation, you make it so that you can change the way you represent numbers. As you change the way you represent the numbers, you can solve the equation for specific values.

An equation, then, consists of a relation you establish between numbers. When you establish the relation, you assert that a balance or condition exists between the representations you provide of the numbers.

You balance equations by manipulating their terms. As the discussion in Chapter 2 emphasized, you manipulate the terms of an equation using the properties of addition, subtraction, multiplication, and division. When you manipulate the terms and expressions of an equation, the goal of your activity is to preserve the equality of the terms.

Addition and Subtraction

Solving equations using addition and subtraction provides what proves to be the easiest approach to viewing how equations work. Here's an equation:

$$x + 3 = 7$$

This equation involves one unknown term (x). If you solve the equation, you find the value of the unknown term. To find this value, you can subtract 3 from both sides of the equation:

$$x + 3 - 3 = 7 - 3$$

$$x + 0 = 4$$

$$x = 4$$

As you carry out the operation, you preserve the equality. In the end, you eliminate enough terms from the equation to find the lone value of x.

Subtraction constitutes a form of addition (adding the inverse). You can begin with an equation of a slightly different form:

$$x - 3 = 7$$

$$x - 3 + 3 = 7 + 3$$

$$x = 10$$

In this instance, the actions you take amount to undoing or reversing the actions you take when you perform the subtraction. Still, by adding the same value to both sides, you eliminate terms to the point that you are left with only x and its value.

With both forms of the equation, when you substitute your final answer back into the original equation, you can check your solution. Here is the equation involving addition:

$$x + 3 = 7$$

$$(4) + 3 = 7$$

$$7 = 7$$

Here is the equation involving subtraction:

$$x - 3 = 7$$

$$(10) - 3 = 7$$

$$7 = 7$$

Exercise Set 5.1

a. $x + 5 = 45$

b. $x - 12 + 25 = 415$

c. $6x - 12 + 25 = 2x + 3$

d. $5b - 125 = 2b + 33$

e. $t + 9 = -4$

f. $-5 = t + 8$

g. $w - 8 = 5$

h. $y - 6 = -14$

i. $4c - 5 = 5c + 8$

j. $35 = 6y - 5$

Multiplication and Division

When you work with multiplication and division to solve equations, your actions proceed along lines similar to those you use when you work with addition and subtraction. Because division often involves work with fractions, however, your activities take on greater complexity. Still, the essential work of maintaining equality between expressions remains the same. Here is an equation you solve using division:

$$2x = 10$$

To or undo the relationship between 2 and x, you divide the expression by 2. When you divide by 2, you employ the multiplicative inverse of 2. The effect of this activity is to transform the coefficient of x into 1 while dividing 10 in a way that equates with this action. Here is how you proceed:

$$\frac{2x}{2} = \frac{10}{2}$$ Multiply by the multiplicative inverse of 2, or $\frac{1}{2}$

$$1x = 5$$

$$x = 5$$

The multiplication brings about a division of 10 by 2. At the same time, it isolates x.

When you undo a relation between two terms, you are able to isolate one of the terms to discover its value. As Figure 5.3 illustrates, as long as the operations you perform on both sides of the equation result in equal changes, you can proceed with such activities until you reach the solution of the equation.

What applies to division also applies to multiplication. Here is an equation that begins with a division:

$$\frac{x}{3} = 7$$

Undoing relationships

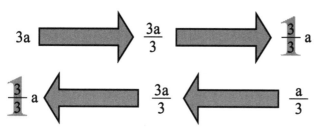

Figure 5.3
Equations allow you to do and undo operations.

Solving this equation involves undoing the division that characterizes the value of x. To undo the division, you can multiply by a value that results in $1x$. Accordingly, you can multiply by 3:

$$3 \times \frac{x}{3} = 3(7) \qquad \text{Multiply by the multiplicative inverse of } \frac{1}{3}, \text{ or } 3$$

$$\frac{3}{3}x = 21$$

$$1x = 21$$

$$x = 21$$

As you proceed, then, you preserve the equality of the terms on both sides of the equation and isolate the unknown term on the one side so that in the end you can identify its value on the other side.

As with addition and subtraction, you can check your division and multiplication activities by substituting the values you arrive at back into the original equations. Accordingly, for the equation you solve using division:

$$2x = 10 \qquad \text{The original equation.}$$

$$2(5) = 10 \qquad \text{Substituting the solution.}$$

$$5 = 5$$

Likewise, for the equation you solve using multiplication:

$$\frac{x}{3} = 7 \qquad \text{The original equation.}$$

$$\frac{21}{3} = 7 \qquad \text{Substituting and dividing.}$$

$$7 = 7$$

Exercise Set 5.2

a. $\dfrac{3x}{2} = 60$

b. $\dfrac{4x}{2} = 42$

c. $\dfrac{6x}{2} = 30$

d. $\dfrac{6b}{2} - 12 = 2$

e. $\dfrac{2}{7} = \dfrac{x}{3}$

f. $\dfrac{-r}{5} = 9$

g. $-\dfrac{6}{7}t = \dfrac{6}{7}$

h. $\dfrac{r}{4} = 13$

i. $b - \dfrac{1}{6} = -\dfrac{2}{3}$

j. $\dfrac{1}{5} + x = -\dfrac{3}{10}$

Combining Operations

Your ability to solve equations substantially increases when you combine addition and multiplication. With the combination of operations, you can proceed to undo relations that have bound numbers to each other in several ways. Here is an equation that combines numbers through addition and multiplication. You use division and subtraction to undo the relations. You begin by working with the addition:

$$2x + 3 = 7$$

$$2x + 3 - 3 = 7 - 3 \qquad \text{Undo the addition.}$$

$$2x + 0 = 4$$

$$\dfrac{2x}{2} = \dfrac{4}{2} \qquad \text{Then undo the multiplication.}$$

$$x = 2$$

When you work with an expression such as $2x + 3$, to solve for x you begin by removing the integer 3 from the left side of the equation. You then remove the coefficient of x, 2. To remove the 3 from the right side, you subtract it from both sides of the equation. To remove the coefficient of x, you divide both sides by 2.

Along a slightly different path, consider the same equation you just worked with. There is more than one way to solve it. Instead of starting by undoing the addition, you can start by undoing the multiplication. In this case, you can begin by dividing. You start off by dividing both sides of the equation by 2:

$$2x + 3 = 7$$

$$\frac{2x + 3}{2} = \frac{7}{2} \qquad \text{Undo the multiplication.}$$

$$\frac{2}{2}x + \frac{3}{2} = \frac{7}{2}$$

$$x + \frac{3}{2} = \frac{7}{2}$$

$$x + \frac{3}{2} - \frac{3}{2} = \frac{7}{2} - \frac{3}{2} \qquad \text{Undo the addition.}$$

$$x = \frac{4}{2}$$

$$x = 2$$

When you divide by 2, you end up with fractions. The fraction associated with the unknown, x, however, is 2/2, which is equal to 1. In this way, then, you isolate the variable x. You can then use subtraction to deal with the fraction that remains on the left side. To verify that the solution you reached is correct, you insert it into the original equation:

$$2x + 3 = 7$$

$$2(2) + 3 = 7$$

$$4 + 3 = 7$$

$$7 = 7$$

Approaching Equations in Different Ways

The previous section reveals that you can approach solving equations in different ways. The specific approach you use can be a matter of figuring out the approach you find easiest. Consider, for example, this approach to solving the problem presented previously:

$$\frac{x}{2} - 4 = 7$$

$$\frac{x}{2} - 4 + 4 = 7 + 4 \qquad \text{Undo the addition.}$$

$$\frac{x}{2} = 11$$

$$2\left(\frac{x}{2}\right) = (11)2 \qquad \text{Undo the division.}$$

$$x = 22$$

In this case, multiply by 2 to remove the fraction. When you remove the fraction, at the same time you first add 4 to both sides, and then multiply both sides by 2. You might just as well have started out by multiplying both sides by 2 but by first adding 4 you reduce the amount of work. To check the solution, you substitute it into the original equation:

$$\frac{x}{2} - 4 = 7$$

$$\frac{22}{2} - 4 = 11 - 4$$

$$\frac{22}{2} - 4 = 7$$

Here is another problem that involves multiple stages of undoing before you reach a solution. When you start off, the denominator of the fraction on the left consists of added terms. The most direct approach to dealing with this situation involves multiplying both sides right off by 7:

$$\frac{3x + 2}{7} = 4$$

$$7\left(\frac{3x + 2}{7}\right) = 7(4) \qquad \text{Multiply by 7 to "clear" the equation of fractions.}$$

$$3x + 2 = 28 \qquad \text{Now the fraction is gone.}$$

$$3x + 2 - 2 = 28 - 2 \qquad \text{Undo the addition.}$$

$$3x = 26 \qquad \text{Undo the multiplication.}$$

$$x = \frac{26}{3}$$

To check this solution, you substitute it back into the original equation:

$$\frac{3x + 2}{7} = 4$$

$$\frac{3\left(\dfrac{26}{3}\right) + 2}{7} = 4 \qquad \text{Substituting the value for } x.$$

$$\frac{\dfrac{78}{3} + 2}{7} = 4 \qquad \text{Divide 78 by 3.}$$

$$\frac{26 + 2}{7} = 4 \qquad \text{Add 26 and 2.}$$

$$\frac{28}{7} = 4 \qquad \text{Divide 28 by 7.}$$

$$4 = 4 \qquad \text{The solution is correct.}$$

Exercise Set 5.3

a. $\dfrac{3x}{2} = 60 - 10$

b. $\dfrac{4x}{2} + 3 - \dfrac{1}{2} = 42$

c. $\dfrac{6x}{2} - 4 = 30$

d. $\dfrac{6b}{\frac{2}{4}} - 12 = 2$

e. $y - \dfrac{5}{6} = \dfrac{7}{8}$

f. $b + \dfrac{1}{3} = \dfrac{8}{3}$

g. $\dfrac{1}{8} + s + \dfrac{3}{8} = \dfrac{5}{8}$

h. $-\dfrac{1}{5} + e = -\dfrac{1}{4}$

i. $a - \dfrac{3}{4} = \dfrac{5}{6}$

j. $\dfrac{8x}{2} + 3 - x = 24$

Least Common Denominators and Clearing Fractions

In the previous section, you multiplied by given values (such as 7) to get rid fractions. This activity is known generally as clearing an equation of fractions. To clear a fraction in an efficient way, you often make use of least common denominators. The least common denominator (LCD) is the number you get if you multiply together the denominators of the terms of the equation.

The least common denominator allows you to evaluate the terms of an equation according to a common denominator value. From there, you can then proceed to cancel terms. Here is an equation worked with on this basis:

$$\frac{x}{3} + \frac{4}{7} = \frac{2}{3}$$

$$21\left(\frac{x}{3} + \frac{4}{7}\right) = 21\left(\frac{2}{3}\right)$$

$$\frac{21x}{3} + \frac{21(4)}{7} = \left(\frac{21}{1}\right)\left(\frac{2}{3}\right) \qquad \text{LCD is 21.}$$

$$\left(\frac{\overset{7}{\cancel{21}}x}{\cancel{3}} + \frac{\overset{3}{\cancel{21}}(4)}{\cancel{7}}\right) = \left(\frac{\overset{7}{\cancel{21}}}{1}\right)\left(\frac{2}{\cancel{3}}\right) \qquad \text{Clearing the fraction.}$$

$$7x + 12 = 14$$

$$7x + 12 - 12 = 14 - 12 \qquad \text{Undoing the addition.}$$

$$7x = 2$$

$$\frac{7x}{7} = \frac{2}{7} \qquad \text{Undoing the multiplication.}$$

$$x = \frac{2}{7}$$

With this equation, you multiply by 21, which you arrive at using the common multiples of 3 and 7. This is the least common denominator. After multiplying the terms of the equation by 21, you cancel terms and reduce the fractions. By first carrying out the work involving the fractions, you can more easily attend to the operations related to addition and multiplication.

Once again, when you substitute the solution back into the original equation, you can test the solution for validity. In this case, you also work with the least common denominator to reduce the resulting fraction to its most simple form:

$$\frac{x}{3} + \frac{4}{7} = \frac{2}{3} \qquad \text{Original equation.}$$

$$x \times \frac{1}{3} + \frac{4}{7} = \frac{2}{3} \qquad \text{Original equation rewritten.}$$

$$\frac{2}{7} \times \frac{1}{3} + \frac{4}{7} = \frac{2}{3} \qquad \text{Substitute solution into equation.}$$

$$\frac{2}{21} + \frac{4}{7} = \frac{2}{3} \qquad \text{Do the multiplication first.}$$

$$\frac{2}{21} + \frac{4(3)}{7(3)} = \frac{2}{3} \qquad \text{Find LCD on left side.}$$

$$\frac{2}{21} + \frac{12}{21} = \frac{2}{3}$$

$$\frac{14}{21} = \frac{2}{3}$$

$$\frac{\cancel{7} \cdot 2}{\cancel{7} \cdot 3} = \frac{2}{3} \qquad \text{Finding the most simple form.}$$

As has been discussed previously, with many equations you make your work easier if you perform some preliminary activities involving addition or subtraction. Here's an example of a problem in which you start off by reversing an addition operation and then moving on to clear a fraction and solve for x:

$$\frac{2x}{3} + 4 = 21$$

$$\frac{2x}{3} + 4 - 4 = 21 - 4 \qquad \text{Undoing the addition.}$$

$$\cancel{3}\left(\frac{2x}{\cancel{3}}\right) = (17)3 \qquad \text{Clearing the fraction.}$$

$$2x = 51$$

$$x = \frac{51}{2}$$

Substituting the solution back into the original equation allows you test the validity of your solution:

$$\frac{2 \times \dfrac{51}{2}}{3} + 4 = 21 \qquad \text{Substituting the solution.}$$

$$\frac{102}{2} \times \frac{1}{3} + 4 = 21 \qquad \text{Multiplying by 2 and dividing by 3.}$$

$$\frac{102}{6} + \frac{24}{6} = 21 \qquad \text{Finding a common denominator.}$$

$$\frac{126}{6} = \frac{\cancel{6}}{\cancel{6}} \cdot \frac{21}{1} = 21 \qquad \text{Canceling and clearing.}$$

Here is one final example. You begin by clearing the fraction on the right side of the equation. To accomplish this, you multiply both sides of the equation by the value 6. This is a value you find in the denominator on the right side of the equation. Having cleared the right side of the equation, you can then more easily work to isolate the variable on the left side of the equation.

$$\frac{2x}{3} + \frac{4}{3} = \frac{5}{6}$$

$$6\left(\frac{2x}{3} + \frac{4}{3}\right) = \cancel{6}\left(\frac{5}{\cancel{6}}\right) \qquad \text{Multiply by 6 to clear the fraction.}$$

$$\frac{12x}{3} + \frac{24}{3} = 5 \qquad \text{Carry out the multiplications.}$$

$$\frac{12x}{3} + \frac{24}{3} = 5$$

$$4x + 8 = 5$$

$$4x + 8 - 8 = 5 - 8 \qquad \text{Undo the addition.}$$

$$\frac{4x}{4} = \frac{-3}{4} \qquad \text{Undo the multiplication.}$$

$$x = -\frac{3}{4}$$

As with the previous examples, you can now substitute the solution back into the original equation to test its validity.

$$\frac{2x}{3}+\frac{4}{3}=\frac{5}{6}$$

$$\frac{2\left(-\frac{3}{4}\right)}{3}+\frac{4}{3}=\frac{5}{6} \qquad \text{Substituting the solution.}$$

$$\frac{\frac{-6}{4}}{3}+\frac{4}{3}=\frac{5}{6} \qquad \text{Multiplying by 2.}$$

$$\frac{\frac{-3}{2}}{3}+\frac{4}{3}=\frac{5}{6} \qquad \text{Simplifying.}$$

$$\frac{-3}{2}\cdot\frac{1}{3}+\frac{4}{3}=\frac{5}{6} \qquad \text{Dividing by 3.}$$

$$\frac{-3}{6}+\frac{4}{3}=\frac{5}{6} \qquad \text{Multiplying.}$$

$$\frac{-3}{6}+\frac{4(2)}{3(2)}=\frac{5}{6} \qquad \text{Finding the common denominator.}$$

$$\frac{-3}{6}+\frac{8}{6}=\frac{5}{6} \qquad \text{Simplifying.}$$

$$\frac{5}{6}=\frac{5}{6} \qquad \text{The solution is correct.}$$

Exercise Set 5.4

a. $\dfrac{x}{3}+\dfrac{2}{7}=\dfrac{4}{6}$

b. $\dfrac{4x}{2}+\dfrac{1}{5}=\dfrac{4}{20}$

c. $\dfrac{4x}{3}+\dfrac{6}{3}=\dfrac{4}{6}$

d. $\dfrac{6b}{\frac{2}{4}}-\dfrac{2}{8}=\dfrac{2}{4}$

e. $\dfrac{5}{4}m + \dfrac{1}{4}m = 2m + \dfrac{1}{2} + \dfrac{3}{4}m$

f. $\dfrac{3}{4}\left(3y - \dfrac{1}{2}\right) - \dfrac{2}{3} = \dfrac{1}{3}$

g. $\dfrac{1}{2} + 4t = 3t - \dfrac{5}{2}$

h. $\dfrac{7}{8}b - \dfrac{1}{4} + \dfrac{3}{4}b = \dfrac{1}{16} + b$

i. $\dfrac{4}{3}(5a + 1) = 8$

j. $\dfrac{2}{3} + \dfrac{1}{4}x = 6$

More on Absolute Values

When you work with absolute values, recall that the absolute value of a number is its distance from zero. Given the use of the number line, any number and its additive inverse possess the same absolute value. You represent this situation as follows:

$$|3| = 3$$
$$|-3| = 3$$

When you translate this set of relations so that you explicitly identify the values of x in a formal way, you can create an expression that assumes this form:

$$\text{If } |x| = 3 \Rightarrow x = 3, -3.$$

Such a statement reads, "Given that the absolute value of some number x is 3, then x can be either 3 and -3." As Figure 5.4 illustrates, if you employ a number line, you can easily show the two values.

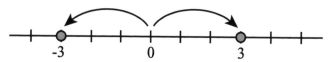

Figure 5.4
You can associate negative and positive numbers with a statement involving an absolute value.

With the use of a number line, you distinguish the absolute value with respect to the origin of the number line, which is zero. The absolute value of a number is its distance from the origin.

Given such an understanding, when you solve an equation that involves an absolute value, then you deal with two absolute distances. Consider this equation:

$$|x - 2| = 5$$

Working with this problem involves two solutions. You arrive at these solutions by anticipating that $|x - 2|$ can be equal to either a positive or negative number. The positive or negative number in this instance is 5 or -5. Given this situation, your solution involves two equations:

$$
\begin{array}{cc}
x - 2 = 5 & x - 2 = -5 \\
x - 2 + 2 = 5 + 2 & x - 2 + 2 = -5 + 2 \\
x = 7 & x = -3
\end{array}
$$

To verify the correctness of these solutions, you substitute them back into the original equation:

$$|7 - 2| = |5| = 5 \quad |-3 - 2| = |-5| = 5$$

Here is a second example. It works the same way. You begin with an equation that includes an expression that embodies an absolute value. You then solve the equation for the two values the absolute value allows:

$$|x + 7| = 8$$

You then proceed with solutions as follows:

$$
\begin{array}{cc}
x + 7 = 8 & x + 7 = -8 \\
x + 7 - 7 = 8 - 7 & x + 7 - 7 = -8 - 7 \\
x = 1 & x = -15
\end{array}
$$

As with the previous example, to test the correctness of these solutions, you substitute them back into the original equation:

$$|1 + 7| = |8| = 8 \quad |-15 + 7| = |-8| = 8$$

Exercise Set 5.5

a. $\left|\dfrac{x}{3}+\dfrac{2}{7}\right|=\dfrac{4}{6}$

b. $|x+27|=85$

c. $\left|x-\dfrac{2}{3}\right|=\dfrac{8}{6}$

d. $|x+7-4|=8-3$

e. $\left|\dfrac{2x-1}{3}\right|=5$

f. $\left|\dfrac{4-5x}{6}\right|=3$

g. $\left|\dfrac{3x-2}{5}\right|=2$

h. $|7x-2|=-9$

i. $|x-7|+1=4$

j. $7|x|+2=16$

Inequalities

Figure 5.5 illustrates the four types of relations that describe inequalities. The relationships that characterize inequalities can unfold in inclusive and exclusive (or non-inclusive) ways. When you use a number line, representing inclusion or exclusion involves two basic activities:

- A range of numbers can be greater than a given value on a number line. To show that the range of numbers is greater than a given number, you employ an open circle. The circle excludes the circled number from the range.

- A range of numbers can be greater than or equal to a given value on a number line. To show that the number is included in the range, you use a filled circle.

The same approaches apply to ranges of numbers that are less than or equal to a given value.

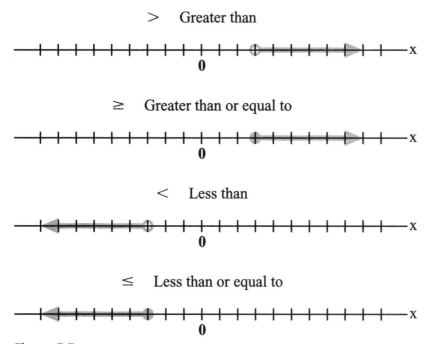

> Greater than

≥ Greater than or equal to

< Less than

≤ Less than or equal to

Figure 5.5
Open circles exclude values while closed circles include them.

When you work with equations that deal with inequalities, you solve them in largely the same way you solve equations that involve equalities, but a few differences apply. Subsequent sections discuss these differences in detail.

Addition and Subtraction of Values

When you add values to both sides of an equation that involves inequalities, you do not alter the relation of the inequality between the two expressions. In other words, the relations

$$a < b \quad \text{and} \quad a \leq b$$

remain the same if you extend them through addition:

$$a + c < b + c \quad \text{and} \quad a + c \leq b + c$$

Likewise, the relations

$$a > b \quad \text{and} \quad a \geq b$$

remain the same if you extend them through addition:

$$a + c > b + c \quad \text{and} \quad a + c \geq b + c$$

Given that you can extend these relations to include the addition of additive inverses, you can safely add or subtract values to remove or isolate values on both sides of the inequality without changing the relation.

Here is an equation that involves inequalities and addition:

$$x + 4 < 6$$
$$x + 4 - 4 < 6 - 4 \qquad \text{Undoing the addition of 4.}$$
$$x < 2$$

You can represent this inequality by graphing it on a number line. The filled circle indicates that valid solutions are any numbers less than 2. In other words, 2 and any number greater than 2 are not members of the solution set.

As with equations involving relations of equality, you can substitute your solution into the original equation to test its validity. In this instance, the solution consists of a range of numbers less than 2, which you can designate as $x \,|\, x < 2$. This expression reads that the solution is any number x such that x is less than 2. Using this expression as a guide, you can arbitrarily designate the following set:

$$\{-2, 0, 1, 1.5\}$$

Given this set, you can substitute the solutions into the original equation:

$$(-2) + 4 < 6 = 2 < 6$$
$$(1.5) + 4 < 6 = 5.5 < 6$$
$$(0) + 4 < 6 = 4 < 6$$
$$(1) + 4 < 6 = 5 < 6$$

In each instance, the expression proves true, verifying the validity of your solution set.

Multiplication and Division of Values

Addition and subtraction of terms in an equation involving inequality renders no change in the relation of inequality. This situation changes with multiplication and division. Specifically, it changes in instances in which you multiply and divide by negative numbers. Why this is so relates the properties of real numbers. As was discussed in an earlier chapter, if you multiply a negative number by a negative number, a positive number results. Likewise, if you divide a negative number by a negative number, a positive number results:

$$-a \times -a = a$$

$$\frac{-a}{-a} = a$$

The effect of such activity is that when you work with an inequality, you must reverse the inequality sign if you divide or multiply a negative number by a negative number. Here is an example of how this happens:

$8 - 4x > 6$	Original inequality
$8 - 8 - 4x > 6 - 8$	Remove the 8. No change in sign.
$-4x > -2$	Simplify.
$\dfrac{-4x}{-4} < \dfrac{-2}{-4}$	Divide by -4 and reverse the inequality sign.
$x < \dfrac{1}{2}$	Simplify.

When you divide by -4, the result of the division on the right side is a positive value, 1/2. This changes the inequality. You must reverse sign to compensate for this fact.

To test the validity of members of your solution set, substitute them into the original equation. You can graph the primary solution on a number line. The graphical representation shows that the solution is less than 1/2, so you use an open circle.

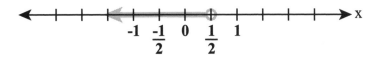

As an example of the effect of multiplying by a negative number, consider this inequality:

$$\frac{-6}{5} \le -4x$$

$$(5)\frac{-6}{5} \le (5)(-4x)$$ Multiply by (5) to clear the fraction.

$$(-1)(-6) \ge (-1)(-20x)$$ Multiply by (-1) and reverse inequality to clear the negative.

$$6 \ge 20x$$ Simplify.

$$\frac{6}{20} \ge x$$ Divide by a positive number. No change.

$$\frac{3}{10} \ge x$$ Reduce.

When you multiply by -1 to make the inequality easier to work with, you render the values on both sides of the inequality positive. This change makes it necessary to reverse the inequality sign.

As in the previous example, to verify the correctness of the solution set, you can first graph it on a number line.

To check the inequality, you can substitute the primary solution into the original inequality:

$$\frac{-6}{5} \le -4\left(\frac{3}{10}\right)$$

$$\frac{-6}{5} \le \frac{-12}{10}$$

$$\frac{-6}{5} \le \frac{-6}{5}$$

Exercise Set 5.6

a. $x + \dfrac{2}{7} \le \dfrac{4}{6}$

b. $\dfrac{4x}{2} + \dfrac{1}{5} < \dfrac{4}{20}$

c. $\dfrac{4x}{3} + 3 > \dfrac{4}{6}$

d. $\dfrac{6b}{2} - 10 \geq 20$

e. $-\dfrac{3}{4}x \geq \dfrac{5}{8}$

f. $x < -3$

g. $x \geq -4$

h. $x - 20 \leq -6$

i. $5z + 13 > 28$

j. $9z < -81$

Conclusion

In this chapter, you have examined different ways to solve equations. You started out with the notion that an equation involves a relation of equality or balance. To solve an equation, you engage in a process of changing the equation in a way that sustains the balance but at the same time allows you to isolate a given variable so that you can determine its value. To solve equations, you use the properties of addition and multiplication. You use these properties to "undo" operations that the equation contains. In addition to working with addition and multiplication (which includes subtraction and division), you also dealt with the use of least common denominators to clear fractions from equations. You also worked with absolute values, which leave you with equations that have two solutions, and inequalities, which often leave you with extended sets with an indefinite number of elements.

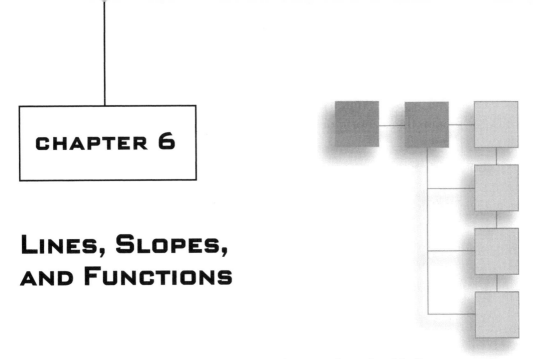

CHAPTER 6

LINES, SLOPES, AND FUNCTIONS

This chapter introduces how to generate lines and work with linear equations. You can use the slope-intercept equation to characterize a linear equation. When you make use of this equation, you examine how the slope of a linear equation changes, depending on whether its slope is positive or negative. You also explore how the y-intercept value is associated with the slope-intercept equation. The slope of a linear equation does not change. To determine a slope, you use the ratio of rise to run of the line. If you know the slope of a line and have one set of coordinates for the line, then you can use the point-slope equation to create an equation for the line. Among the topics this chapter covers are the following:

- Further explorations of domains, ranges, and ordered pairs

- How the slopes of lines change

- How a line shifts depending on its y-intercept

- How you can use the rise and run of a line to determine the slope

- How to use the slope and a coordinate to create an equation

- Combining several functions into one

Reviewing Domain and Range

Chapter 4 provided a discussion of how domain and range values can be understood in the context of relations. When you can establish a relation between a set you designate as a domain and another set you designate as a range, then you can usually create a function that defines the relation. A function constitutes a formalized relation between the values in the domain and the values in the range. As Figure 6.1 illustrates, you can depict this formalization using set notation. The expression $f(x)$ reads, "the function of x" or, more briefly, "f of x." It formally designates an equation that relates the domain and range. When you use such a function, you employ the values of the domain to generate the values of the range.

As discussed in Chapter 4, you identify an equation as a function. Here is an example of how to accomplish this:

$$f(x) = 3x + 2$$

You identify $f(x)$ with the value the expression $3x = 2$ generates. You might just as well write the function as $y = 3x + 2$. Expressed as a function, $(f(x))$ generates the value of y. It remains, however, that y is a variable that stands for the result of the application of $f(x)$.

When you define a function, you can designate or describe its permissible domain and range values. For example, a function can serve as a way to relate an element from the set of real numbers to another element in the set of real numbers. With $f(x) = 3x + 2$, you can arrive at the following generalizations:

$$\text{Domain} = \{\text{All real numbers}\}$$
$$\text{Range} = \{\text{All real numbers}\}$$

Along narrower but equally formal lines, for an equation such as $y = \sqrt{x}$, you can qualify the value of y so that it must be 0 or greater:

$$\text{Domain} = \{\text{All real numbers}\}$$
$$\text{Range} = \{y \mid y \geq 0\}$$

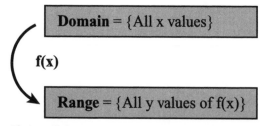

Figure 6.1
Set notation allows you to formalize how you express relations.

The goal here is to designate that you cannot solve the equation for y if the value of x is less than 0.

Note

For much of the discussion in this book, consider *function* and *equation* to be nearly synonymous. Not all equations can be interpreted as functions, however. Generally, a function and an equation both relate the values of a range to the values of a domain.

Linear Functions

Certain functions are linear. A linear function is a function that generates a straight line. Here are a couple of examples of linear equations:

$$y = 2x + 3$$

$$4a - 3a = 12$$

Generally, when you formally identify such equations, you use the following expressions:

$$y = mx + b$$

$$Ax + By = C$$

In these equations, y and x represent variables. You can view x as representing the domain value and y as representing the range value. In both cases, these are variable values. The other letters (m, b, A, B, and C), represent constant values. A constant value is a value you see literally expressed. In the first equation, 2 and 3 serve as constants. In the second equation, 4 and 3 furnish the constants.

The equation $y = mx + b$ is known as the slope-intercept equation. The variable m identifies the slope. The letter b identifies the y-intercept. Here's yet another rewriting of the equation:

$$value\_of\_range = slope\,(value\_of\_domain) + y\text{-}intercept$$

Table 6.1 provides discussion of the primary features of the slope-intercept equation. Subsequent sections discuss the features of the equation in detail.

Slope

To understand how the slope-intercept equation works, consider the graph that Figure 6.2 illustrates. At the top of the figure, the equation allows you to see how constants and variable values combine to generate a straight line. When you set

Table 6.1 The Slope-Intercept Equation

Item	Discussion
$y = mx + b$	The standard way you can express the equation. This is a linear equation if you generate range values (y) using domain values (x).
$f(x) = mx + b$	You can designate the equation as a function.
Graphical form	The graph of the slope-intercept equation is a straight line.
m	The constant m designates the slope of the line.
b	The constant b designates the point at which the line crosses the y axis of the Cartesian plane. You refer to this point as the y-intercept.
(0,b)	If you want to designate the position of the y-intercept using an ordered pair, then you set the domain value (x) to 0 and assign b to the domain value (y).

$$y = mx + b$$

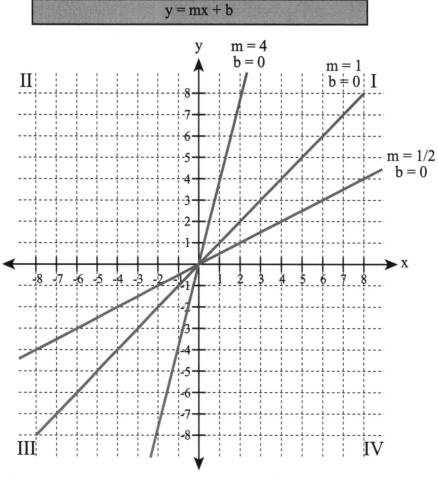

Figure 6.2
The constant m establishes how much the line rises as it extends relative to the x axis.

the value of the slope (m) to 1 and the value of the intercept (b) to 0, then you generate a line that crosses the y axis at 0. If the value of m is positive, then the line slopes up and to the right of the y axis.

When you set the slope (m) to 1, you multiply the value of the domain (x) by 1, so as you move into quadrant I, for each unit on the x axis, you generate a corresponding and equal unit on the y axis. For example, when the line with slope 1 reaches the dashed graph line for the value of 4 on the x axis, it also reaches the dashed graph line for the value of 4 on the y axis.

The situation changes when you set the slope (m) to 4. When you set the slope to 4, then each unit in a positive direction on the x axis corresponds to a movement of 4 units on the y axis. In the Cartesian plane Figure 6.2 illustrates, you increase the value of the slope until you reach 8, at which point the "rise" of the line has progressed at a rate of 8 units for every 1 unit in the "run" (1, 8). At this point, you are out of room for expansion. Given a larger coordinate system, you could continue to increase the slope indefinitely.

In the same way, when you set the slope to $\frac{1}{2}$, then for each unit on the x axis, you find only half a unit on the y axis. When the line with a slope of $\frac{1}{2}$ reaches the dashed line for the value of 6 on the x axis, it has climbed only to the value of 3 on the y axis (3, 6). The larger the value of the denominator of the slope, the smaller the rise of the line. For a slope of $\frac{1}{8}$, for example, when the line reaches the dashed line corresponding to the value of 8 on the x axis, you find that it has climbed only to 1 on the y axis (8, 1).

y-Intercept

As mentioned previously, the constant b in the slope-intercept equation designates the point at which the line crosses the y axis of the Cartesian plane. Figure 6.3 illustrates lines with the same slopes as shown in Figure 6.2. In this instance, however, you change the value of the y-intercept (b). When you assign a value other than 0 to the y-intercept, the line no longer crosses the x axis at its origin. When you set the y-intercept to a positive value, it crosses the y axis above the x axis.

When you set the value of the y-intercept (b) to 4 in Figure 6.3, the line crosses the y axis at 4. When you set it at 2, it crosses the y axis at 2. For the line with a slope of $\frac{1}{2}$, when you set the y-intercept value (b) to 1, then you shift the line upward by 1, so it crosses at 1. In each chase, changing the y-intercept does not alter the slope of the line. It affects only the position at which the line crosses the y axis.

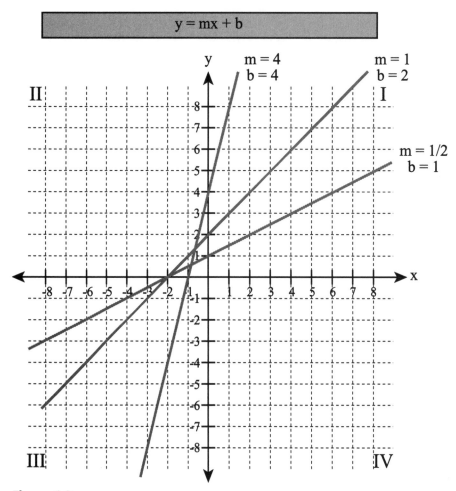

Figure 6.3
The value of the y-intercept (*b*) increases the value of the product of *mx*.

Negative Slopes

As Figure 6.4 shows, when you assign a negative number to the slope value of the slope-intercept equation, you reverse the slope. The slope now slants from the upper left (quadrant II) toward the lower right (quadrant IV). The general relations between values you see with positive slopes continue to apply, however. If you set the slope to -1, then the *y* value that corresponds to 1 on the *x* axis becomes -1. If you set the slope to -4, then the *y* value that corresponds to 1 on the *x* axis becomes -4. Similarly, for 6 on the *x* axis, if you set the slope to $-\frac{1}{2}$, you find that

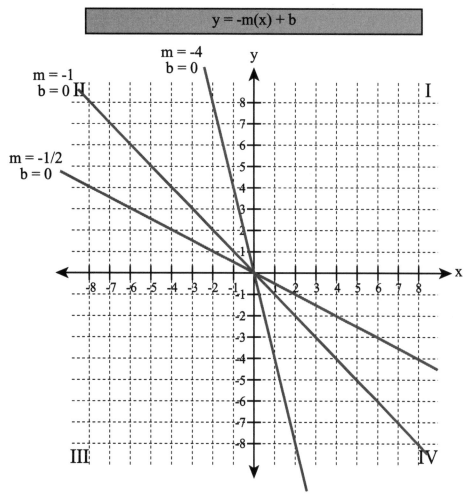

Figure 6.4
When you use a negative value for the slope, the line slopes from quadrant II to IV.

the corresponding value on the y axis is -3. The same applies to the y-intercept values. A value of 2 for the y-intercept causes the line to cross the y axis at 2.

As the lines in quadrant II of Figure 6.4 reveal, when a domain (x) value is negative, multiplying by a negative slope generates a positive range value. As a result, the value of y continues to grow as x becomes more negative. On the other hand, since the values of x are positive, multiplying by a negative slope generates a negative number, so the range values become more negative in quadrant IV as the positive value of x increases.

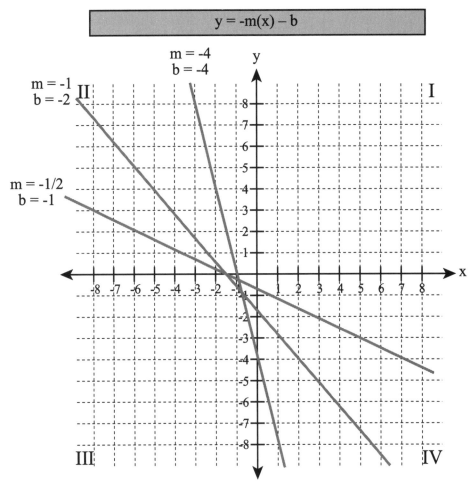

Figure 6.5
With a negative slope and a negative y-intercept, the line slopes toward quadrant IV.

Negative Shifts

You can define linear equations so that the y-intercept is negative. As Figure 6.5 illustrates, when you combine a negative slope value with a negative y-intercept, the line shifts down on the y axis and slopes downward toward quadrant IV. It no longer passes through quadrant I. When you set the slope to -1 and the y-intercept to -2, then the line crosses the y axis at -2. The value of y when x equals 2 is -4. On the other side of the y axis, when x is equal to -2, y is equal to 0. Multiplying a negative value of x by the negative slope generates a positive value, so the value of y continues to increase as the negative values of x increase.

Exercise Set 6.1

For each line, find the slope and y-intercept. Graph the line.

a. $y = 4x + 3$

b. $y = -2x - 2$

c. $y = -2x + 3$

d. $y = 3x - 2$

e. $y = -5x + 5$

f. $y - 3 = 5$

g. $y = \frac{3}{7}x + 5$

h. $y = \frac{9}{4}x - 7$

i. $y = -\frac{2}{5}x$

j. $y = -\frac{3}{8}x + 6$

What Makes a Function Linear?

In the graphs presented in the previous sections, you worked with straight lines defined by different slope and y-intercept values. In each instance, the line you generated sloped upward into quadrant I or downward into quadrant IV, depending on whether you assigned a negative or positive value to the slope constant (m). The slope of a function is defined as the ratio between its rise and run. As Figure 6.6 illustrates, a key defining feature of functions identified as linear is that regardless of the position at which you examine a line you generate using a linear function, the ratio of the rise to the run remains the same.

You can express the ratio of the rise to the run of a linear function using the capital letter delta (Δ) from ancient Greek:

$$slope = m = \frac{rise}{run} = \frac{\Delta y}{\Delta x}$$

In Figure 6.6, to make it easier to view the ratio, you measure the rise and the run of the line with triangles with a height of 2 and a base of 2, but the slope (m) throughout remains 1. In other words, for each rise of 1 unit, the line runs by

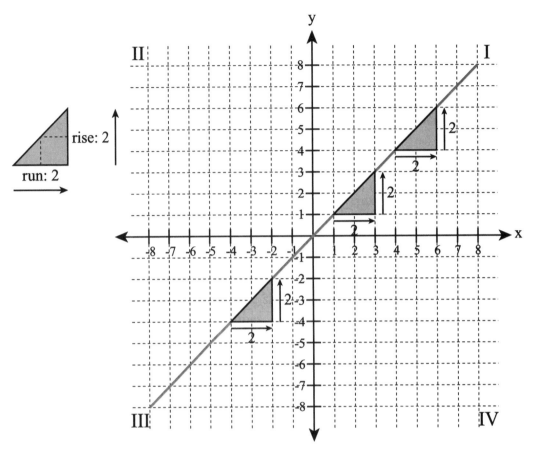

Figure 6.6
The ratio of the rise to the run of a linear function does not change.

1 unit. As Figure 6.7 illustrates, as long as the slope does not change, whether the slope is 1, −1, 4, or −4 makes no difference. The function remains linear.

Slopes That Do Change

As a momentary contrast with linear functions, consider at this point the graph of a function that generates a line with a slope that does change. Figure 6.8 illustrates a curve that you can generate using a quadratic equation. The lower part of the curve reveals a slope of approximately 1. For every one unit on the *y* axis, the lower part of the curve moves one unit on the *x* axis. However, after the line climbs past 1 on the *y* axis, the slope changes. For one unit on the *x* axis, the line climbs 3 units on the *y* axis. The slope for this part of the curve is approximately 3. In this respect, then, the line does not reveal the work of a linear function.

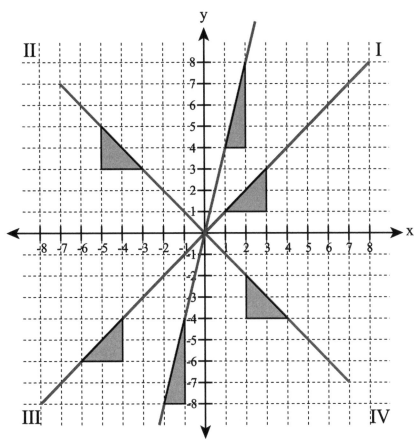

Figure 6.7
The slopes of linear functions do not change.

Note

A linear function generates a line that possesses a slope that remains constant throughout. A non-linear function does not.

Points, Intercepts, and Slopes

Figure 6.9 illustrates the rise and run of a line you generate with a linear equation. To identify the slope, consider first that you can identify a line using two points.

In Figure 6.9, you create three lines using unique sets of coordinates. Each line starts at the origin of the Cartesian plane. For the middle line, the coordinate set is as follows:

$$(0,0) \quad (2,2)$$

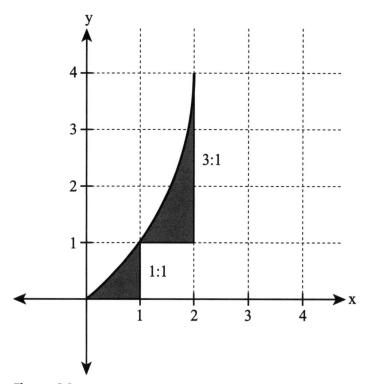

Figure 6.8
The line of a non-linear function reveals a slope that changes, depending on the segment of the line you investigate.

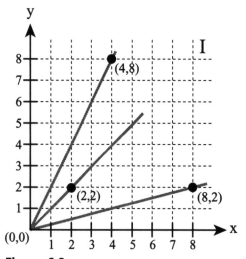

Figure 6.9
You use two sets of coordinates to identify a slope.

Given this set of coordinates, you can then determine the slope of the line if you establish the ratio of the rise (y) to the run (x). Here is the equation and work that accomplishes this task:

$$m = \frac{\Delta y}{\Delta x} = \frac{y_2 - y_1}{x_2 - x_1} = \frac{2 - 0}{2 - 0} = \frac{2}{2} = 1$$

The slope, then, is 1.

For the upper line, you start with this set of coordinates:

$$(0, 0) \quad (4, 8)$$

As with the middle line, you determine the slope of the upper line if you establish the ratio of the rise (y) to the run (x):

$$m = \frac{\Delta y}{\Delta x} = \frac{y_2 - y_1}{x_2 - x_1} = \frac{8 - 0}{4 - 0} = \frac{8}{4} = 2$$

The slope is 2.

For the bottom line, you follow the same approach as before. Your starting coordinates are these:

$$(0, 0) \quad (8, 2)$$

As with the middle and lower lines, you can determine the slope of the line if you establish the ratio of the rise to the run:

$$m = \frac{\Delta y}{\Delta x} = \frac{y_2 - y_1}{x_2 - x_1} = \frac{2 - 0}{8 - 0} = \frac{2}{8} = \frac{1}{4}$$

For each unit the line rises, it runs 4 units. The slope is $\frac{1}{4}$.

Using the slope-intercept equation, you can shift the line you generate for a linear equation above or below the x axis by using a constant to designate the y-intercept:

$$y = mx + b$$

The letter b designates the y-intercept. A line by definition connects two points. To establish one of these two points, as Figure 6.9 reveals, you can use the coordinate values of the origin. On the other hand, if the line does not pass through the origin, you can work with the coordinates that define the y-intercept.

In both instances, after you calculate the slope of the line, you can use the slope to calculate other coordinates.

When you work with the y-intercept, the first coordinate that defines the intercept is 0, which establishes the value of the run (x). The second coordinate establishes the value of the y-intercept. Here is a representative equation containing a y-intercept:

$$y = 2x + 3$$

Given this equation, you know that the line generated includes one coordinate pair in which x equals 0 and y equals 3.

As Figure 6.10 illustrates, using the y-intercept as a starting point, you can use the slope information to determine new points. The slope is 2. If you move to the right by 1 unit along the x axis, you know that you move upward by 2 units on

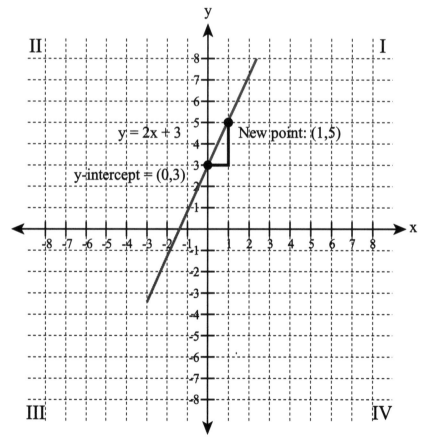

Figure 6.10
The slope and y-intercept allow you to generate points on the line.

the *y* axis. If you start at the y-intercept, you can then arrive at a coordinate of (1, 5). Here is how you calculate this value using the slope-intercept equation:

$$y = 2x + 3$$
$$y = 2(1) + 3$$
$$y = 2 + 3$$
$$y = 5$$

The Point-Slope Equation

The previous sections reveals that if you start with the y-intercept and the slope of a line, you can generate additional coordinate sets. When you determine points in this way, you work with differences between the two sets of coordinates (the deltas). As Figure 6.11 illustrates, you can always employ the differences you find between the run and rise values of two coordinates to calculate the slope of the line. At the same time, you can make use of a given point along with the slope to determine the position of another point.

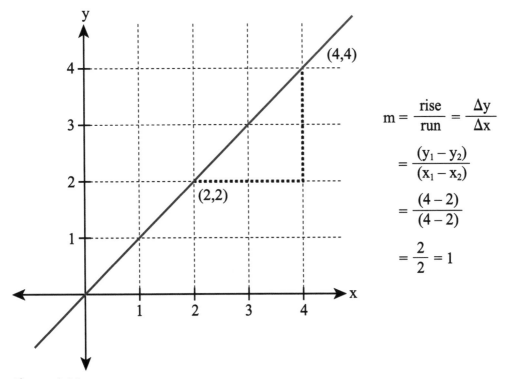

$$m = \frac{rise}{run} = \frac{\Delta y}{\Delta x}$$

$$= \frac{(y_1 - y_2)}{(x_1 - x_2)}$$

$$= \frac{(4 - 2)}{(4 - 2)}$$

$$= \frac{2}{2} = 1$$

Figure 6.11
The slope remains a ratio between the rise and the run of a line.

To examine relating the point to the differences of the values of two points, consider that if you take the ratio shown in Figure 6.11, you develop this equation. On the top, you present the ratio and the slope:

$$\frac{(y_2 - y_1)}{(x_2 - x_1)} = m$$

$$(y_2 - y_1) = m(x_2 - x_1)$$

When you rewrite the equation in the second form, the result is known as the *point-slope equation*. This equation gives a formal definition to the notion that if you know the coordinates of a point on a line and the slope of the line, then you can create an equation for the line.

Consider the line shown in Figure 6.12.

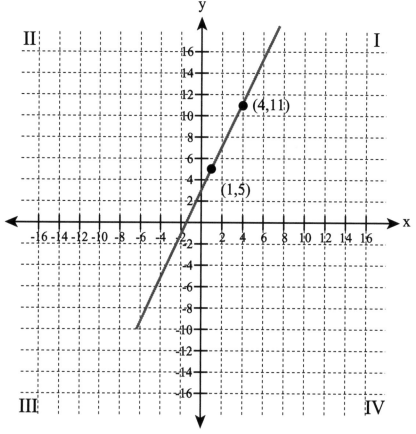

Figure 6.12
Two points allow you to create an equation.

Given the points in the graph featured in Figure 6.12, you can determine the slope if you substitute coordinate values into the point-slope equation:

$$m = \frac{\Delta y}{\Delta x} = \frac{11 - 5}{4 - 1} = \frac{6}{3} = 2$$

Note

It is important to retain a specific ordering of the coordinate values when you determine the slope. Figure 6.13 illustrates a situation in which the order of the x coordinates is the reverse of the order of the y coordinates:

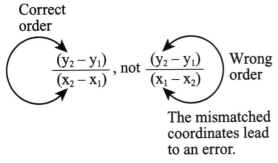

Correct order

$$\frac{(y_2 - y_1)}{(x_2 - x_1)}, \text{ not } \frac{(y_2 - y_1)}{(x_1 - x_2)}$$

Wrong order

The mismatched coordinates lead to an error.

Figure 6.13
Preserve the order of the pairs.

When you know the slope of the line that connects the two points, you can proceed to find the equation of the line. To accomplish this, you make use of the point-slope equation. This equation reads as follows:

$$(y_2 - y_1) = m(x_2 - x_1)$$

You now substitute the slope and values from one of the coordinate pairs. Using the values from Figure 6.12, this leaves you with this form of the equation:

$$y - (5) = 2(x - 1)$$

If you solve for y, you arrive at the standard form of a linear equation:

$$y - 5 = 2(x - 1)$$
$$y = 2x - 2 + 5$$
$$y = 2x + 3$$

This, then, is the equation for the line shown in Figure 6.12.

Exercise Set 6.2

Determine the line's slope-intercept equation for the line containing the given pair of points.

   a. (1, 4) and (3, −4)

   b. (4, −5) and (0, 5)

   c. (6, −2) and (4, 5)

   d. (0, 3) and (5, 12)

   e. (4, −3) and (−2, 4)

   f. (3, 7) and (4, 8)

   g. (−3, 5) and (−1, −3)

   h. (−1, 2) and (3, 8)

   i. (2, 2) and (−1, 4)

   j. (−3, 6) and (4, −2)

Using Visual Formula

Among many other things, you can use Visual Formula to explore negative slopes. You create a negative slope when you make the m (slope) value of the line's slope-intercept equation negative. The equation then assumes the form $y = -m(x) + b$. Here are a few equations to try:

   a. $y = -4x + 3$

   b. $y = -6x + 1$

   c. $y = -5x + 2$

To implement equation a, work in the upper composition area and use the following steps:

   1. Click the Value menu item and then to position the Value field, click in the upper equation composition area. This is the field that corresponds to the coefficient m. Click in the field and then type −4.

2. Click the Multiply menu item. Click to the right of the Value field to position the multiplication sign.

3. Click the Value field item. This time, click to the right of the multiplication sign to position the field. Click in this field and type *x*.

4. Click the Add menu item and position the plus sign to the right of the *x* field.

5. Click the Value menu once again. This time position the Value field after the plus sign. This is the field for the y-intercept value. Click in this field, and then type 3.

6. Now in the lower-right panel find the From and To fields for the X Range setting beneath the Chart for Formula 1 button. Click the From control and set the value to −10. Click the To control and set the value to 10.

7. Now click the Chart for Formula 1 button. As Figure 6.14 illustrates, the negative slope slants down to the right.

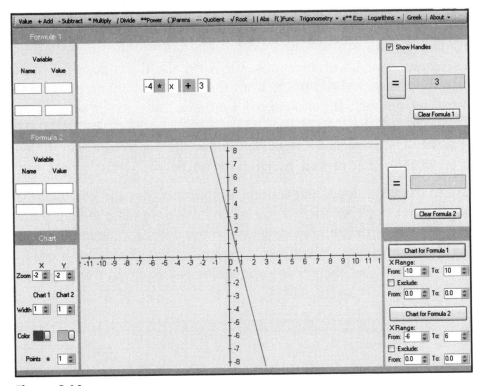

Figure 6.14
Negative slopes slant down and to the right.

8. To show more of the graph, place the cursor on the top border of the graph and drag it to the top of the lower equation composition area by holding down the left mouse button and moving the mouse up.

9. To show more values on the graph, in the lower-left panel find the Zoom fields for X and Y. Click the X control and set the value to −2. Click the y control and set the value to −2.

After implementing the first equation, try the others or improvise to explore different slopes and intercept values.

Conclusion

In this chapter, you have explored how relations between domain and range values allow you to understand linear equations. In your explorations of linear equations, you generated lines that have slopes that do not change. A line with a slope of 2 maintained its slope for its entire length, which might have extended indefinitely. In contrast, you explored how lines for other types of equations, such as parabolas, do not maintain the same slope throughout.

In your exploration of linear functions, you used the line's slope-intercept equation. This equation allowed you to bring the slope and y-intercept of a line into a formal relationship. If you assigned a negative value to the slope of an equation, you forced the line to slope downward into quadrant IV of the Cartesian plane. If you assigned a negative value to the y-intercept, you shifted the point at which the line of your equation intersected the y axis.

In addition to changing slopes and shifting y-intercepts, you also explored the way to use the point-slope equation. If you know the slope of a line and one point on it, then you can use the point-slope equation to create an equation for your line. This chapter provides preparation for more work with linear equations in the next chapter, and that chapter in turn equips you to begin working with non-linear equations.

CHAPTER 7

DISTANCES AND OTHER THINGS

In this chapter, you extend the work begun in the last chapter to investigate different types of linear and non-linear relationships. You start with a review of the slope-intercept equation and how you can use the pattern it provides to quickly establish equations if you are given two points in a coordinate plane that define a line. From there, you work with different properties of lines, such as how to shift them up and down. As you go, you also explore perpendicular lines and lines you create using absolute values. From there, you proceed to explore how a line can be symmetrical to a point or another line. In addition, you look briefly at how you can invert the values of an equation. You also explore absolute values using Visual Formula. Here are some representative topics:

- Simplifying approaches used to create equations

- How to apply the Pythagorean theorem

- Exploring how you can find a line perpendicular to another

- Moving lines up and down

- The effect of absolute values on lines

- How lines are symmetrical with respect to lines, axes, and points

More Slopes

In Chapter 6, you investigated the slope-intercept and point-slope equations. These equations allowed you to become familiar with a number of activities you can perform to explore relationships between sets of numbers. You can view such equations as functions. As explained previously, you can view a function as a formal mechanism for interpreting or transforming the values of a domain into those of a range.

Making It Easy

When you create a linear equation, you can make use of the point-slope equation. As the discussion in Chapter 6 indicates, expressed in its entirety, this equation takes this form:

$$(y - y_1) = m(x - x_1)$$

This equation is for a line with slope m that contains the point (x_1, y_1). The slope-intercept equation also uses a slope and a point. The point is called the y-intercept. The equation appears in one of two forms:

$$y = mx + b$$

$$Ax + By = C$$

Drawing on the discussion in Chapter 6, consider a situation in which you know the slope of a line is 2. You can then write the following, preliminary equation of a line:

$$y = 2x + b$$

If you know the coordinates of a point on the line, then you can substitute the x and y values that define the point into the slope-intercept equation. Assume, for example, that you are working with the point (4, 11). You can substitute the x and y values of this point into the standard slope-intercept equation in this way:

$$11 = 2(4) + b$$

Having made this substitution, you can then solve for b:

$$11 = 8 + b$$

$$11 - 8 = b$$

$$3 = b$$

Having solved the equation for b, you can then substitute the values of the slope and b (the y-intercept) into the original slope-intercept equation to create the equation for your line:

$$y = 2x + 3$$

Making It Still Easier

In Chapter 6, you also dealt with the ratio that exists between the rise and run of a line. You expressed that ratio in this way:

$$m = \frac{\Delta y}{\Delta x} = \frac{y_2 - y_1}{x_2 - x_1}$$

The Greek letter delta signifies changes in the ratio. The ratio works for all ordered pairs on a line. If you return to the ordered pair you dealt with in the previous section (4, 11), you can substitute as follows:

$$m = \frac{y - 11}{x - 4}$$

Since you know the slope of the function is 2, you can set up this equation:

$$m = \frac{y - 11}{x - 4} \Rightarrow 2(x - 4) = y - 11$$

You can then solve the equation for y:

$$2(x - 4) = y - 11$$
$$2x - 8 = y - 11$$
$$2x - 8 + 11 = y$$
$$2x + 3 = y$$

Again, given the basic versions of the point-slope form of a linear function,

$$m(x_2 - x_1) = (y_2 - y_1)$$

or

$$(y_2 - y_1) = m(x_2 - x_1),$$

you can then proceed to develop different equations with relative ease. You derive the slope using a ratio of the values you find in two points anywhere on the line:

$$\frac{(y_2 - y_1)}{(x_2 - x_1)} = m$$

You then proceed to take any ordered pair on the line and substitute it into a version of the point-slope equation. If you are working with a line that has a slope of -3, for example, and you know that the ordered pair $(2, -7)$ lies on the line, then you substitute in this way:

$$y - (-7) = -3(x - 2)$$

or

$$y + 7 = -3(x - 2)$$

You then solve these for y to arrive at the slope-intercept form:

$$y + 7 = -3x - 3(-2)$$

$$y + 7 = -3x + 6$$

$$y = -3x - 1$$

Exercise Set 7.1

Write the slope-intercept equation for the line containing the given pair of points.

a. (0, 0) and (12, 4)

b. (0, 2) and (12, 8)

c. (0, 4) and (10, 12)

d. (0, 0) and (2, 10)

e. (0, 2) and (12, 6)

Write the point-slope equation for the line passing through each pair of points.

f. (−2, 7) and (4, −3)

g. (1, 2) and (3, 7)

h. (−3, 1) and (4, 3)

i. (2, 1) and (7, 2)

j. (−1, 2) and (3, 4)

The Distance Between Points

To take the preceding discussion a step further, consider once again the distance between two points on a line. In Figure 7.1, you establish a relationship between two ordered pairs, (4, 9) and (1, 5). As the figure reveals, the distance between the two points can be viewed in terms of the differences between the corresponding elements of the two ordered pairs. Accordingly, the difference between 9 and 5 is 4 and the difference between 4 and 1 is 3. The figure uses the delta character to show this difference (or change).

Applying the Pythagorean Theorem

The two points in Figure 7.1 define two of three points in a triangle. The difference between the corresponding x values of the two points gives you the distance that defines the base of the triangle. The difference between the corresponding y values

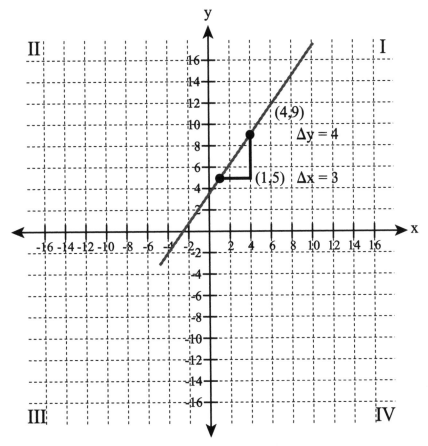

Figure 7.1
The change in the rise is 4 and the change in the run is 3.

of the two points gives you the distance that defines one side of the triangle. Given the measurements of the base and a side of a triangle, you can then draw upon the Pythagorean theorem to find out more about the triangle.

According to the Pythagorean theorem, the square of the hypotenuse of a right-angled triangle is equal to the sum of the squares of the remaining two sides. The theorem is usually expressed along the following lines:

$$c^2 = a^2 + b^2$$

where c represents the hypotenuse and a and b represent the remaining two sides. If you know that one side of a triangle is equal to 2 and another is equal to 4, then proceed to solve the equation in this manner:

$$3^2 + 4^2 = d^2$$

$$9 + 6 = d^2$$

$$25 = d^2$$

$$\sqrt{25} = d$$

$$5 = d$$

Exercise Set 7.2

Using the Pythagorean theorem, use these values for the sides of triangles and calculate the length of the hypotenuse.

a. 12, 5

b. 32, 24

c. 3, 4

d. 24, 10

e. 12, 9

The Distance Formula

Given the grounding the previous section provides, you can set up an equation to calculate the distance between two points in this way:

$$\Delta x^2 + \Delta y^2 = d^2$$

The d is the distance between the two points. From the perspective afforded by the Pythagorean theorem, the difference the delta sign signifies is the difference between the corresponding elements in the coordinate pairs you use in your calculations.

To return to the discussion of the point-slope equation, you can revise it slightly using what you know about the Pythagorean theorem. Consider a line on which you have identified two points, (x_1, y_1) and (x_2, y_2). Drawing upon the formulation of the Pythagorean theorem introduced in the previous section

$$\Delta x^2 + \Delta y^2 = d^2$$

you can then proceed to establish a specific formula, called the distance formula, for determining the distance between two points:

$$(y_2 - y_1)^2 + (x_2 - x_1)^2 = d^2$$
$$d = \sqrt{(y_2 - y_1) + (x_2 - x_1)}$$

Having attended to these preliminaries, you can then ascertain the distance between any two points on a line in a fairly ready manner. Assume, for example, that you begin with two ordered pairs $(2, -3)$ and $(4, 7)$. You substitute these values into the primary terms of the equation:

$$\Delta y = 7 - (-3) = 10$$
$$\Delta x^2 = 4 - 2 = 2$$
$$d = \sqrt{10^2 + 2^2}$$
$$d = \sqrt{104}$$

Exercise Set 7.3

Use these ordered pairs with the distance formula to find the distance between points.

a. (1, 0) (13, 4)

b. (2, 1) (14, 9)

c. (0, 4) (10, 16)

d. (0, 0) (2, 10)

e. (1, 2) (13, 8)

Perpendicular Lines

Figure 7.2 provides an illustration of a basic linear function $y = 3x + 2$. The y-intercept is 2. The slope is 3. The line extends upward into quadrant I since the slope is positive. You see three coordinates on the line, the top of which is (2, 8). At the same time, the graph features a second line, one that slopes downward into quadrant IV. This second line runs perpendicular to the first line. It intersects the x axis at (6, 0).

To create an equation that generates a line that is perpendicular to another line, consider in Figure 7.2 the equation that generates the line with the positive slope. The y-intercept is at (0, 2). The line slopes up into quadrant I. In addition to this

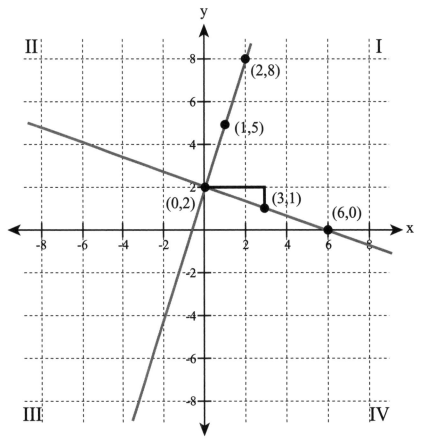

Figure 7.2
The inverse creates a perpendicular line.

line, you see another line. The second line has a negative slope. It slopes downward, into quadrant IV. It passes through the y-intercept (0, 2). Among the points in its path are (3, 1) and, as mentioned previously, (6, 0). The second line is perpendicular to the line with the positive slope.

To investigate the features of the perpendicular line, consider the expression you use to determine the slope of a line:

$$\frac{y_2 - y_1}{x_2 - x_1}$$

To make use of this expression, you can substitute the values given by the two ordered pairs as follows:

$$\frac{2 - 1}{0 - 3} = \frac{1}{-3}$$

This gives you the slope of the second line $(-\frac{1}{3})$, and given that you know the slope of the second line, you can then write the following slope-intercept equation:

$$y = -\frac{1}{3}x + 2$$

You then have at hand an equation you can use to determine the point at which the line crosses the x axis. Toward this end, you can rewrite the equation so that you set y to 0 and solve for x:

$$-\frac{1}{3}x + 2 = 0$$

$$-\frac{1}{3}x = -2$$

$$(-3)\left(-\frac{1}{3}\right)x = (-2)(-3)$$

$$x = 6$$

To explore this notion from a slightly different perspective, here is an equation that provides the following negative slope:

$$y = \frac{-2}{3}x + 4$$

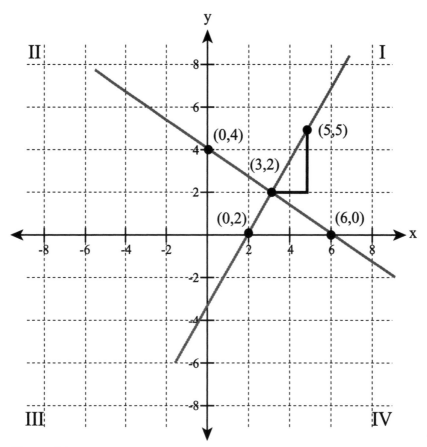

Figure 7.3
The multiplicative inverse of the slope allows you to generate a perpendicular line.

As Figure 7.3 indicates, the y-intercept for this line is (0, 4). If you solve the equation for the point at which the line crosses the x axis, you arrive at (6, 0). If you set x to 3 for this equation, you find that the value of y is 2.

To create a perpendicular line beginning at the coordinate (3, 2), you can an add 2 to the run value and 3 to the rise value. In other words, you invert the values you obtain from the original slope, and then add them to the original slope. This gives you a point at (5, 5). Now you draw a line from the your initial set of coordinates to your new set of coordinates. You can then find a slope for the new line. You proceed along this path:

$$m = \frac{y_2 - y_1}{x_2 - x_1} = \frac{5 - 2}{5 - 3} = \frac{3}{2}$$

The multiplicative inverse of $\frac{3}{2}$ is $\frac{2}{3}$. Your first slope was $-\frac{2}{3}$, however, so when you carry out the multiplication, you end up with -1.

$$\frac{-2}{3} \cdot \frac{3}{2} = -1$$

Exercise Set 7.4

Write the equations for the lines perpendicular to the given lines.

a. $y = \dfrac{3}{4}x + 2$

b. $y = 3x - 2$

c. $y = \dfrac{1}{4}x + 3$

d. $y = \dfrac{2}{3}x + 2$

e. $y = -3x$

Determine whether each set of equations represents perpendicular lines.

f. $y = 4x - 5,$
$4y = 8 - x$

g. $2x - 5y = -3,$
$2x + 5y = 4$

h. $y = 5 - 3x,$
$-y + 3x = 8$

i. $x - 2y = 5,$
$2x + 4y = 8$

j. $2x + 3y = 1,$
$3x - 2y = 1$

Depicting Absolute Values

You can view a given absolute value as representing two values, one positive and one negative. Consider, for example, that you begin with an equation such as $y = |x|$. If you solve this equation for values ranging from 0 to 14, you end up with the graph Figure 7.4 illustrates. The values of x extend in positive and negative directions that reflect distances of the value from zero. The distances can be negative or positive.

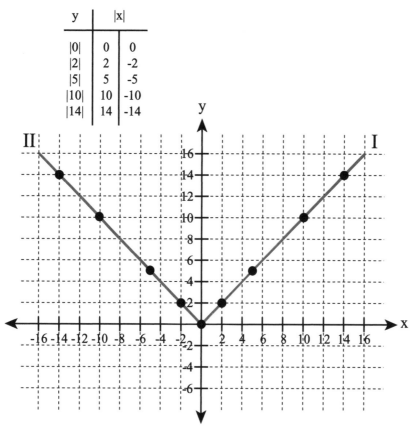

y		|x|
|0|	0	0
|2|	2	-2
|5|	5	-5
|10|	10	-10
|14|	14	-14

Figure 7.4
The graph of an absolute value rises to the left and right of the y axis.

When you create a graph in which the points are at equal positions across a given line, they are symmetric with respect to the line. For example in Figure 7.4, the y axis is a line of symmetry for the two values you generate as you work with the absolute values of x. You can also refer to points you generate in this way as reflections of each other. As reflections, they are *mirrored* across the y axis.

Translation and Shift

You can alter functions that incorporate absolute values so that you move your graph along the x or y axis. This activity is known as translation. To see how this is so, consider again the equation used to generate a graph that is symmetrical to the y axis (see Figure 7.4):

$$f(x) = |x|$$

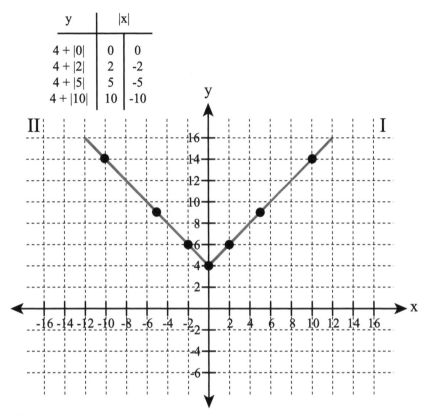

y	$|x|$	
$4 + |0|$	0	0
$4 + |2|$	2	-2
$4 + |5|$	5	-5
$4 + |10|$	10	-10

Figure 7.5
Translation preserves the symmetry of the graph across the y axis.

If you add a value to the absolute value of x, you can move the resulting graph up or down the y axis. A positive value moves it up. A negative value moves it down. To see how this is so, consider an equation that involves translating the graph up by 4:

$$y = 4 + |x|$$

Even if x is a negative value, the absolute value sign makes it positive. For this reason, adding 4 to the value of x always increases the corresponding y value by 4. As Figure 7.5 illustrates, on both the positive and negative sides of the y axis, then, the slope of the line remains consistent but is shifted upward. Both lines are translated in a consistent, symmetrical way.

As Figure 7.5 reveals, adding a value to the absolute value of x, you translate coordinates vertically upward. On the other hand, if the value you add is negative, the translation moves the line downward.

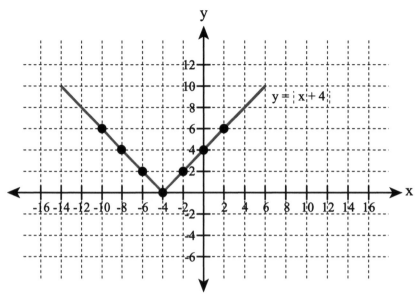

Figure 7.6
The expression |x + 4| translates the graphs to the left.

Horizontal translation differs from vertical translation because the addition or subtraction you perform is within the absolute value signs. You are changing the value of *x,* as such, before you determine its absolute value. The effect of such an addition is that you move along the *x* axis to the right if you subtract a value. You move to the left if you add a value.

This equation shifts the graph to the left:

$$y = |x + 4|$$

This equation shifts the graph to the right:

$$y = |x - 4|$$

For Figure 7.6, you replace *x* with the expression x + 4. This activity moves to graph to the left.

Exercise Set 7.5

Graph the results of the following equations.

a. $y = 3 + |x|$

b. $y = -2 + |3|$

c. $y = (-3)|4|$

d. $y = \left| \dfrac{4}{3}x \right|$

e. $y = |4 + x|$

Slopes

If you change the slopes of functions that involve absolute values, you still preserve the symmetry of the lines that result. Consider, for example, the effect of altering the value of the slope from $\frac{1}{2}$ to 2. Here are the resulting functions:

$$f(x) = (2)|x|$$

$$f(x) = \left(\dfrac{1}{2}\right)|x|$$

For the first equation, when you set the slope to 2, for every 1 unit of run, you generate 2 units of rise. On the other hand, when the slope is $\frac{1}{2}$ for every 1 unit of run, you generate only half a unit of rise. When you explore these slopes with respect to absolute values, then the lines illustrated by Figure 7.7 result.

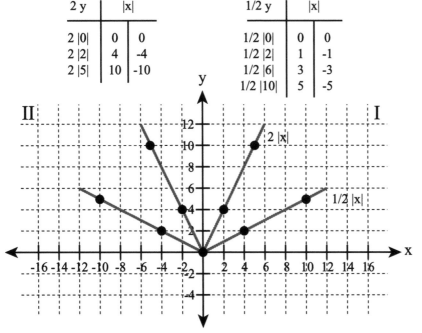

2 y	$|x|$	
2 |0|	0	0
2 |2|	4	-4
2 |5|	10	-10

1/2 y	$|x|$	
1/2 |0|	0	0
1/2 |2|	1	-1
1/2 |6|	3	-3
1/2 |10|	5	-5

Figure 7.7
Slopes sustain symmetry.

More on Symmetry

When you work with functions that involve absolute values, the slopes of lines allow them to be symmetric relative to either the y axis or some other line. Such a line is known as the line of reflection. As is evident from the discussion of lines generated with absolute values, you can create a set of such lines such that each point on one line corresponds to a point on another line. When you create such sets of lines, you can mirror them horizontally, vertically, or at other angles. If you mirror them horizontally, they are symmetric with respect to the x axis. If you mirror them vertically, the are symmetric with respect to the y axis.

A parabola provides a mirrored graph that you create with an equation that is not linear. A parabola provides a graphical form that you can manipulate in largely the same ways that you manipulate the mirrored lines of an equation containing absolute values. Here are equations that create parabolas mirrored across the y and x axes:

$$x^2 = y \qquad \text{Generates a line mirrored across the } y \text{ axis.}$$
$$y^2 = x \qquad \text{Generates a line mirrored across the } x \text{ axis.}$$

Figure 7.8 illustrates lines you can generate from these two equations.

Note

A parabola that is symmetrical to the x axis is not properly a function if you apply the horizontal line rule.

Alternate Forms of Symmetry

The use of an even-numbered exponent in the previous section resulted in parabolas that are symmetrical across an axis. Yet another form of symmetry occurs when you use an odd-numbered exponent. In this case, the graph that results is symmetrical to a given point. The origin of the Cartesian plane lies at point (0,0). You can draw many geometrical figures that are symmetrical to this point. Drawn symmetrical to this point, a line is said to be symmetrical to the origin.

Figure 7.9 illustrates a line generated using the cube of x, (x^3). The line slopes down from quadrant I, across the origin, and into quadrant III. The points you map in the two quadrants mirror each other, but the coordinate pairs in quadrant III contain negative x and y values while those in quadrant I do not. The resulting graph is symmetrical with respect to the origin.

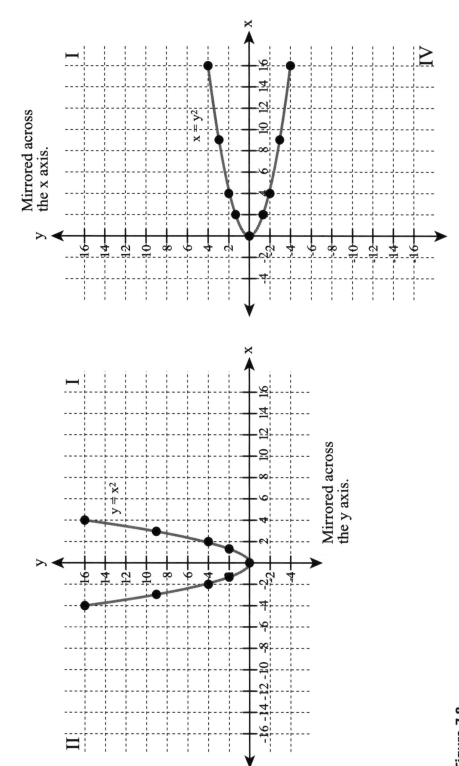

Figure 7.8
Exponents generate lines mirrored across the *x* and *y* axes.

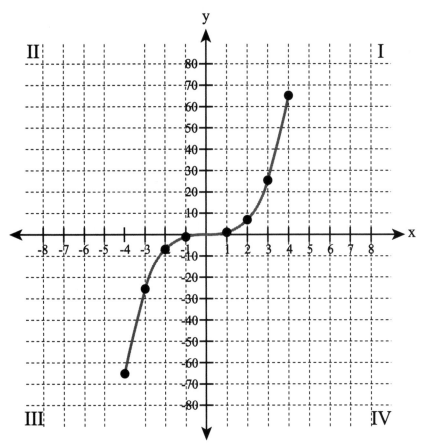

Figure 7.9
A cube generates a line symmetrical to the origin.

Exercise Set 7.6

Plot coordinate pairs for these equations and determine whether they are symmetrical to the x axis, the y axis, or a point.

   a. $2y = x^2 + 6$

   b. $4y = 4x^2 - 3$

   c. $2y^3 = 3x^2$

   d. $4y = 5x + 4$

   e. $3y^2 + 4 = x^2$

Inverses Generally

In previous sections, you have explored how the multiplicative inverse of a slope creates a line that is perpendicular to the line the slope defines. When a function is the inverse of another function, the situation differs. In such a case, as Figure 7.10 illustrates, the values of the x and y coordinates that make up the

$4y + 4x = 6$	$4x + 4y = 6$
(-0.5, 1)	(1, -0.5)
(-1.5, 3)	(3, -1.5)
(-3.5, 5)	(5, -3.5)
(-8.5, 10)	(10, -8.5)

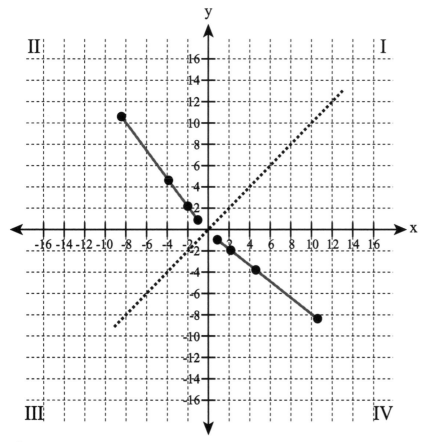

Figure 7.10
Equations that are the inverse of each other generate inverted ordered pairs.

coordinate pairs of the two lines occur in reversed order. Rather than being perpendicular to each other, the lines are symmetrical.

At the top of Figure 7.10, there is a table in which the coordinate pairs on the left are the reverse of those on the right. Above the table you see equations that represent the inverses of each other. The graph shows the two lines.

When you solve the inverse equations using the set of values, the lines that you generate mirror each other. The line of symmetry can be identified if you use the equation $y=x$, as the dashed line in Figure 7.10 reveals.

Exercise Set 7.7

Plot values for the following equations to determine if the lines that result are symmetrical to the line you get when you plot $x=y$.

a. $x + y = 6$

b. $3x + 3y = 5$

c. $yx = 12$

d. $xy = 4$

e. $y = |x|$

Using Visual Formula

Use Visual Formula to implement a linear equation involving an absolute value. Toward this end, generate a graph that shifts the vertex of the graph to the left on the x axis 4 units. Here is the equation that accomplishes this task:

$$y = |4 + x|$$

To implement the equation, refer to Figure 7.11 and use the following steps:

1. Double click the menu item for absolute values (‖ Abs). Then click in the equation composition area to position the absolute value bars. Use the mouse cursor to pull the bars for the absolute value area far enough apart to accommodate two value fields and a plus sign (see Figure 7.11).

2. Click the Value menu item. Position the field just to the right of the left absolute value bar. Click in the field and type 4.

3. Click the Add menu item and position the plus sign to the right of the Value field.

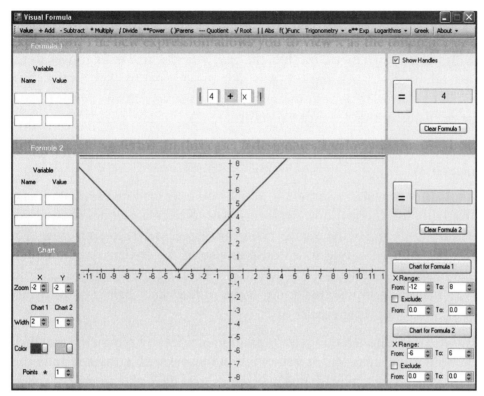

Figure 7.11
Adding to the number inside the absolute value bars shifts the graph to the left.

4. Click the Value menu item again and position the field after the plus sign and inside the absolute value bars. Click in the field and type *x*.

5. In the lower part of the Visual Formula window, move the cursor to the top of the Cartesian plane so that it turns into parallel bars. Pull the Cartesian plane up until it is even with the bottom of the top equation composition area.

6. In the lower-right panel find the From and To fields for the X Range setting beneath the Chart for Formula 1 button. Click the To control and set the value to −12. Click the From control and set the value to 8.

7. In the lower-left-panel, find the Zoom label. Click the controls for the X and Y fields for the Zoom label, and set both fields to −2.

8. In the Chart 1 area, set the Width field to 2.

9. Click the Chart for Formula 1 button. You see the graph shown in Figure 7.11.

To experiment, insert the following values in the field preceding the plus sign and observe the results: 2, 3, 5, 6. In each instance, the distance you shift the graph to the left on the x axis changes. To shift the graph so that its vertex moves to the right, use values of -2, -3, and -6. As you go, remember to click on the Chart for Formula 1 button to refresh the graph each time you change a value. Also, increase the value of the X Range To control to 12.

Conclusion

This chapter has provided a context in which you have explored several types of work related to linear equations. Exploring how to calculate slopes allowed you to gain a stronger sense of the way that coordinate pairs relate to each other. You extended this understanding to encompass use of the Pythagorean theorem, which allowed you to calculate the distances separating points on a line. From there, you moved on to investigate the slopes of lines and their inverses, which enabled you to find perpendicular lines.

You also worked with such things as translation of lines and symmetry, and these activities will prove important as you move on to work with quadratic and other equations. When you explored absolute values, you were able to generate symmetrical lines by mirroring positive and negative values. In your explorations of symmetry relative to points, axes, and lines, you saw that if you generate values that are the square of x, you arrive at a line that is symmetrical to the y axis. If you generate values that are the cube of x, you arrive at a line that is symmetrical to the *origin* of the Cartesian plane. Still other lines are symmetrical to the line you create with the equation $x = y$.

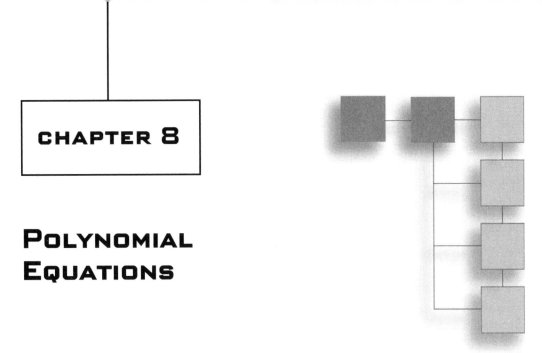

CHAPTER 8

POLYNOMIAL EQUATIONS

In this chapter, you examine a number of operations you can perform to solve polynomial equations. To start things off, you review the definition of a polynomial. To identify polynomials, you also examine monomial, binomial, and trinomial expressions. Given a basic definition of what counts as a polynomial, you then proceed to work with different operations that pertain to polynomials. Among the more involved of these operations are those dealing with multiplication and division. One approach to dividing one polynomial by another involves using long division. Among helpful approaches to multiplication is the FOIL approach. Along with the FOIL approach, it is helpful to be familiar with equations dealing with the sums and differences of binomials. Among the topics covered in this chapter are the following:

- Why a monomial usually does not feature a negative exponent

- Working with curves characteristic of nonlinear functions

- Terms that are important to know when you work with polynomials

- How to use a model from arithmetic to perform multiplication

- Dealing with terms in a formalized manner

- How to use long division for polynomials

Polynomials

Polynomials constitute what you can regard as a superset that contains other types of expressions, such as monomials, binomials, and trinomials. A monomial consists of a constant coefficient and a single variable. The coefficient must be a real number. The variable often possesses an exponent. If it does, then the exponent must be an integer, and it may not be negative. Here are a few examples of monomials:

$$5x^2, \quad 2x^2, \quad -2, \quad 0, \quad 3x^4, \quad 2$$

Monomials are polynomials, as are binomials and trinomials. A binomial consists of two monomials. A trinomial consists of three monomials. A polynomial, generally, can consist of a monomial or a combination of monomials. If you combine monomials to create a polynomial, you use only addition and subtraction to do so. To put it differently, a polynomial provides a sum or difference of monomials, not the quotient or a product. Here are some examples of polynomials:

$$2x^2 + 2x, \quad 15a^3 + 2a, \quad 15a^3, \quad a^3, \quad -15a, \quad 6x + \frac{1}{2}x, \quad 0$$

Adding or subtracting monomials creates a polynomial. If you multiply or divide monomials, however, you do not create a polynomial. Also, if the variable in an expression contains a negative number, then it is not considered a monomial. Here are a few examples of terms that are not monomials or polynomials:

$$\frac{1}{x} + 2x, \qquad \frac{2x}{x^2 + 3}, \qquad \frac{2 + x}{2 - x}$$

In the first expression, $1/x$ represents a negative exponent (x^{-1}). The second expression contains two monomial expressions ($2x$ and $x^2 + 3$), but dividing one by the other does not create a relation based on addition and subtraction. With the third example, the situation is the same. Although the expression includes two monomials, the relation between them is that of division.

Exercise Set 8.1

Determine whether the following expressions constitute polynomials, monomials, or neither polynomials nor monomials.

a. $\frac{1}{2}x^2 + 2x^2$

b. $3x$

c. $3x^{-2}$

d. $\dfrac{a+2}{a+2}$

e. $\dfrac{1}{3x^2}$

f. $-9x^2$

g. 17

h. $s^3 + 4$

i. $4x^3 - 2x^2 + \dfrac{1}{x}$

j. $6a + 7$

Working with Polynomials

Given a review of how to identify a polynomial, it is also appropriate to review a few of the characteristic activities you perform in association with polynomials. First, when you replace the variable in a polynomial with a number, you find the *value* of the polynomial. Along the same lines, when you employ operations to determine the value of the variable in a polynomial, then you *evaluate* the polynomial.

When you state a polynomial so that you represent the variable of the polynomial on one side of an equal sign, and then place another variable on the other side to represent the value of the polynomial, then you create a *polynomial equation*. Many of the equations you have dealt with in preceding chapters have been, in this respect, polynomial equations.

As you have seen repeatedly, to evaluate such an equation, a standard approach involves supplying a value to the variable of the expression, and then solving the equation for the value of the variable. The value of the equation corresponds to the value of the variable, so in this way, you create an ordered pair. When you have generated two or more ordered pairs in this way, you can plot them in the Cartesian plane to create a graph of the equation.

In previous chapters, you have extensively explored graphs of linear equations. In a few instances, you explored graphs that did not involve linear equations. As mentioned previously, a linear equation generates a line that possesses a slope that does not change. In contrast, a non-linear equation generates a line that possesses a slope that does change.

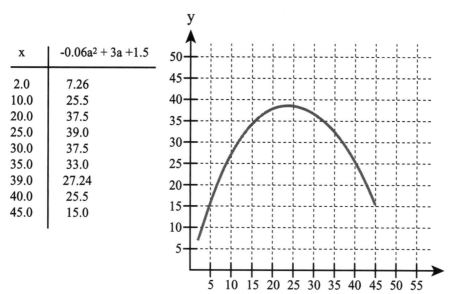

x	$-0.06a^2 + 3a + 1.5$
2.0	7.26
10.0	25.5
20.0	37.5
25.0	39.0
30.0	37.5
35.0	33.0
39.0	27.24
40.0	25.5
45.0	15.0

Figure 8.1
A polynomial establishes a hypothetical trend for the effect of a mosquito repellent.

To review the notion of a changing slope, consider Figure 8.1. To generate the values for the graph shown in the figure, you use this equation:

$$0.06a^2 + 3a + 1.5$$

As the figure illustrates, the curve that results from calculating representative values of x creates something akin to an arc tracing the path of an arrow. Along its ascending path, the slope is consistent and resembles that of the graph of a linear equation. Then the path changes and with it the slope. The slope evens out and then turns downward.

The graph of this polynomial might represent the effectiveness of a given brand of mosquito repellent in relation to the number of hours that elapse after you apply it. Accordingly, for the first few hours, the number of mosquitoes that alight and immediately retreat without biting increases consistently. After around 25 hours, however, this trend changes. At a declining rate, the mosquitoes fail to retreat, and the trend shows that after roughly 50 hours, the effects of the repellent completely disappear.

A polynomial function allows you to trace such changing trends because its slope does not remain consistent throughout its extent. In the instance of the mosquito repellent, the slope changes from one moving in a positive direction to one moving in a negative direction. It shows a trend characterized by a moment of maximum effectiveness preceded and followed by periods of increasing and declining effectiveness.

Solving Equations

In previous chapters, when you have solved equations, you have put to work a variety of tools that have allowed you to manipulate the expressions and terms equations contain. These tools can be brought forward and extended as you solve polynomial equations. Table 8.1 lists a few of the fundamental concepts you work with as you solve polynomial equations. Subsequent sections of this chapter elaborate on these concepts.

Addition and Subtraction Activities

When you add the terms that a polynomial contains, one of the first steps is to group like terms. Like terms identify what you are adding. Here is an equation with like terms:

$$2x + 3x$$

In this instance, the terms of the equation constitute like terms because each term consists of the variable x. Each of the like terms is associated with an integer coefficient. To solve for x, you put the distributive property to work:

$$(2 + 3)x = 5x$$

Here is an extended example of the same type of operation:

$$\begin{aligned}
6x + 7x &- 4x + 8x - x \\
&= (6x + 7x) - 4x + 8x - x \\
&= (13x - 4x) + 8x - x \\
&= (9x + 8x) - x \\
&= (17x - x) \\
&= 16x
\end{aligned}$$

For each step, you successively group like terms, and then carry out additions or subtractions. In the end, you have combined all terms in the polynomial and are left with the final term.

Table 8.1 Concepts Related to Solving Polynomial Equations

Practice	Discussion
Addition	The addition property allows that if you begin with an equation such as $a = b$, then you can add equal values to both sides of the equation: $a + c = b + c$.
Multiplication	The multiplication property allows that if you begin with an equation such as $a = b$, then you can multiply both sides of the equation by equal values to obtain an equivalent equation: $a \times c = b \times c$. When you multiply the sides of an equation by an expression that contains a variable, you must take a few precautions. One involves checking whether you are multiplying by a value that is equal to zero.
Coefficients	With a term such as $3a^2$, the constant (3) preceding the variable a is the coefficient of the term. In a polynomial, you often find several coefficients for any given variable: $4b^2 + 3b^3 + 4b^4$. In this polynomial, you find three coefficients for three separate instances of the variable b.
Like Terms	If you find terms that are raised to the same power, such terms are *like terms*. You can also refer to them as *similar terms*.
Degrees	The degree of a term is the value of its exponent. For the term $3x^5$, the variable x possesses an exponent of 5, and this is the degree of the term. For the term $3x$, the degree is 1. Each term of a polynomial that contains a variable also possesses a degree. When a polynomial contains several terms, each with a different degree, then the degree of the polynomial is the largest degree of the constituent terms. For example, with $3x^2 + 4x^3 + 3x^4$, the degree of the polynomial is 4, because the highest degree of the terms is 4.
Order	You can organize the terms in a polynomial according to ascending or descending order. To organize the terms of a polynomial in ascending order, begin on the left with the term that contains the smallest exponent ($3x^2 + 4x^3 + 3x^4$). To organize the terms of a polynomial in descending order, begin on the left with the term that contains the largest exponent ($3x^4 + 4x^3 + 3x^2$).
Zero Products	If you begin with two numbers, and one of the numbers is equal to 0, then the product is zero. Along the same lines, if you start with either $a = 0$ or $b = 0$, then you can create an equivalent equation that reads $ab = 0$.
Missing Terms	If you want to write expressions in standard ways, you can use the coefficient 0 to identify terms that are absent or missing from a polynomial. For example, you can rewrite $a^2 + a^4 + a^5$ as $a^2 + 0a^3 + a^4 + a^5$.
Classification	A polynomial consisting of one term is a monomial. A polynomial consisting of two terms is a binomial. A polynomial consisting of three terms is a trinomial.

You can also group terms with exponents. Here are a couple of expressions that you can more easily view as monomials if you combine the like terms they contain:

$$x^2 \cdot x^5 = x^{2+5} = x^7 \qquad \text{Add the exponents with the same base value.}$$
$$x^3 \cdot x^{-2} = x^{3-2} = x^1 = x$$

If you consider that the commutative and associate properties of numbers allow you to express exponents in different ways, you can extend the work you perform by grouping like terms. Consider this expression:

$$6x^2y \cdot 8xy^3$$
$$6 \cdot 8 \cdot x^2 x^1 \cdot y^1 y^3 \quad \text{Group like terms.}$$
$$48x^3y^4$$

Here is an example that incorporates negative exponents. While the grouping creates a fraction, it still serves to simplify the terms:

$$-2xy^{-4} \cdot 5x^3y = (-2 \cdot 5)(x^1 x^3)(y^{-4} y^1)$$
$$= -10x^4 y^{-3} = \frac{-10x^4}{y^3} \quad \text{Rewrite to make the negative exponent positive.}$$

Using the distributive property, you can regroup like terms along the following lines:

$$6x^1 y^2 (3x^4 - 5xy^2)$$
$$= 6x^1 y^2 (3x^4) - 6x^1 y^2 (5x^1 y^2) \quad \text{Distribute the multiplications.}$$
$$= 18x^5 y^2 - 30x^2 y^4$$

With this expression, you begin by using the distributive property to extract the terms beginning with the coefficients 3 and 5 from the parentheses. You can then group the resulting line terms and multiply the variables. To perform the multiplications, you add the exponents.

Note

You employ an exponent of 1 (x^1) to make operations clearer. Normally, you do not need to use an exponent of 1 because a number with an exponent of 1 equals itself ($x = x^1$).

Multiplication and Division Activities

When you approach situations in which you must divide one polynomial by another, grouping like terms allows you to use the properties of exponents more readily. Often, such work begins with expressions or terms that involve combinations of positive and negative exponents. Here is such an expression.

$$\frac{18x^5y^{-3}}{3x^{-4}y^2}$$

$$\frac{18}{3} \cdot \frac{x^5}{x^{-4}} \cdot \frac{y^{-3}}{y^2}$$ Rearrange so that like terms are visible.

$$6 \cdot x^{5-(-4)} \cdot y^{-3-2}$$ Rearrange so that you can perform operations.

$$6 \cdot x^9 \cdot y^{-5}$$

$$\frac{6x^9}{y^5}$$ Rearrange to remove the negative exponent.

In each step above, you avoid most of the complexity the division might involve by rearranging the expression so that you can carry out the divisions using exponential arithmetic.

Here is another expression that involves exponents. In this instance, the numerator contains a binomial that you approach by making the denominator explicit for each of the terms in the binomial.

$$\frac{6x^2y^3 - 4x^5y}{2xy^3}$$

$$= \frac{6x^2y^3}{2xy^3} - \frac{4x^5y}{2xy^3}$$ Distribute the division.

$$= \frac{6}{2}(x^{2-1}y^{3-3}) - \frac{4}{2}(x^{5-1}y^{1-3})$$ Rearrange with negative exponent.

$$= 3x - 2(x^4y^{-2})$$ Carry out the divisions.

$$= 3x - \frac{2x^4}{y^2}$$ Rearrange to remove the negative exponent.

Here is another problem that appears involved until you rearrange its terms so that you can view them in relative isolation:

$$\frac{2x^2y^3z}{6x^3y^5z^{-3}} \times \frac{8x^1y^{-4}z^{-5}}{10x^2y^3}$$

$$\frac{(2\cdot8)(x^2x^1)(y^3y^{-4})z^1z^{-5}}{(6\cdot10)(x^3x^2)(y^5y^3)(z^{-3})} \qquad \text{Group like terms.}$$

$$\frac{16x^{2+1}y^{3-4}z^{1-5}}{60x^{3+2}y^{5+3}z^{-3}} \qquad \text{Perform multiplications.}$$

$$\frac{16x^3y^{-1}z^{-4}}{60x^5y^8z^{-3}} \qquad \text{Simplify.}$$

$$\frac{16}{60}\cdot\frac{x^3}{x^5}\cdot\frac{y^{-1}}{y^8}\cdot\frac{z^{-4}}{z^{-3}} \qquad \text{Group like terms.}$$

$$\frac{4}{15}\cdot x^{3-5}\cdot y^{-1-8}\cdot z^{-4-(-3)} \qquad \text{Perform divisions.}$$

$$\frac{4}{15}\cdot x^{-2}\cdot y^{-9}\cdot z^{-1} \qquad \text{Simplify.}$$

$$\frac{4}{15x^2y^9z^1} \qquad \text{Remove negative exponents.}$$

To work with this problem, you proceed in two distinct phases. For the first phase, you group like terms and carry out the multiplications. For the second phase, you again group like terms, but this time you carry out the divisions.

Monomial and Binomial Expressions

As emphasized previously, the distributive property proves important when carrying out multiplication operations. When you multiply a polynomial by an expression consisting of only one term, you apply the single term to each of the terms in the polynomial expression. Here is an example:

$$3x(4x + 2)$$
$$(3x)(4x) + 3x(2) \qquad \text{$3x$ applied to both of the terms in the binomial.}$$
$$12x^2 + 6x \qquad \text{Completing the multiplications.}$$

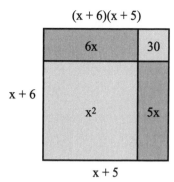

$(x+6)(x+5)$

Figure 8.2
Blocks allow you to visualize the values involved in a multiplication problem.

When you work with binomial expressions, the same practice applies. You must apply both of the terms in the first expression to both of the terms in the second expression. A common form of binomial multiplication problem involves two binomials that add terms:

$(x+6)(x+5)$ Binomial expressions.

$x(x+5)+6(x+5)$ Distribute the multiplications.

$x^2+5x+6x+30$ Carry out the multiplications.

$x^2+11x+30$ Simplify.

As Figure 8.2 illustrates, you can visualize a binomial multiplication problem if you use a series of blocks to represent the values the multiplication involves.

You also commonly encounter binomial problems in which the first expression adds terms, while the second expression subtracts one term from another. You employ the same procedure as before. Using distribution, you multiply each term in the second expression by each term in the first:

$(5m+4)(m-3)$

$5m(m)-5m(3)+4(m)-4(3)$

$5m^2-15m+4m-12$

$5m^2-11m-12$

In this instance, the two middle terms are of opposite signs, and whether the final middle term is positive depends on the values of the terms combined.

A third form of binomial that occurs commonly involves two expressions that are characterized by subtraction. Here is an example:

$$(3x - 5)(4x - 3)$$
$$3x(4x) - 3x(3) - 5(4x) - (5)(-3)$$
$$12x^2 - 9x - 20x + 15$$
$$12x^2 - 29x + 15$$

In such expressions, the multiplication of a negative by a negative value generates a positive value. The middle term, likewise, is negative, because when you create the values for the middle term, you combine two negative terms.

Sums, Differences, and Squares

Table 8.2 provides a summary of operations involving a few of the most common forms of binomial expressions. The discussion that follows examines a few expressions that illustrate the application of these generalized approaches to working with binomials.

As an illustration of the product of the sum and difference of the same binomial, consider this expression:

$$(m + 3)(m - 3)$$
$$= m^2 - 3m + 3m - 9 \quad \text{The middle terms cancel out.}$$
$$= m^2 - 9 \quad\quad\quad\quad\quad \text{The difference of the squares remains.}$$

Here is an example of the square of the sum of two terms:

$$(m + 3)^2$$
$$= m(m) + 3m + 3m + 3(3)$$
$$= m^2 + 6m + 9$$

Table 8.2 Sums, Differences, and Squares

Item	Discussion
$(a - b)(a + b) = a^2 - b^2$	The product of the sum and the difference of the same two terms consists of the square of the second term subtracted from the square of the first term.
$(a + b)^2 = a^2 + 2ab + b^2$	The square of the sum of two terms consists of the sum of the square of the first term, twice the product of the two terms, and the square of the second term.
$(a - b)^2 = a^2 - 2ab + b^2$	The square of the difference of two terms consists of the square of the first term minus twice the product of the first and second terms, plus the square of the second term.

Finally, here is an example of the square of the difference of two terms:

$$(m - 3)^2$$
$$= (m - 3)(m - 3)$$
$$= m(m) - 3m - 3m + 3(3)$$
$$= m^2 - 6m + 9$$

Exercise Set 8.2

Identify each expression as a sum, difference, or square (see Table 8.2).

a. $(x^2 + 1)(x^2 - 1)$

b. $(4x + 3)(4x^2 - 3)$

c. $(3m^2 + 2)^2$

d. $(3m^2 - 2)^2$

e. $(6 + \frac{1}{2})^2$

FOIL Strategies

As the examples in the previous section reveal, you can proceed methodically when you multiply binomial terms. The most universally adopted method in this respect is identified with the acronym FOIL (First, Outer, Inner, and Last). Figure 8.3 illustrates how the FOIL approach to multiplication works.

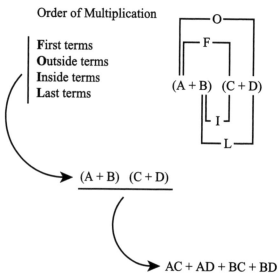

Order of Multiplication

First terms
Outside terms
Inside terms
Last terms

$(A + B) \quad (C + D)$

$(A + B) \quad (C + D)$

$AC + AD + BC + BD$

Figure 8.3
The FOIL approach allows you to work more effectively with multiplication of binomials.

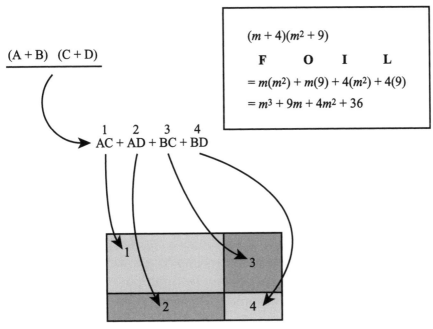

Figure 8.4
A set of rectangles allows you to visualize the FOIL approach.

As an example of the application of the FOIL technique of multiplying binomials, consider this problem:

$$(m + 4)(m^2 + 9)$$

$$\text{F} \qquad \text{O} \qquad \text{I} \qquad \text{L}$$

$$= m(m^2) + m(9) + 4(m^2) + 4(9)$$

$$= m^3 + 9m + 4m^2 + 36$$

Figure 8.4 illustrates the relationships that exist between the values generated using the FOIL approach and the areas of a rectangle that represent the values.

Polynomial Multiplication

When you explore multiplication of polynomials consisting of trinomial expressions, the process does not vary from those of other types of polynomial multiplications, but they do become more involved. Here is a multiplication problem involving a binomial and a trinomial. You must multiply each term of the first expression by each term of the second expression.

$(x^2 + 3x - 4)(2x^2 + 3)$	Trinomial and binomial.
$x^2(2x^2 + 3) + 3x(2x^2 + 3) - 4(2x^2 + 3)$	Distribution.
$x^2(2x^2) + x^2(3) + 3x(2x^2) + 3x(3) - 4(2x^2) - 4(3)$	Multiplying.
$2x^4 + 3x^2 + 6x^3 + 9x - 8x^2 - 12$	Collect terms.
$2x^4 + 6x^3 + 3x^2 - 8x^2 + 9x - 12$	Group like terms.
$2x^4 + 6x^3 - 5x^2 + 9x - 12$	Simplify.

When you deal with polynomials that consist of several terms, you can use approaches drawn from arithmetic. When you use such approaches, ordering the terms in a polynomial by degree constitutes an important step. You can then arrange the expressions in columns and carry out the multiplications. Here is an example involving a trinomial and a binomial:

$$4x^2y - 3xy + 2y$$

$$\underline{ xy + 3y}$$

$8x^2y^2 - 9xy^2 + 6y^2$	Multiply by the $3y$.
$\underline{3x^3y^2 - 3x^2y^2 + 2xy^2}$	Then multiply by xy.
$3x^3y^2 - 5x^2y^2 - 7xy^2 + 6y^2$	Add the products.

Exercise Set 8.3

Solve each equation.

a. $4x^5 \cdot 4x^3$

b. $3n^2 \cdot (2n + 3)$

c. $-2x^2(2x - 2)$

d. $(2z^2 + 2)(3z^2 + 4)$

e. $(3t^2 - 3)(t^2 + 2t + 5)$

f. $(a + 4)(a + 4)$

g. $(2a - 1)(3a + 1)$

h. $(3z^2 - 2)(z^4 - 2)$

i. $(-5t^3)(t^2 + 5t + 25)$

j. $(a + 1)(a^2 - a + 1)$

Reviewing Long Division

You can perform division operations involving polynomial expressions using the procedures employed for long division in arithmetic. Here is a typical progression of steps for a long division problem involving whole numbers.

$$
\begin{array}{r}
2 \\
41{\overline{\smash{\big)}\,8642}} \\
-8200 \\
\hline
442
\end{array}
$$

You divide 8600 by 41. It goes 200 times. To indicate that it goes 200 times, you place the 2 in the hundreds place. You multiply 41 by 200 and subtract the product from 8642.

$$
\begin{array}{r}
21 \\
41{\overline{\smash{\big)}\,8642}} \\
-8200 \\
\hline
442 \\
-410 \\
\hline
32
\end{array}
$$

You divide 442 by 41. It goes 10 times. To indicate that it goes 10 times, you place the 1 in the tens place. You multiply 41 by 10 and subtract the product from 442.

$$
\begin{array}{r}
210 \\
41{\overline{\smash{\big)}\,8642}} \\
-8200 \\
\hline
442 \\
-410 \\
\hline
32
\end{array}
$$

At this point, you discover that you cannot divide 32 by 41 and produce a whole number. For this reason, you place a 0 in the 1's place. To indicate that the division has resulted in a remainder, you show a fraction of 32/41.

Long Division in Algebra

When you perform divisions involving polynomials, you use an approach similar to the one you employ for arithmetic. To perform such divisions, you group like terms and combine them. You also order the terms relative to their degree in descending order. Likewise, it is helpful if you remove fractions and in other respects simplify the expressions as much as possible before attempting the division.

As an example of a polynomial division problem, consider this expression:

$$\frac{2x^2 + 3x + 7}{x + 3}$$

The terms in the numerator appear in descending order with respect to the degrees of their exponents. In this case, the largest degree is that of the square of x. The same applies to the terms of the denominator, where the highest degree is 1.

To set up the division, you proceed in the same manner you did when you performed long division involving whole numbers:

$$x + 3 \overline{)\, 2x^2 + 3x + 7} \quad \overset{2x}{}$$

To perform the division, you concentrate first on the term with the exponent of the highest degree. Carrying out such a division is analogous to long division in arithmetic. You can envision 8642 in this way:

$$8 \cdot 10^3 + 6 \cdot 10^2 + 4 \cdot 10^1 + 2 \cdot 10^0$$

In the previous section, for example, in essence you first divide 8×10^3 by 41. Ten raised to the power of 3 constituted the highest degree of ten as given in the problem. Having dealt with the highest degree of 10, you then move on to the second highest degree.

In this instance, you concentrate first on the highest power of x, which is 2. Isolating the terms involved, the division takes this form:

$$\frac{2x^2}{x} = 2x^{2-1} = 2x$$

You then multiply $x+3$ by $2x$ to arrive at the expression you subtract from the dividend. The multiplication proceeds as follows:

$$2x(x+3) = 2x^2 + 6x$$

Given this term, you then subtract the term from the dividend and find the remainder:

$$
\begin{array}{r}
2x \\
x+3{\overline{\smash{\big)}\,2x^2 + 3x + 7}} \\
-(2x^2 + 6x) \\
\hline
\end{array}
$$

To carry out the subtraction, it is necessary to consider the signs of the terms in the subtracted expression. To prevent errors, you can treat the subtraction as an addition problem and change the signs of all terms in the subtracted expression:

$$
\begin{array}{r}
2x \\
x+3{\overline{\smash{\big)}\,2x^2 + 3x + 7}} \\
+(-2x^2 - 6x) \\
\hline
-3x + 7
\end{array}
$$

You then carry out the next step, which involves dividing $-3x+7$ by $x+3$. To carry out this division, you again concentrate on x, this time with an exponent of 1:

$$\frac{-3x}{x} = -3$$

When you perform the long division, you multiply $x + 3$ by -3, to obtain $-3x - 9$:

$$
\begin{array}{r}
2x \;\; -3 \\
x+3{\overline{\smash{\big)}\,2x^2 + 3x + 7}} \\
+(-2x^2 - 6x) \\
\hline
-3x + 7 \\
+3x + 9 \\
\hline
16
\end{array}
$$

After you carry out the subtraction, the remainder in this instance is 16, so the answer is $2x - 3 + \frac{16}{x+3}$.

Exercise Set 8.4

Solve each equation using long division.

  a. $(2x^2 + 11x - 5) \div (x + 6)$

  b. $(a^2 + 4a - 12) \div (x - 2)$

  c. $(y^2 - 10y - 20) \div (y - 5)$

  d. $(3b^2 - 2b - 13) \div (b - 2)$

  e. $(12a^4 - 3a^2) \div (a - 3)$

Using Visual Formula

Use Visual Formula to test the values you generate when you square the sum of two terms. Here is the equation for working with the square of the sum of two terms:

$$(a + b)^2 = a^2 + 2ab + b^2$$

Assume that you are dealing with the expression $(3 + 4)^2$ and that you want to test whether both sides of the standard equation for quadratics of this type does, indeed, render equal values.

To implement the left side of the equation, refer to Figure 8.5 and use the following steps:

1. For starters, position the cursor on the top of the Cartesian plane. When it turns into parallel bars, pull the Cartesian plane down so that you do not see it. You are interested in this session only in the values that appear in the Solution panels on the right side of the equation composition areas.

2. Click the ( )Parens menu item and position the parentheses in the upper equation composition area. Pull the parentheses far enough apart to accommodate two fields and a plus sign.

3. Click the Value menu item. Position the field just to the right of the left parentheses. Click in this field and type 3.

4. Click the Add menu item and position the plus sign to the right of the Value field.

5. Click the Value menu item again and position the field after the plus sign and inside the closing parenthesis after the plus sign. Click in this field and type 4.

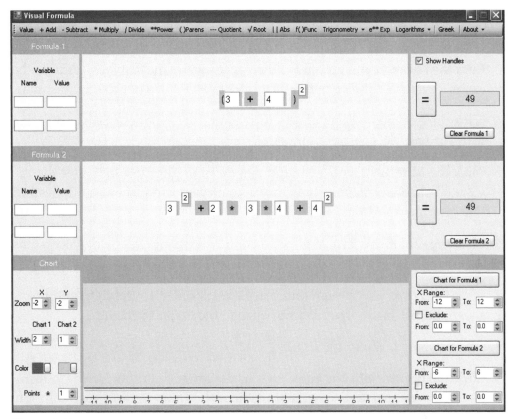

Figure 8.5
Confirm the equations used to work with the square of the sum of two terms.

6. Click the Power menu item and position the exponent field to the upper right of the closing parenthesis. By default, you see a 2 in this field. Do not change this value.

7. Click the equal button to the right of the upper composition field. You see 49 in the field.

Now implement the right side of the equation in the lower equation composition area. The form the expression on the right assumes is $a^2 + 2ab + b^2$. Refer to Figure 8.5 and follow these steps:

1. For five fields in succession, click on the Value menu item, and then place the field in the lower equation composition area. Position the fields so that you leave space for an exponent field and an operator between the first and second fields.

2. Starting on the right, type 3 in the first field, 2 in the second, 3 in the third, and 4 in the fourth and fifth fields. Verify your work with Figure 8.5.

3. Click the Power menu item and to the upper right of the first field, position the exponent field. The value in this field is by default 2. Do not change this value.

4. Click the Add menu item, and to the right of the exponent field and in line with the base field, position the plus sign.

5. Click the Multiply menu item and place a multiplication sign after the second field. Click the Multiply menu item again and place a multiplication sign after the third field.

6. Click the Add menu item, and between the fourth and last field, place a plus sign.

7. Click the Power menu item and place the exponent to the right and just above the last menu item. Do not change the default value of 2.

8. Set the Chart 1 Width field to 2.

9. Click the button with the equal sign in the lower Solution panel. Confirm that the value you see in the field matches the value in the upper Solution panel.

Conclusion

In this chapter, you have reviewed a number of activities relating to polynomial expressions. A polynomial expression consists of a monomial expression or two or more monomial expressions combined through operations involving addition or subtraction. When you work with polynomials, it helps to be able to distinguish them according to whether they are binomials. Among commonly used binomials are those that involve squares or the sum and difference of the same terms. In addition to using standard equations to work with such binomials, you can also use the FOIL approach. This approach allows you to quickly combine terms. For polynomials involving several variables, you can use forms of multiplication and division derived from arithmetic. When you perform operations of these types, it is important to order the terms of the polynomials according to the degrees of their exponents.

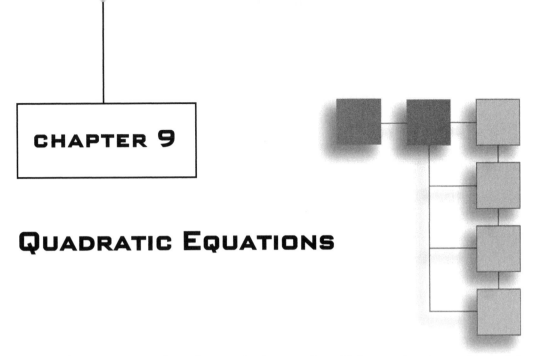

CHAPTER 9

QUADRATIC EQUATIONS

In this chapter, you explore the quadratic equation. This equation is a polynomial of the second degree and generates a parabola. The standard form of the quadratic equation reads $ax^2 + bx + c$. In the same way that you could change the shape and position of sets of lines used to graph absolute values, you can also change the shape and position of the parabolas you create using quadratic equations. You can make the parabola narrower or wider by changing the coefficient of the x variable. You translate the parabola along the x axis by interpreting x as $x - h$, where h establishes the line of symmetry for the parabola. You can also shift the parabola up and down the y axis by using a value that corresponds to c in the standard formula. To solve for the x-intercepts of a quadratic equation, you can start by completing the square. You can also use the quadratic formula. Such topics provide many interesting ways to interpret events mathematically. Among the topics that you examine as you explore how this is so are the following:

- How to define a quadratic equation in its standard form

- Reviewing the notions of constant and changing slopes

- How to make a parabola narrower or wider

- Translating a parabola along the x axis

- Making a parabola so that it opens downward

- Completing squares and the quadratic formula

Quadratic Equations

A quadratic equation is a polynomial of the second degree. In other words, one of its terms possesses an exponent of 2. A quadratic equation usually consists of three terms. Here is the standard form of a quadratic equation:

$$ax^2 + bx + c = 0$$

In such an equation, the constant a cannot be equal to 0, because then the variable x is also 0. As already mentioned, the degree of the quadratic equation is based on the value of the exponent for the variable x, which is 2. On the other hand, the constants c and b can be zero.

To solve quadratic equations, you can employ a set of techniques. Using this set of techniques provides a much easier way to solve quadratic equations than if you approach them intuitively. To understand how to use these techniques, consider working with the following equation:

$$x^2 = 36$$

Such an equation falls into the standard quadratic category, but to see it as such, you must realize that b and c are equal to zero. Think of the equation as

$$x^2 + 0x - 36 = 0$$

Since little is accomplished by using the second term, you can drop it. You are then left with this equation:

$$x^2 - 36 = 0$$

To solve for the value of x, you can draw from the discussion in Chapter 8 and factor the equation. To factor the equation, you draw on observations concerning the difference of two squares. You take the square roots of both of the terms in the expression. Accordingly, while $x \cdot x = x^2$, it also stands that $\sqrt{36} \cdot \sqrt{36} = 36$. If you then rearrange the resulting term so that you show the difference of two squares, your work appears as follows:

$$x^2 - 36 = 0 \qquad \text{Set equal to 0.}$$

$$(x - \sqrt{36})(x + \sqrt{36}) = 0 \qquad \text{Factor.}$$

$$x - \sqrt{36} = 0 \quad \text{or} \quad x + \sqrt{36} = 0 \qquad \text{Solve for each factor.}$$

$$x = \sqrt{36} \quad \text{or} \quad x = -\sqrt{36} \qquad \text{Possible solution set.}$$

To generalize then, solving for the two terms, $\sqrt{a}$ and $-\sqrt{a}$, it is necessary to consider a set of observations that apply to the solutions of all quadratic equations. These observations are as follows:

- If the value of a is greater than zero, then there are two solutions ($\pm\sqrt{a}$).

- If the value of a equals zero, then only one solution is correct.

- If the value of a is less than zero, no solution exists. (You cannot in this situation find the square root of a negative number.)

Quadratic Appearances

You can draw on the discussion that previous chapters provided to explore a few basic ideas that apply to representing quadratic equations. Consider, for example, that quadratic equations possess a degree of 2. A variable with an exponent of 2 represents a square. When you graph values you generate using a square, the values you generate are positive. For this reason, in the functional form of a quadratic equation, the values of a domain (x) generate positive values of a range (y). The resulting geometrical representation for this graph is a parabola. Figure 9.1 illustrates a parabola generated by the equation $y = x^2$.

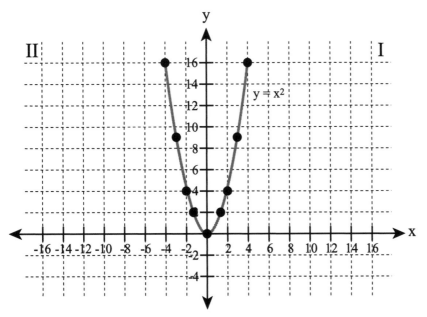

Figure 9.1
A rudimentary quadratic function generates a parabola.

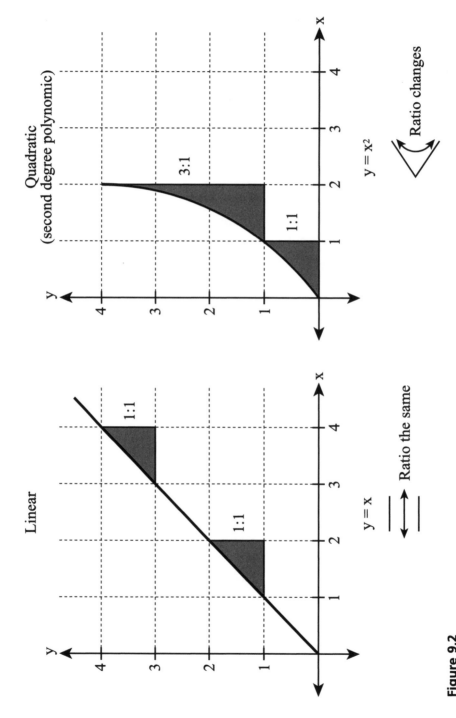

Figure 9.2
The slope changes, becoming more pronounced due to work of the exponent.

The graph you generate using a quadratic equation differs from the graph you generate using a linear equation. The most fundamental characteristic of this difference is that the slope of a parabola changes, whereas that of a straight line defined by a linear equation does not.

To review this notion, consider the slopes shown in Figure 9.2. The slope of the parabola tends to become steeper the larger the value of y becomes. On the other hand, the slope of the linear equation remains constant throughout. The capacity to show the change in the slope of a line provides you with a powerful tool with which to examine rates of change. Central to this idea is that, as the value of the x axis increases, you can discern a continuously steeper or more accentuated change in the value of the y axis. With change comes a change in the rate of change.

As Figure 9.2 reveals, the change of the slope reveals a changing relationship between the base number and the resulting value of y. Contrast what happens if you add 2 to 2 or 3. Each time, you perform the same action. You add 2 to a number. The slope of the graph that represents this activity stays the same. This activity differs from what happens when you employ an exponent.

When you employ an exponent, if you raise 2 to the power of 2, the relation between 2 and the base number changes as you increase the value of the exponent. With each successive exponential operation, the ratios between the values of x and y change, and the shape of the curve changes. When you can change the slope in this way, you arrive at a way of representing or describing phenomena that significantly expands the work you perform using linear equations.

Changing Appearances

The work you performed in Chapter 7 when examining absolute values anticipates the work you perform with quadratic equations. As Figure 9.3 illustrates, you can view the V shape of the graph you generate when working with absolute values as similar to the rounded U shape you generate when you work with quadratic equations. In both cases, the graph is symmetrical with respect to an axis. Two lines meet to form the vertex of an angle. In the same way the point that corresponds to the lowest (or highest) reach of the parabola is called the vertex of the parabola.

In most cases, the figures you generate are symmetrical with respect to the y axis, but you can also generate graphs that are symmetrical with respect to the x axis. Generally, however, if you apply the vertical line rule to the graph of a quadratic equation, then functions you define using quadratic equations remain symmetrical with respect to the y axis.

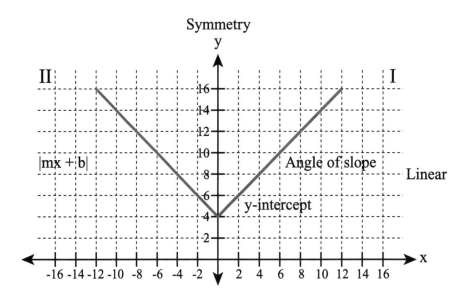

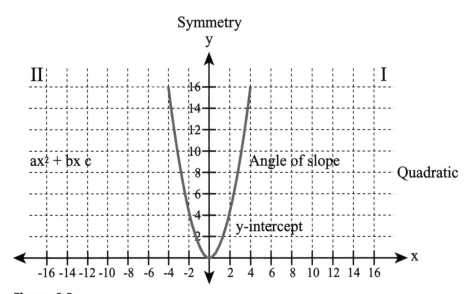

Figure 9.3
You can adjust the appearance of a graphical representation of a quadratic equation in a number of ways.

Positive and Negative

As with a linear equation generated using absolute values, a quadratic equation possesses attributes that allow you to adjust the appearance of the graph in a number of ways. In the most basic form of a quadratic equation, the vertex of the parabola opens upward and the parabola is symmetrical to the *y* axis. You can alter

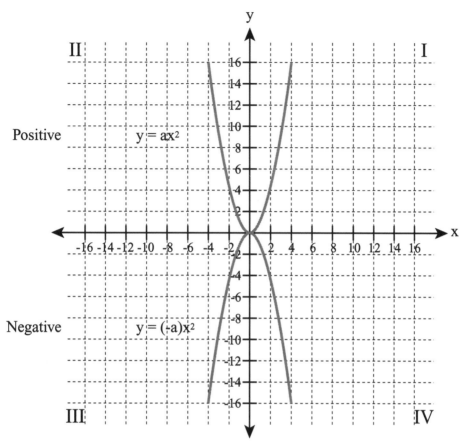

Figure 9.4
A negative coefficient establishes a downward slope.

this situation if you apply a negative coefficient to the x variable of the quadratic. Figure 9.4 illustrates the effect of a negative coefficient. On the top, the parabola opens upward. The coefficient of x establishes a positive slope, so the parabola opens upward. On the bottom, the coefficient is negative, and the result is that the values you generate establish a negative slope. The parabola opens downward.

Widening a Parabola

As you can change a quadratic equation so that its vertex opens up or down, so you can change the width of a parabola. As with direction of the vertex, you adjust the coefficient of the x in a quadratic to change the width. If you make the value of the equation less than 1, then the parabola becomes less steep. Its mouth widens. Its rate of climb becomes less pronounced. Figure 9.5 illustrates this

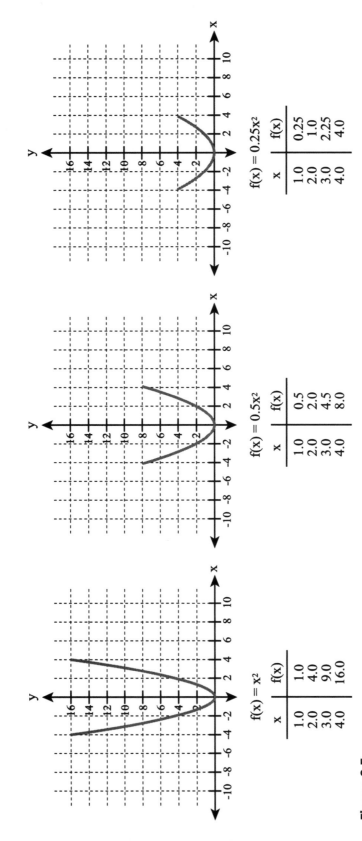

f(x) = x²

x	f(x)
1.0	1.0
2.0	4.0
3.0	9.0
4.0	16.0

f(x) = 0.5x²

x	f(x)
1.0	0.5
2.0	2.0
3.0	4.5
4.0	8.0

f(x) = 0.25x²

x	f(x)
1.0	0.25
2.0	1.0
3.0	2.25
4.0	4.0

Figure 9.5
If the coefficient is less than one, the climb becomes more gradual.

situation. On the left, you see a parabola defined with a coefficient of 1. In the middle, the value of the coefficient becomes $\frac{1}{2}$. On the right, the value of the coefficient becomes $\frac{1}{4}$. As the value of the coefficient decreases, the slope of the line tends to become more gradual.

Narrowing a Parabola

As you might expect after experimenting with values less than 1 in relation to the coefficient of x in a quadratic equation, when you make the coefficient of x greater than 1, you increase the steepness of the parabola's climb (or slope). Figure 9.6 illustrates how this happens. On the left, the parabola you see is defined by an equation in which the coefficient of x is 1. In the center, the value of the coefficient increases to 2. The steepness of the climb increases. On the right, the value of the coefficient increases to 3. The steepness of the climb becomes even greater. In each case, as the value of the coefficient increases, the steepness of the parabola becomes more pronounced.

Translation Along the x and y Axes

When you graph a quadratic equation, in many instances, you find that the vertex of the parabola you generate corresponds to the origin of the Cartesian plane (0, 0). The discussions of linear equations in Chapter 7 and elsewhere emphasize that while many linear equations cross or intersect with the origin of the Cartesian plane, by shifting an intercept value, you can raise or lower the intercept point. The same situation arises when you work with quadratic equations.

When you consider the coordinate pair that defines the vertex of a parabola, you deal with the minimum value of the parabola if it opens upward. You deal with the maximum value of the parabola if it opens downward. You can shift this value so that it moves along the x axis or along the y axis. If you move it along the x axis, you translate it horizontally. If you move it along the y axis, you translate it vertically. You translate the vertex in a positive fashion if you shift it up or to the right. You translate the vertex in a negative fashion if you translate it downward or to the left.

To understand the mechanics of translating the vertex of a parabola along the x axis, consider an expression of the following form:

$$ax^2$$

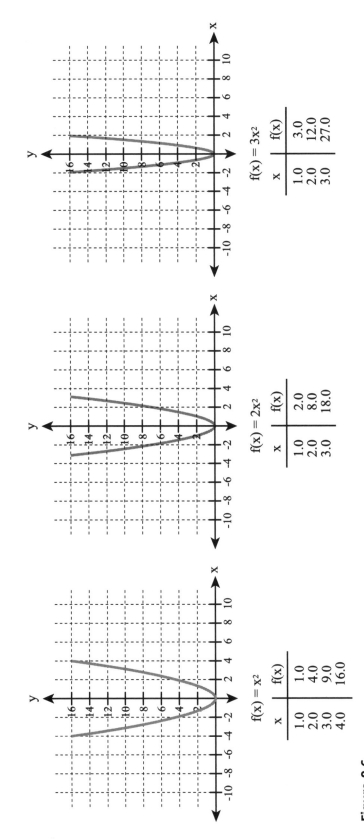

Figure 9.6
If the coefficient is greater than 1, the climb becomes more pronounced.

174

You can rewrite this expression so that you replace the variable x with a different expression. The new expression allows you to view x as the difference or sum of two other values. Accordingly, you might rewrite the expression in this way:

$$a(x - h)^2 \qquad \text{Replacing } x \text{ with } x - h$$

You now have a situation in which you are dealing with the square of the difference of two terms. In this case, h designates a value you can use to translate the vertex of a parabola along the x axis.

Translating to the Right

As Figure 9.7 shows, when h is a positive number, then the translation is to the right. On the left of the figure, the value of h is set to 0, so no shift occurs. On the right, the value is set to 4, so the shift is four units to the right. As you can see from the figure, if the equation is of the form $a(x - h)^2$, and the constant a is a positive number, the vertex of the parabola opens upward. The position of the vertex is defined by the ordered pair $(h, 0)$. Given this position on the x axis, you can locate the line of symmetry at the position on the x axis that corresponds to the value of h. Since a has a positive value, the vertex of the parabola opens up, so the minimum value of the parabola is 0.

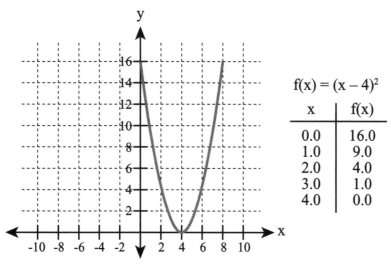

$f(x) = (x - 4)^2$

x	f(x)
0.0	16.0
1.0	9.0
2.0	4.0
3.0	1.0
4.0	0.0

Figure 9.7
A positive value creates a difference of two terms and shifts the vertex to the right.

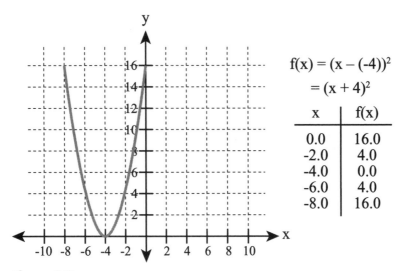

Figure 9.8
A negative value creates a difference of two terms and shifts the vertex to the left.

Translating to the Left

If you again rewrite the expression ax^2 so that x can be defined by the difference of two values, you arrive at an expression that reads $a(x - h)^2$. If you then substitute a negative value for h, you end up with an expression that appears as $a(x - (-h))^2$. Figure 9.8 illustrates a situation in which you use a negative value in a quadratic equation in this way. The basic effect of this operation is the same as if you carried out an addition of the form $(x + h)^2$. The result in the graph is that the vertex of the parabola is shifted to the left of the origin on the x axis by 4 units.

As with the previous example, the position of the vertex is defined by a coordinate pair in which the value of the first coordinate is 0. In this instance, the value of the second coordinate is a negative number $(0,-4)$. The location of the line of symmetry on the x axis is the value of -4. As in the previous example, since the value of a is positive, the parabola opens upward.

Inverting and Translating

As you might expect, no restriction prevents you from both inverting and translating a parabola. To accomplish this, you set the slope value (a) to a negative number. As in the previous sections, you can also continue to substitute the expression $x - h$ for x to shift the vertex along the x axis. For example, if you

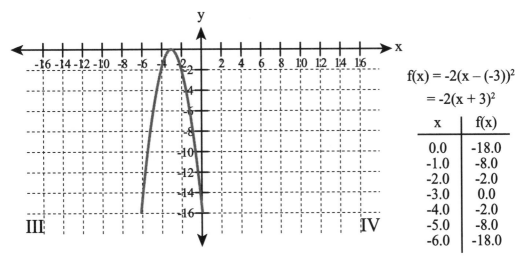

$$f(x) = -2(x - (-3))^2$$
$$= -2(x + 3)^2$$

x	f(x)
0.0	-18.0
-1.0	-8.0
-2.0	-2.0
-3.0	0.0
-4.0	-2.0
-5.0	-8.0
-6.0	-18.0

Figure 9.9
You can translate and invert parabolas simultaneously.

set h to -2, you invert the parabola, and if you set a to -3, you shift it to the right. You arrive at a parabola similar to the one Figure 9.9 illustrates.

In Figure 9.9, since the value of a is a negative value (-3), the parabola has a negative slope. The coordinates defining the vertex are $(0, -3)$, so -3 is the line of symmetry.

Arbitrary Vertex Positions

In addition to translating the vertex of the parabola along the x axis, you can move it vertically, along the y axis. Toward this end, consider what happens if you add a constant k to the basic quadratic equation you have worked with in the previous sections. Here is the new form of the equation:

$$a(x - h)^2 + k$$

This form of the equation allows you to adjust the y-intercept of the parabola. When you assign a value to k, you can translate the position of the vertex of the parabola up or down relative to the y axis.

As Figure 9.10 illustrates, if you assign a positive value to k, then you translate the vertex of the equation upward on the y axis. If the value of a is positive, then the vertex of the parabola opens upward, so the coordinates $(x, y + k)$ establish

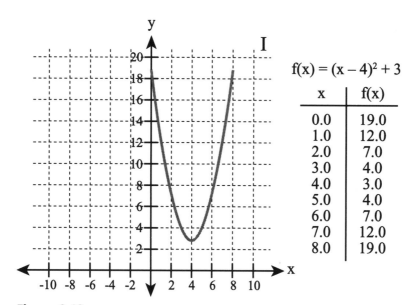

$$f(x) = (x - 4)^2 + 3$$

x	f(x)
0.0	19.0
1.0	12.0
2.0	7.0
3.0	4.0
4.0	3.0
5.0	4.0
6.0	7.0
7.0	12.0
8.0	19.0

Figure 9.10
By setting the values of a, k, and h to positive numbers, you position the parabola so that it opens upward in quadrant I of the Cartesian plane.

the minimum vertex value. Since k is a positive value, the vertex is translated upward along the y axis.

As Figure 9.10 illustrates, since the equation also includes the expression x − 4, the parabola is shifted to the right along the x axis. The vertex lies on the x axis, and the parabola opens up into quadrant I of the Cartesian plane. Note that since you have shifted the position of the vertex, the parabola intercepts the y axis when y equals 19.

You achieve a different effect if you employ negative numbers to define the a and h constants of the quadratic equation. Consider the following equation:

$$-2[x - (-4)]^2 + 3$$

This equation unfolds so that the coefficient or slope of x is negative. For this reason, the vertex of the parabola points downward. Since the value of h is negative (−4), you shift the vertex to the left of the y axis. While you make the first two constants negative, you set the value that corresponds k to 3. This action, as in the previous example, translates the vertex upward. As Figure 9.11 illustrates, the vertex of the parabola lies in quadrant II of the Cartesian plane. The maximum value lies at (−4, 3).

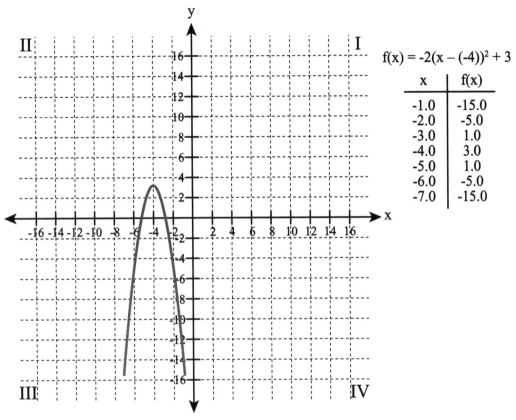

$$f(x) = -2(x - (-4))^2 + 3$$

x	f(x)
-1.0	-15.0
-2.0	-5.0
-3.0	1.0
-4.0	3.0
-5.0	1.0
-6.0	-5.0
-7.0	-15.0

Figure 9.11
A negative slope and a negative shift value invert the parabola and move it to the left, but you still shift it upward 3 units.

The x-intercepts

The points at which the graph of the quadratic equation cross the x axis are known as the x-intercepts. If you can determine the vertex of the parabola, and know whether the parabola opens upward or downward, then you are in an excellent position to calculate the x-intercepts. As the previous examples reveal, not all quadratic equations have x-intercepts. For example, if a parabola opens upward and is shifted upward from the x axis, it does not intercept the x axis.

Figure 9.12 provides a summary view of a few possibilities with respect to quadratic equations. Accordingly, parabola A has one x-intercept because its vertex lies on the x axis. The same is true of parabola C. Parabolas B and D have

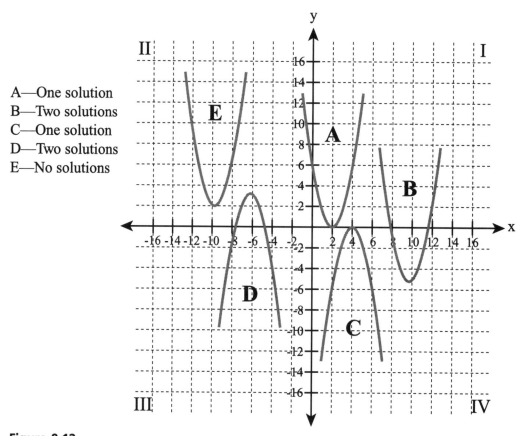

A—One solution
B—Two solutions
C—One solution
D—Two solutions
E—No solutions

Figure 9.12
When you solve for the values of a quadratic equation, you determine if the parabola the equation generates intersects with the x axis.

two solutions each because they intersect the *x* axis in two places. Parabola E has no solutions because its origin lies above the *x* axis and it opens upward.

Standard Forms

If you consider the examples quadratic equations offered in the previous sections, you find that the standard form of the equation can prove useful as a way to easily discern the basic features of the parabola the equation generates. To recapitulate, consider again the extended form of the equation:

$$a(x - h)^2 + k$$

If you know the value of *a*, then you can determine how wide or narrow the parabola is likely to appear. If *a* is positive, the parabola opens upward. If *a* is negative, the parabola opens downward. If the value of h is positive, then the vertex of the parabola shifts to the right, or positive, direction on the x axis. If it is negative, then the vertex of the parabola shifts to the left, or negative, direction on the x axis. If the value of k is positive, then the vertex shifts upward on the y axis. If the value of k is negative, then the vertex shifts downward on the y axis.

The equation in this form proves so valuable that it is worthwhile knowing how to convert quadratic equations so that they appear in this form. Toward this end, consider again the standard form of a quadratic equation:

$$ax^2 + bx + c$$

To alter an equation you find in this form so that you can discern its component variables, you perform an operation known as completing the square. The next section covers in detail the procedure for completing the square of a quadratic equation. For now it remains important to focus on the notion that the extended form of the equation consists of a restatement of the standard form of the equation. Table 9.1 provides a summary of the features of the extended form of the equation. Subsequent sections of this chapter discuss features not covered in the previous sections.

Table 9.1 Features of the Standard Form

Item	Discussion
$ax^2 + bx + c$	Standard form of a quadratic equation. You can set the constants b and c to 0, resulting in an expression of the form ax^2, but you may not set the constant a to 0. By definition, the quadratic equation is an equation of the second degree, so if you eliminate the term with the coefficient corresponding to the second-degree variable, you change the equation so that it no longer corresponds to the definition of a quadratic equation.
$a(x - h)^2 + k$	This is the form a quadratic equation can assume if you rewrite it by completing the square.
(h, k)	This coordinate pair establishes the position of the vertex. If h is negative, then the vertex lies to the left of the y axis. If h is positive, then the vertex lies to the right of the y axis. If the variable k is positive, then the vertex is above the x axis. If the variable k is negative, then it lies below the x axis.
h	The value of h defines the line of symmetry for the parabola. If this is a positive value, then the line of symmetry shifts to the right of the y axis. If the value is negative, then the line of symmetry shifts to the left of the y axis.
a	The value of a determines how sharply the parabola rises. If the value is greater than 1, then the parabola narrows and rises more precipitately. If the value is less than 1, then the parabola becomes wider and rises less precipitately.
k	The constant k establishes the y intercept for the parabola. If the value of k is positive, then the vertex moves upward relative to the x axis. If the value of k is negative, then the vertex shifts downward.

Completing the Square

Working with the basic form of the quadratic equation the previous section afforded, you gain some sense of what it is to complete the square of an expression to solve a quadratic equation. For starters, recall that these two equations represent standard forms of polynomials that incorporate squares:

$$(a + b)^2 = a^2 + 2ab + b^2$$

$$(a - b)^2 = a^2 - 2ab + b^2$$

Generally, completing the square begins with examining an equation to discover whether you can rewrite it in a way that allows you to make a perfect square on the left side of the equal sign. To understand how this works, consider the following equation:

$$a^2 - 6a - 12 = 0$$

This is a standard quadratic equation. To make it so that it represents the square of two expressions, you begin by considering the first two terms. The first term is a square. The second term might represent the combined square roots of two squares. (The variable a, for example, is the square root of a^2.) The third term, however, does not easily fit into this scheme. For this reason, you move 12 to the right side of the equal sign:

$$a^2 - 6a = 12$$

You then find a term that you can add to the left side of the equation that allows you to create a perfect square. To arrive at this number, you use an expression you derive from the standard form of the quadratic equation. Accordingly, the second term of the standard equation is bx. If you divide b, the coefficient of x, by 2 and square the result, then you arrive at an expression that completes the square. Here is how this approach unfolds for the equation at hand:

$$a^2 - 6a + \left(\frac{6}{2}\right)^2 = 12 + \left(\frac{6}{2}\right)^2 \qquad \text{Add half the coefficient squared.}$$

$$a^2 - 6a + 3^2 = 12 + 3^2$$

$$a^2 - 6a + 9 = 12 + 9$$

$$a^2 - 6a + 9 = 21$$

$$(a - 3)^2 = 21$$

You can then solve the last form of the equation using the approaches rehearsed previously:

$$\sqrt{(a-3)^2} = \pm\sqrt{21}$$

$$a - 3 = \pm\sqrt{21}$$

$$a = 3 \pm \sqrt{21}$$

Since the value of a is greater than zero, two solutions exist. The solution set is as follows:

$$\left\{3 + \sqrt{21}, 3 - \sqrt{21}\right\}$$

Figure 9.13 reviews the general technique you use to complete squares.

In many instances, completing the square involves working with coefficients of the first term that are greater than 1. Consider, for example, the following equation:

$$2x^2 - 3x - 1 = 0$$

In this instance, the coefficient of the first term is 2. To alter the equation so that you proceed as before with completing the square, you multiply the equation by

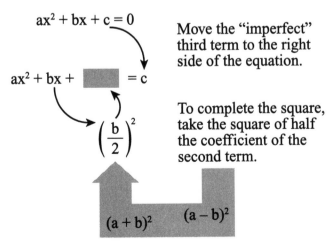

Figure 9.13
To complete the square, divide the coefficient of the second term by 2 and square the result.

the inverse of the coefficient. In this case, the inverse of 2 is $\frac{1}{2}$, so your work takes the following form:

$$\frac{2x^2}{2} - \frac{3x}{2} - \frac{1}{2} = 0 \qquad \text{Multiply by } \frac{1}{2}.$$

$$x^2 - \frac{3}{2}x = \frac{1}{2}$$

$$x^2 - \frac{3}{2}x + \left(\frac{\frac{3}{2}}{2}\right)^2 = \frac{1}{2} + \left(\frac{\frac{3}{2}}{2}\right)^2$$

$$x^2 - \frac{3}{2}x + \frac{9}{16} = \frac{1}{2} + \frac{9}{16}$$

$$x^2 - \frac{3}{2}x + \frac{9}{16} = \frac{8}{16} + \frac{9}{16}$$

$$x^2 - \frac{3}{2}x + \frac{9}{16} = \frac{17}{16}$$

$$\left(x - \frac{3}{4}\right)^2 = \frac{17}{16}$$

$$x - \frac{3}{4} = \pm\sqrt{\frac{17}{16}}$$

Having proceeded this far, you can then rationalize the denominator of the expression on the left side of the equation. This gives you

$$x - \frac{3}{4} = \pm\frac{\sqrt{17}}{4}$$

The solution set for the equation is as follows:

$$\left\{\frac{3 + \sqrt{17}}{4}, \frac{3 - \sqrt{17}}{4}\right\}$$

Exercise Set 9.1

Solve by completing the square.

a. $p^2 + 5p - 3 = 0$

b. $q^2 - 10q - 22 = 0$

c. $4a^2 + 8a + 3 = 0$

d. $2a^2 + 5a + 2 = 0$

e. $a^2 - 6a = 0$

f. $b^2 + 6b = 7$

g. $b^2 + 10 = 6b$

h. $2x^2 - 5x - 3 = 0$

i. $9x^2 + 18x + 8 = 0$

j. $6t^2 - t = 15$

The Quadratic Formula

Completing the square provides a reliable approach to solving quadratic equations, but you can also use an approach that involves applying the quadratic formula. To use the quadratic formula, you first put the equation you are dealing with in a standard form. As mentioned before, the standard form of a quadratic equation is as follows:

$$ax^2 + bx + c = 0$$

It is not absolutely necessary that you set up the equation in this way, but if you do, then it becomes easier to use the quadratic formula to work with it. The quadratic formula is stated as follows:

$$x = \frac{-b \pm \sqrt{b^2 - 4ac}}{2a}$$

Consider the following quadratic equation:

$$2x^2 + 3x = 7$$

To rewrite the equation in standard form, you add -7 to both sides:

$$2x^2 + 3x - 7 = 0$$

You can then identify a, b, and c as follows: $a = 2$, $b = 3$, and $c = -7$.

Substituting these values into the quadratic formula, you arrive at this equation:

$$x = \frac{-3 \pm \sqrt{3^2 - 4(2)(-7)}}{2(2)}$$

$$x = \frac{-3 \pm \sqrt{9 + 56}}{4}$$

$$x = \frac{-3 \pm \sqrt{65}}{4}$$

For a solution set, you can use a calculator to arrive at a decimal value that represents the root or an approximation of the root:

$$x \approx \frac{-3 - 8.06}{4} \approx \frac{-11.06}{4} \approx -2.756$$

$$x \approx \frac{-3 + 8.06}{4} \approx \frac{5.06}{4} \approx 1.265$$

The Discriminant

In the quadratic equation, you refer to the expression $\sqrt{b^2 - 4ac}$ as the discriminant. The result of the expression allows you to determine the values that are acceptable as solutions of the quadratic formula:

▪ If you find that $b^2 - 4ac = 0$, then the equation possesses only one real number solution.

▪ If you find that $b^2 - 4ac > 0$, then two real number solutions satisfy the equation.

▪ If you find that $b^2 - 4ac < 0$, then no real number solution exists for the equation.

As mentioned previously, the values you arrive at when you examine the discriminant allow you to determine whether the lines of the parabola the equation generates intersect with the x axis.

Exercise Set 9.2

Solve the following equations using the quadratic formula. After you solve the equation, use the value of the discriminant to determine which solutions are valid.

a. $3x^2 - 8x = 4$

b. $x^2 + 7x - 3 = 0$

c. $9u^2 - 8u + 3 = 0$

d. $x^2 - 5x + 6 = 0$

e. $2x^2 - x = -6$

f. $3a^2 - 18a = 4$

g. $r^2 + 4 = 6r$

h. $h^2 + h + 1 = 0$

i. $12b^2 + 9b = 1$

j. $3x - x(x - 2) = 4$

Using Visual Formula

Use Visual Formula to implement a quadratic equation. Then use this equation to test different values for quadratic. Set up the quadratic equation using the standard form of a quadratic equation:

$$f(x) = ax^2 + bx + c$$

Here is an equation you can use for practical purposes of implementation:

$$f(x) = 3x^2 + 3x - 1$$

To implement this equation, use the upper equation composition area. Refer to Figure 9.14 and follow these steps:

1. Click the Value menu item five times in succession and, with each click, position a field in the upper equation composition area. Position the first two fields in close proximity to each other, skip enough space to allow for a field and an operator, and then position the third and fourth fields in close

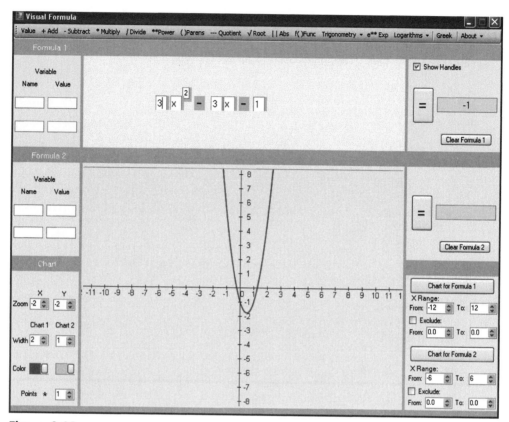

Figure 9.14
Set up a quadratic equation to generate a graph.

proximity. Leave enough space for an operator, and then position the last field.

2. In the first and third fields type 3. In the second and fourth fields type *x*. In the last field type 1.

3. Move the fields apart from each other so that they correspond roughly to the fields shown in Figure 9.14. You will need more room between some of the fields than others. Make enough room so that the fields you place in the next few steps do not overlap. Recall that if you make a mistake, press the Shift key and left click on a field to delete it.

4. Click the Power menu item and to the right and just above the second *x* field position the exponent. The default value is 2. Do not change this value.

5. Click the Subtract menu twice in succession. With the first click, position the minus sign after the exponent field and level with the x field. With the second click, position the minus sign before the final x field.

6. Click on the equal button to the right of the equation composition area.

7. Position the cursor on the top of the Cartesian plane. When it turns into parallel bars, pull the Cartesian plane up to the bottom of the equation composition area.

8. Now proceed to the lower-right panel. Beneath the Chart for Formula 1 button, set the X Range From control to −12. Set the X Range To control to 12.

9. In the lower-left Chart panel, set the Zoom X and Y fields to −2.

10. Set the Width field for Chart 1 to 2.

11. Click the Chart for Formula 1 button to see your work.

To view changes in the behavior of your equation, change its values. Before working with these values, in the Chart panel, click the controls for the X and Y Zoom fields and set the values for both fields to −4. Then work through these values and see how the parabola changes:

4	x^2	−	2	X	−	5
6	x^2	−	6	X	−	8
8	x^2	−	3	X	−	1
1	x^2	−	-5	X	−	8
9	x^2	−	2	X	−	5

Conclusion

This chapter has allowed you to explore how quadratic equations work. A quadratic equation is a second degree equation that generates a parabola. When you generate a parabola using a quadratic equation, three basic possibilities exist with respect to how the parabola relates to the x axis. Both of its arms can intersect the x axis. It's vertex can lie on the axis, or it can open upward or downward and never intersect with the x axis at all. To help you determine the type of quadratic equation you are dealing with, you can use techniques such as completing the square. You can also apply the quadratic formula. When you apply the quadratic formula, you can determine the type of parabola you are dealing with from the values the discriminant of the formula generates.

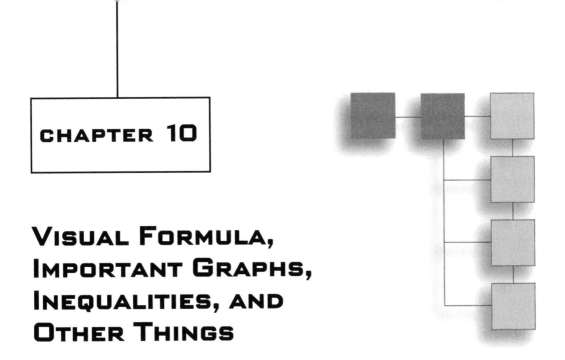

CHAPTER 10

VISUAL FORMULA, IMPORTANT GRAPHS, INEQUALITIES, AND OTHER THINGS

The activities this chapter covers allow you to use Visual Formula to work with many of the equations discussed in previous chapters. Visual Formula equips you to quickly plot the values you generate using various equations. When you do this, you can explore how changing such items as the slopes or y-intercepts of equations changes the shapes of the graphs that result. As you work with Visual Formula in this chapter, first perform the operations the steps guide you through. Then retrace the steps and change the values on your own to broaden and deepen your understanding of the equations and their features. As you go, experiment. If you create equations that do not work, click the Clear Formula 1 or Clear Formula 2 buttons to erase your work. The topics covered in this chapter include the following:

- Changing positive slopes of linear equations

- Charting parallel lines

- Adding y-intercept values to shift linear equations

- Working with absolute values

- Creating parabolas

- Flipping and shifting parabolas

Compare and Contrast

Other chapters of this book discuss in detail several of the graphs you encounter in this chapter. The purpose of this chapter is to expand on material you have already covered by allowing you to experiment with it in a safe, painless way. Visual Formula provides a tool that allows you to go in this direction.

A key activity involves creating pairs of graphs. When you create pairs of graphs, you can explore changes in a relative manner. One graph can serve as a starting point or contrasting point for the other. As you go, keep in mind that instruction sets accompanying each exercise are intended to isolate your activities so that you can easily jump around the chapter and try experiments at random.

When you examine the graphs in this way, you gain a sense of the extent to which graphing the output of functions furnishes a stronger sense of how algebra relates to geometric visualization.

To work with the graphs in this chapter, use Visual Formula to set up the named equations and generate graphs of them. Many of the examples show that when you type an x in the Value field of your equation, Visual Formula automatically generates enough plotted values to draw a graph. In cases in which the default setting for the number of plotted points proves too small and results in a skewed graph, use the Points control in the bottom-left Chart panel of Visual Formula to set the graph so that more points for plotting are available.

Linear Graphs

A linear function generates a graph characterized by a slope that does not change. The line-slope-intercept equation provides a way to experiment with linear equations. Here is the line-slope-intercept equation as you have seen it in previous chapters:

$$f(x) = mx + b \qquad \text{or} \qquad y = mx + b$$

Drawing from Table 10.1, you can use this equation to generate a line with a positive slope of 2 and a y-intercept at 3:

$$y = 2x + 3$$

Table 10.1 Experiments with Linear Equations

Item	Discussion
$y = 2x + 3$	Creates an equation that slopes upward into quadrant I with the y-intercept at 3.
$y = -\frac{1}{2}x + 3$	Creates a line that is perpendicular to the line you create with $y = 2x + 3$.
$y = \frac{1}{2}x + 3$	Reduces the severity of the slope you generate with $y = 2x + 3$.
$y = -2x + 3$	Causes the slope to trail downward from quadrant II to quadrant IV. Passes through quadrant I from the y-intercept at 3.
$y = 2x - 3$	Moves the y-intercept below the x axis. The line you generate in this way parallels the line you generate with $y = 2x + 0$.
$y = -2x - 3$	Reverses the slope and places the y-intercept below the x axis.
$y = 2x + 0$	Causes the line to cross the origin of the Cartesian system (value of the y-intercept is 0). The line remains perpendicular to $y = -\frac{1}{2}x + 3$.

Refer to Figure 10.1 as you go, and implement this equation in Visual Formula using the following steps:

1. Click the Value menu item. To position the field the Value menu activates, click in the top equation composition area. This creates a field for constants that corresponds to the *m* constant. This constant defines the slope of the equation. For the value for the field, click in the box and type 2.

2. Click the Multiply menu item. Then click to place the multiplication symbol immediately after the Value field.

3. Following the multiplication sign, double-click to create a second Value field. Type an *x* in this field. The *x* represents a range of values you use to generate the graph of a line.

4. After setting up the Value field for *x*, click the Add menu item. To place the plus sign in the equation composition area, click just after the *x* Value field.

5. Click the Value menu item. Then click in the composition area after the plus sign to place the Value field for the y-intercept constant. Type 3 in this field.

See the equation composition area of Figure 10.1 for the appearance of the equation after you have implemented it. To test your work, click the button on the right of the composition that contains the equal sign. You see 2 in the field adjacent to it.

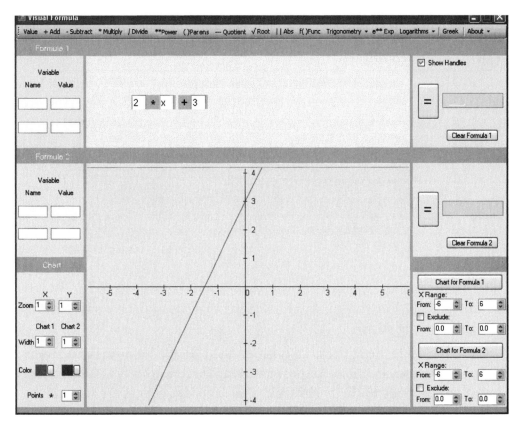

Figure 10.1
Create and graph a linear equation.

Now you can proceed to generate a graphical representation of the equation. Toward this end, first move the cursor to the top of the Cartesian plane. As you do so, the cursor turns into a horizontal line with arrows extending up and down. Press the left mouse button and pull the Cartesian plane upward until its top edge is even with the bottom of the composition area that contains your equation. Figure 10.1 illustrates Visual Formula after you have extended the Cartesian plane.

Having extended the Cartesian plane, you are ready to generate the line. To accomplish this, click on the Chart for Formula 1 button on the lower right panel of the Visual Formula window. You see the line illustrated in Figure 10.1.

Changing the Intercept Value

To work with the linear equation you have set up in the previous exercise, find the y-intercept field in your equation in the composition area. You have assigned

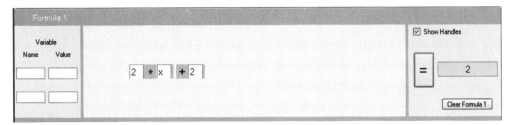

Figure 10.2
The equation allows you to change the slope.

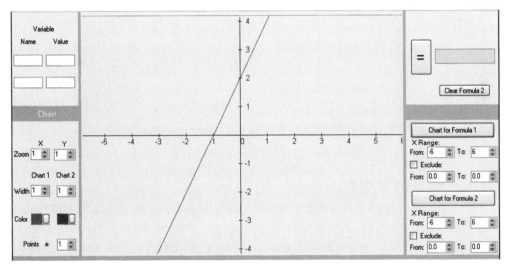

Figure 10.3
When you change your y-intercept value, you change the point at which the line intersects with the *y* axis.

an initial value of 3 to the y-intercept. The value corresponds to the *b* constant in the slope-line-intercept equation. The goal here involves altering this value to see the difference that results in the position of the line.

Referring to Figure 10.2, change the value of the y-intercept to 3. To do so, click to activate the field. Press the back arrow key to delete the previous value. Type 2 to replace it. To verify your value, click the button with the equal sign on the right. The value you see is 2, as Figure 10.2 illustrates.

Now click the Chart for Formula 1 button in the lower-right panel. The position at which the line crosses the *y* axis changes. You see the line intercept with 2 on the *y* axis, as Figure 10.3 illustrates. After changing the y-intercept to 2, change it back to 3. Try other values, such as 1 and 4.

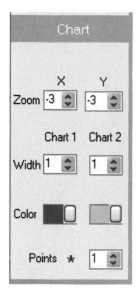

Figure 10.4
Adjust the Zoom fields so that you see more points on the *x* and *y* axes.

Changing the Scale

Prior to proceeding with further operations, find the Zoom fields in the Chart panel (see Figure 10.4). The Zoom fields allow you to adjust the number of crosshatches you see on the *x* and *y* axes. In this instance, adjust the settings of both of the fields so that you see values of −3. Figure 10.5 illustrates the fields after you have adjusted the values. If you compare Figure 10.3 with Figure 10.5, you can see the scale of the lines is now much finer than before. The number of cross hatches on both axes increases.

To explore the use of the Zoom controls, adjust the scale up and down. As long as you adjust the two controls in tandem, the appearance of the slope does not change. Figure 10.5 illustrates the Zoom controls set with values of −3. Positive values draw the crosshatches farther apart. Negative values draw them closer together.

Setting Up a Contrasting Line

To make it so that you can contrast the work of one equation with that of another, you make use of the upper and the lower equation composition areas. If you have performed the exercises in the previous sections, you have pulled the Cartesian plane over the lower composition area. You did this in part to be able

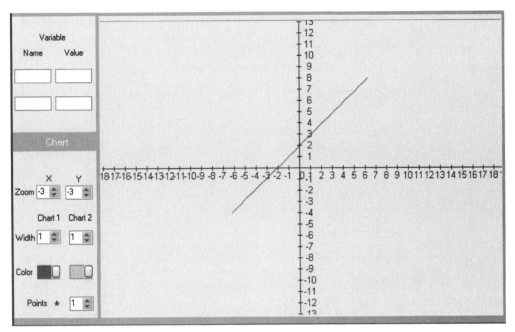

Figure 10.5
Adjust the Zoom fields so that you see more points on the *x* and *y* axes.

to adjust the scale of the crosshatches on the axes. Now that you have adjusted the lines to accommodate your work, you can pull the Cartesian plane back so that it no longer conceals the lower equation composition area.

Toward this end, position the cursor on the top of the Cartesian plane until it appears as a horizontal bar with arrows extending up and down. Then press the left mouse button and pull downward on the bottom edge of the lower composition area. Pull it until it is even with the Chart panel, as shown in Figure 10.6.

Now you have two equation composition areas to work with. The equation you created before is still in the upper equation composition area. The lower composition area remains blank.

To create a contrasting equation, consider another of the equations in Table 10.1:

$$y = \frac{1}{2}x + 3$$

Since the slope of this equation is $\frac{1}{2}$, the line it generates appears more horizontal than a line with the slope of 2. To see how this is so, implement this equation in

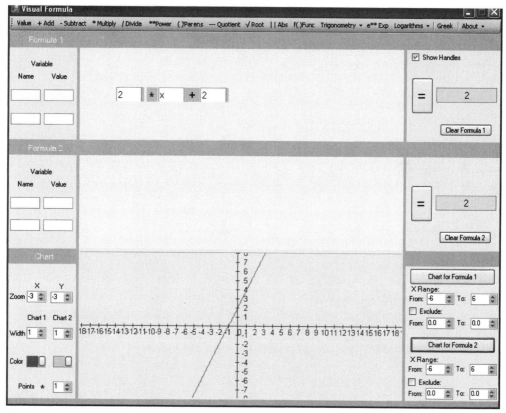

Figure 10.6
Pull the lower equation composition area open above the Cartesian plane.

the lower equation composition area. Refer to Figure 10.7 and use the following steps:

1. Click the Value menu item. Then in the lower equation composition area, click to position the Value field. As in the previous exercise, this field corresponds to the *m* constant. This constant defines the slope of the equation. Type $\frac{1}{2}$ in this field. When you type this value, type 1, a forward slash (/), and then 2.

2. Click the Multiply menu item. Then click to place the multiplication symbol immediately after the Slope field.

3. Following the multiplication symbol, click the Value menu item. To place the second Value field, click to the right of the multiplication sign. Type an *x* in this field. The *x* represents a range of values Visual Formula can use to generate the graph of a line.

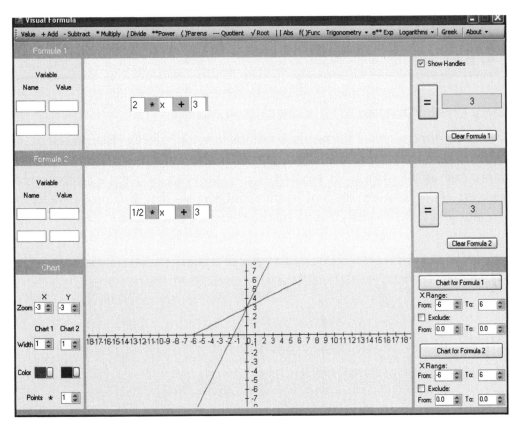

Figure 10.7
Use both composition areas to graph contrasting equations.

4. After setting up the Value field for *x*, click the Add menu item. Then click in the composition area to place the plus sign immediately after the *x* Value field.

5. Now click the Value menu item. To position the corresponding field, click in the composition area to the right of the plus sign. This field is for the y-intercept. Enter 3 in this field.

Having implemented the equation, click the Chart for Formula 2 button. As Figure 10.7 illustrates, the shorter, more gradually sloped line appears. To change the color of the line, click Color option on the Chart panel and select from the color palette.

You can use a similar approach to generate graphs for other linear equations. Table 10.1 provides some of the common forms of linear equations. Work through the examples the table provides.

Note

If you want to delete an element you have placed in the equation composition area, hold down the Shift key and click on the element.

Lines that Parallel the x and y Axes

Some linear functions are known as constant functions. They are characterized by vertical or horizontal lines that run parallel to the y or x axes. These functions assume one of two forms. In the first form, the value of y remains the same regardless of the position you plot relative to the x axis. This line runs parallel to the x axis and is distinguished only by the changing value of x.

$$y = a$$

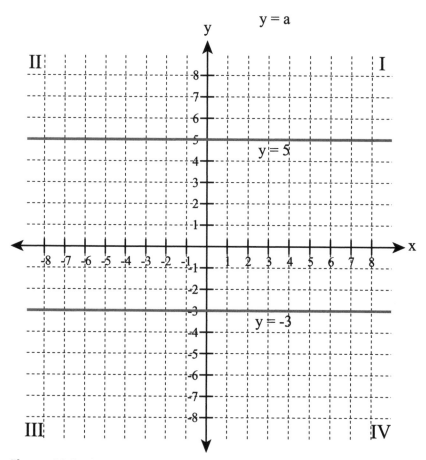

Figure 10.8
A constant value on the y axis creates a line that parallels the x axis.

In $y = a$, a identifies a constant value. When you plot such a function, the graph assumes the form shown in Figure 10.8. You equate the lines this figure shows as a flat slope. In other words, the slope has no rise, only a run. For all values of x, y remains the same.

To use Visual Formula to plot constant values, click on the Value menu item. Then click in the upper equation composition area to position the Value field. Type 5 in the field. The equation you implement takes the form of $y = a$, as is illustrated in Figure 10.8. Click the Chart for Formula 1 button to view the graph. Figure 10.9 illustrates the result.

To generate the lower line in the Cartesian plane, click the Value menu item. Then click in the lower of the two equation composition areas. In the field that results, type −3. Then in the lower-right panel, Click Chart for Formula 2. As Figure 10.9 illustrates, the lower line is beneath and parallel to the x axis.

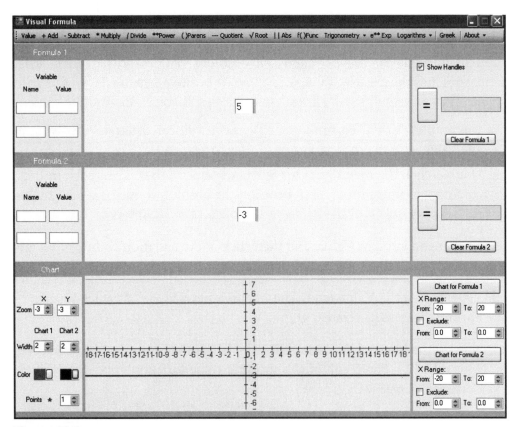

Figure 10.9
Generate parallel lines by setting the y value to a constant.

To set Visual Formula so that the lines and scales resemble those shown in Figure 10.9, type −20 in the From field beneath the X Range label for the Chart for Formula 1 button. In the To field, type 20. In the Chart panel, set the Zoom values to −3. Set the Width fields to 2. If you click the Color fields, you can choose the colors you find preferable from the color palette.

Absolute Values

The absolute value of a number corresponds to two values, one positive, the other negative. Because the graphs you create using absolute values depict both of these values, they are reflected across the y axis.

Here is an equation involving an absolute value that equates the absolute value of x with y:

$$y = |x|$$

For each value on the y axis, you find corresponding negative and positive values of x. Figure 10.10 illustrates a graph of an equation that does not involve an absolute value ($y = x$). To the right of the graph of this equation, you see the graph of an equation that contains an absolute value. The darkened arrow emphasizes how the negative values of x generate positive y values. From this arises a typical V representation of a linear equation that involves an absolute value.

You can employ Visual Formula to implement a linear equation involving an absolute value. Use the following steps (refer to Figure 10.11):

1. Double-click the menu item for absolute values (Abs). Then click in the equation composition area to position the absolute value bars. Use the mouse cursor to pull the bars apart enough to accommodate a field.

2. Click menu item for Value, and then click in the equation composition area to place the Value field between the absolute value bars.

3. Type an x in the Value field. The x represents a range of values Visual Formula uses to generate a graph.

4. Now in the lower-right panel, click the Chart for Formula 1 button. (See Figure 10.12.) The graph of the absolute value function appears in the Cartesian plane.

5. To adjust the lengths of the lines you see graphed, click the X Range number controls.

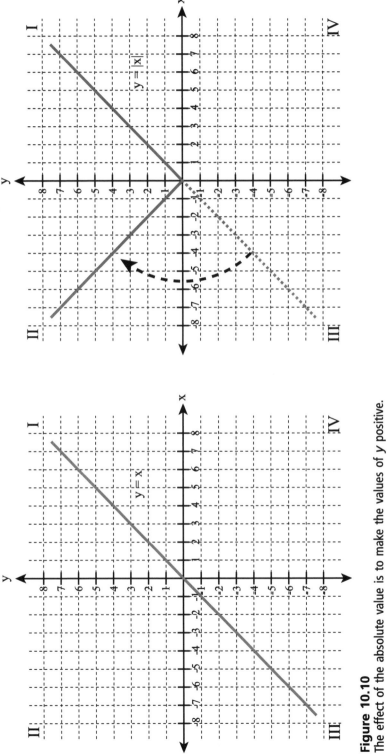

Figure 10.10
The effect of the absolute value is to make the values of *y* positive.

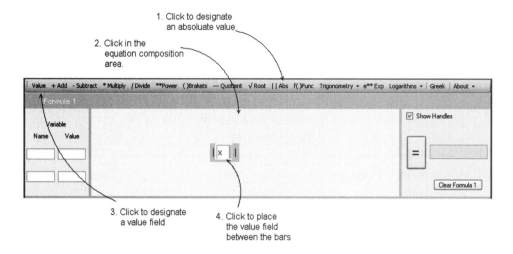

1. Click to designate
   an absoluate value

2. Click in the
   equation composition
   area.

3. Click to designate
   a value field

4. Click to place
   the value field
   between the bars

Figure 10.11
Position the absolute value bars before you position the Value field.

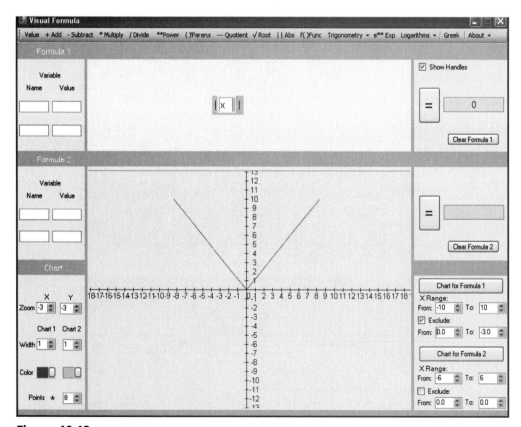

Figure 10.12
A linear equation containing an absolute value generates only positive *y* values.

Non-linear Absolute Values

Equations can contain terms that possess exponents and that are also absolute values. The graph of such an equation in some ways resembles the graph of a linear equation that possesses an absolute value because the values you plot for the y axis are all positive, while those you plot for the x axis are both negative and positive. Here is an example of an equation that requires you to plot the absolute value of the cube of x:

$$y = |x^3|$$

As the graph on the right in Figure 10.13 illustrates, when you do not designate the absolute value of a cube, an equation with a cube can generate negative numbers. This is so because an expression such as $-x \cdot -x \cdot -x$ renders a negative product. The graph of an equation involving a cube for this reason can extend into quadrant III. However, if you perform this operation in the context provided by an absolute value, then the product is positive. The expression $|-x \cdot -x \cdot -x|$ renders positive y values.

To employ Visual Formula to implement an equation that generates values using the absolute value of a cube, use the following steps (refer to Figure 10.14):

1. Click the menu item for absolute values (Abs). Then click in the equation composition area to position the absolute value bars. Verify if the Show Handles check box on the right of the composition area is checked. If it is not checked, then click it.

2. Use the mouse cursor to resize the area between the absolute value bars. To accomplish this, position the cursor on the right absolute value bar and when the cursor turns into a line with arrows on either end, drag the absolute value bar to the right. To make the area longer, position the cursor on the bottom of the area between the absolute value bars and when the cursor turns into a line with arrows on either end, drag the area down.

3. Click on the Value menu item. Then place a Value field in the absolute value area. Type an x in the value field.

4. Click on the Power menu. Then place a field for the exponent to the upper right of the Value field. Type a 3 in the Exponent field.

5. In the lower-right panel, click the Chart for Formula 1 button. The graph of the absolute value function appears in the Cartesian plane (see Figure 10.15).

6. To adjust the lengths of the lines you see graphed, click the X Range number controls.

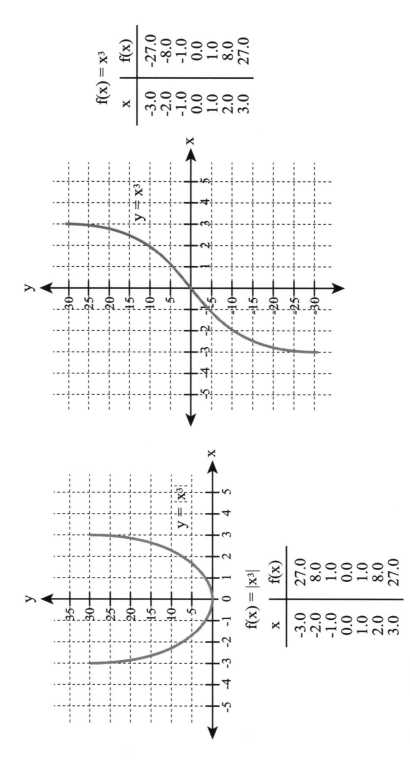

$f(x) = |x^3|$

x	f(x)
-3.0	27.0
-2.0	8.0
-1.0	1.0
0.0	0.0
1.0	1.0
2.0	8.0
3.0	27.0

$f(x) = x^3$

x	f(x)
-3.0	-27.0
-2.0	-8.0
-1.0	-1.0
0.0	0.0
1.0	1.0
2.0	8.0
3.0	27.0

Figure 10.13
The absolute value of a cube renders the values of *y* positive.

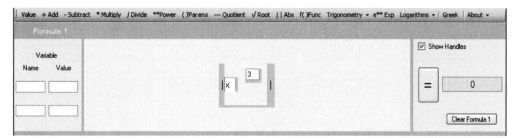

Figure 10.14
Position the absolute value bars before you position the Value field.

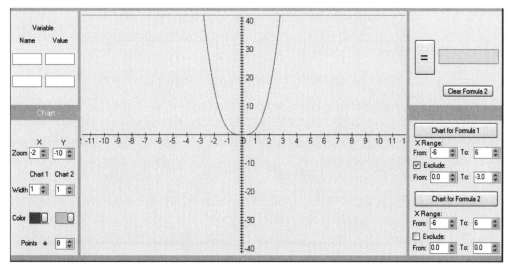

Figure 10.15
The absolute value of a cube generates positive *y* values.

Even and Odd Exponential Values

Plotting the values for the cube of *x* introduces a notion that proves essential to working with the graphs of exponents. As Figure 10.16 illustrates, in situations where the exponent for the number is even, you see graphs that open upward. Such graphs are symmetrical with respect to the *y* axis.

In contrast, in situations where the exponent of the variable is odd, then only one arm of the graph extends upward. As Figure 10.17 shows, the graph that results is symmetrical with respect to the origin of the Cartesian coordinate plane.

You can use Visual Formula to implement two equations at a time and, in this way, compare the actions of even and odd exponents and negative base values.

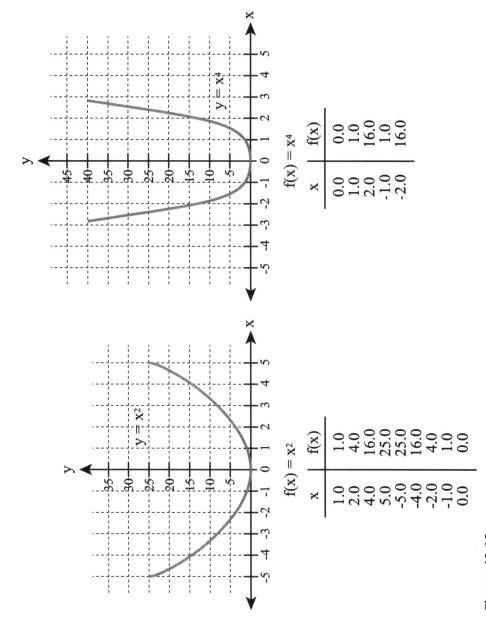

$f(x) = x^2$

x	f(x)
1.0	1.0
2.0	4.0
4.0	16.0
5.0	25.0
-5.0	25.0
-4.0	16.0
-2.0	4.0
-1.0	1.0
0.0	0.0

$f(x) = x^4$

x	f(x)
0.0	0.0
1.0	1.0
2.0	16.0
-1.0	1.0
-2.0	16.0

Figure 10.16
Graphs with even exponents open upward.

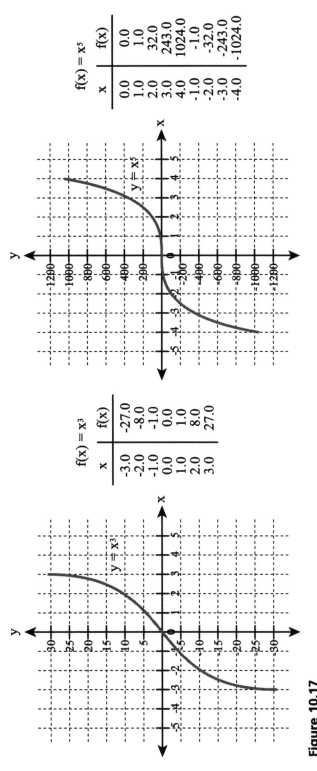

f(x) = x³	
x	f(x)
-3.0	-27.0
-2.0	-8.0
-1.0	-1.0
0.0	0.0
1.0	1.0
2.0	8.0
3.0	27.0

f(x) = x⁵	
x	f(x)
0.0	0.0
1.0	1.0
2.0	32.0
3.0	243.0
4.0	1024.0
-1.0	-1.0
-2.0	-32.0
-3.0	-243.0
-4.0	-1024.0

Figure 10.17
Odd exponents used with negative numbers result in graphs that are symmetrical with respect to the origin.

Refer to Figure 10.18, and use these steps:

1. Create an equation with an even exponent and a negative base value. Click the Parens menu item. Then click in the equation composition area to position the parentheses. Pull the parentheses apart far enough to accommodate a field for a value.

2. Click the Subtract menu item. Then click inside the parens in the equation composition area to create a minus sign (−). Move the minus sign snugly against the left parenthesis.

3. Click on the Value item in the menu. In the equation composition area just after the minus sign, click to place the Value field inside the parens. In this field, type x.

4. Click on the menu item for Power (or exponent). Then place the field for the exponent to the upper right of the closing parenthesis. Type a 6 in the Exponent field.

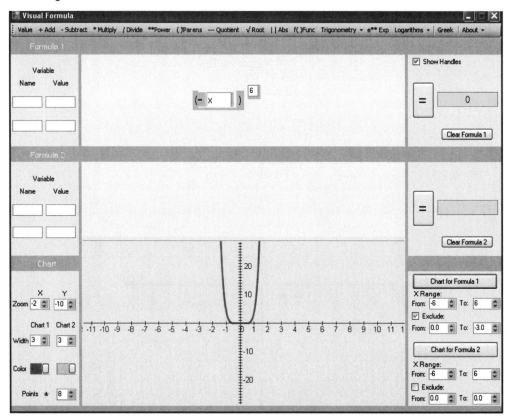

Figure 10.18
A graph of negative values raised to an even power is symmetrical to the y axis.

5. Now in the lower-right panel, click on the Chart for Formula 1 button. The graph shown in Figure 10.18 appears in the Cartesian plane.

6. To thicken the line for the graph so that it appears as shown in Figure 10.18, click on the Chart 1 Width field in the Chart panel. You can also use the Color palette to select a darker color.

Now add a second equation that generates a graph using an odd exponent. When you use a negative sign with the base value in an equation that contains an odd exponent, the upper arm of the graph extends up into quadrant II, while the lower arm extends down into quadrant IV. To see how this is so, refer to Figure 10.19 and use the following steps:

1. If you have not done so, position the mouse cursor on the top edge of the Cartesian plane. When it becomes a horizontal bar with arrows extending up and down, pull the Cartesian plane down so that the lower equation composition area is exposed.

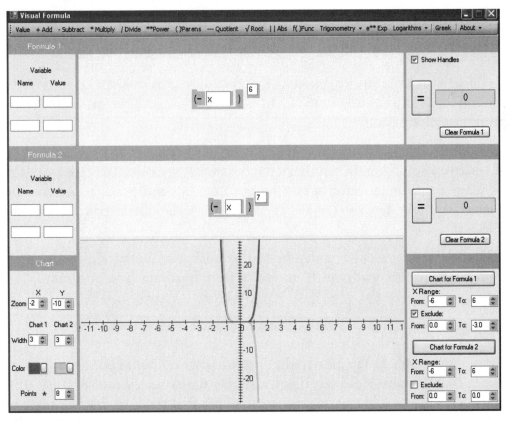

Figure 10.19
The exponent with an odd number generates a graph symmetrical to the origin of the Cartesian plane.

2. Click the Parens menu item. Then click in the lower equation composition area to position the parentheses. Pull them apart far enough to accommodate a field for a negative sign and a Value field.

3. Click the Subtract menu item. Then click inside the parens in the equation composition area to create a minus sign (−). Move the minus sign so that it rests against the left parenthesis.

4. Click on the Value item in the menu. In the equation composition after the minus sign, click to place the Value field. In this field, type x.

5. Now click on the menu item for Power, and place a field for the exponent to the upper right of the closing parenthesis. Type a 7 in the Exponent field.

6. Now in the lower-right panel, click on the Chart for Formula 2 button. As Figure 10.19 reveals, you now see a second graph in the Cartesian plane. Unlike the first, this graph is symmetrical with respect to the origin of the Cartesian plane. Its course is from quadrant II to quadrant IV.

To thicken the lines for the graphs so that they appear as shown in Figure 10.19, click on the Width controls in the Chart panel. To change the color, select a color from the Color palette.

In Figure 10.19, the shape of the graph the negative values generate is the reverse of what you see if you do not make the base value negative. To see how this is so, remove the minus sign from the lower of the two equations. To remove the minus sign, hold down the Shift key and click on the minus sign. This action deletes it.

Then click the Chart for Formula 2 button. The effect is that the odd graph travels from quadrant I to quadrant III instead of from quadrant II to quadrant IV.

Roots

For rational numbers, the use of radicals restricts the output to positive values, as Figure 10.20 reveals. However, if you multiply the extracted root by a negative number, such as −1, then you reverse the values that result so that the curve of the graph falls below the x axis.

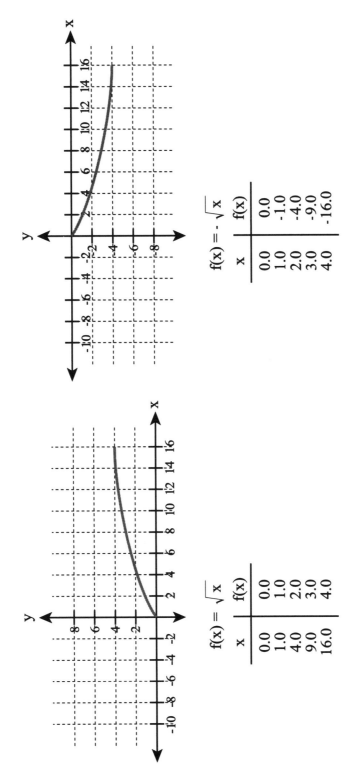

Figure 10.20
Multiplying the root by a negative flips the graph of the root.

213

Graphs of Inverses

When you work with inverse values, such as $\frac{1}{x}$, you create a graph that is undefined at $x = 0$. The domain of such graphs consists of all real numbers except 0. Zero is excluded because division by 0 is not defined. For this reason, when you use Visual Formula to generate a graphical representation of inverse values, you must use the Exclude option to prevent calculations that might involve using 0 as the divisor.

Note

Visual Formula issues a warning if you set up an equation that allows you to divide by 0. To adjust for this situation, use the Exclude option to restrict the range of values you allow for the calculation.

To employ Visual Formula to implement an equation that generates values that are the inverses of the domain values, use the following steps (refer to Figure 10.21):

1. Click the menu item for Value. Then click in the equation composition area to position a Value field. Type a 1 in the Value field.

2. Click the Divide menu item. Then click to the right of the Value field to position the division sign.

3. Again, click on the Value menu item. Place a Value field immediately after the division sign. Type an x in the Value field.

4. Now proceed to the lower-right panel and find the Exclude controls. As mentioned previously, you must exclude 0 from the values that are used in the calculations of the inverse of the domain values. To exclude 0, designate the range of values to exclude. To exclude a range that includes only −0.1 to 0.1, manually type −0.3 in the From field or use the control arrows. Then manually type 0.1 in the To field or use the control arrows.

5. Verify that the Exclude option is checked. If it is not checked, check it.

6. In the Chart panel, set the Zoom values to −3 and the Width values to 3. Set the Points value to 8.

7. Click the Chart for Formula 1 button to generate the graph. Figure 10.21 illustrates the graph of inverse values that results.

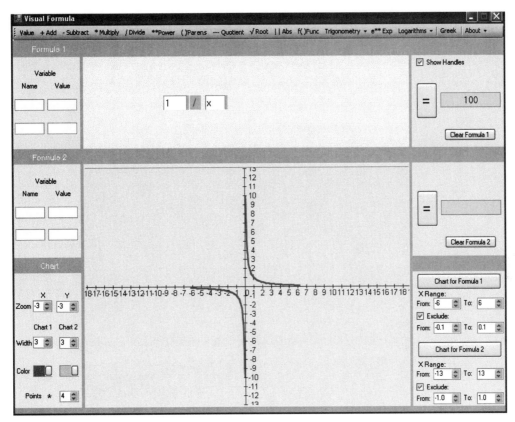

Figure 10.21
Graphs of the inverse values of the domain are undefined at 0.

For the inverses of domain values you define using exponents, the appearance of the graph that results depends on whether the exponent is even or odd. Figure 10.22 illustrates the graph of the inverse of a square. The domain values are all greater than 0 and symmetrical with respect to the y axis.

To implement the equation shown in Figure 10.22, begin with the equation you create for Figure 10.21. Click the Power menu item. To position the exponent, click to the upper right of the x field. Then type 2 in the exponent field. Click the Chart for Formula 1 button to refresh the graph.

Inverse squares generate graphs that are symmetrical to the y axis. Inverses of all domain values with even-numbered exponents are likewise symmetrical with respect to the y axis. With odd-numbered exponents, the situation changes. The

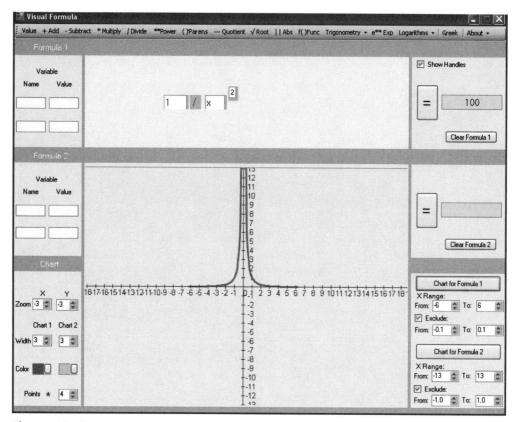

Figure 10.22
Range values using the inverse of a square are greater than zero.

graph that results is symmetrical with respect to the origin of the Cartesian plane. Figure 10.23 illustrates how this is so. As with other graphs of inverse values, these also exclude 0.

Varieties of Translation

Translating the curves generated by equations with exponents entails performing operations similar to those you perform with linear equations. On one basic level, translation involves moving the vertex of a parabola along the y axis. To move a vertex along the y axis, you first consider the position of a parabola with its vertex resting on the origin of the Cartesian plane. You can then add values to this position to shift it up or down the y axis.

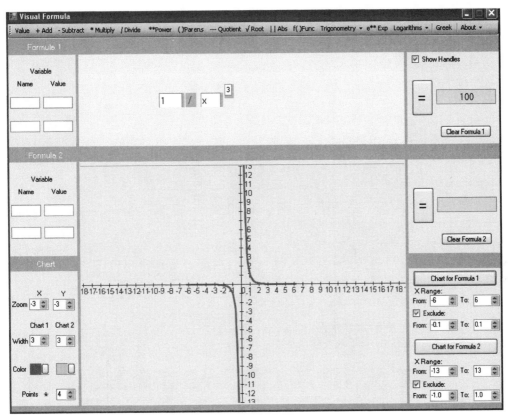

Figure 10.23
Inverse values with numbered exponents generate graphs that are symmetrical with respect to the origin.

Parabolas

When you calculate values for a parabola, you use an exponent of an even value. The result is a graph that is symmetrical with respect to the y axis. A parabola crosses the y axis once, so if you employ an equation of the form $y = x^2 + c$, the value of c provides a translation value that is also the value of the y-intercept. As a translation value, the constant c moves the graph up or down the y axis. Figure 10.24 provides a few examples of translation.

Each parabola shown in Figure 10.24 represents an equation that includes a constant for the y-intercept. In the first use of the equation, you can rewrite it as $x^2 + 0$. When the vertex rests on the coordinates (0,0), the y-intercept value is 0. The other two uses of the equation set the y-intercept at values greater than or less than zero. The first adds 3. The second explicitly subtracts 3.

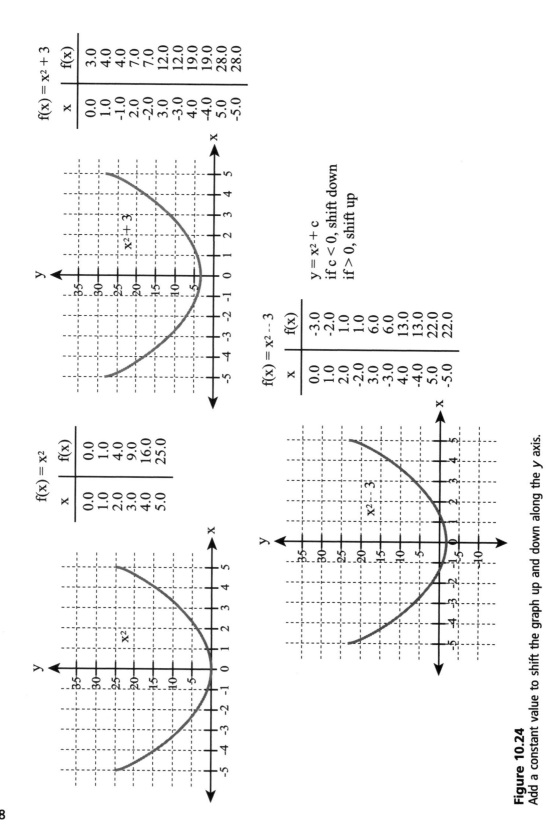

$f(x) = x^2$

x	f(x)
0.0	0.0
1.0	1.0
2.0	4.0
3.0	9.0
4.0	16.0
5.0	25.0

x^2

$f(x) = x^2 + 3$

x	f(x)
0.0	3.0
1.0	4.0
-1.0	4.0
2.0	7.0
-2.0	7.0
3.0	12.0
-3.0	12.0
4.0	19.0
-4.0	19.0
5.0	28.0
-5.0	28.0

$x^2 + 3$

$f(x) = x^2 - 3$

x	f(x)
0.0	-3.0
1.0	-2.0
2.0	1.0
-2.0	1.0
3.0	6.0
-3.0	6.0
4.0	13.0
-4.0	13.0
5.0	22.0
-5.0	22.0

$x^2 - 3$

$y = x^2 + c$
if $c < 0$, shift down
if > 0, shift up

Figure 10.24
Add a constant value to shift the graph up and down along the *y* axis.

218

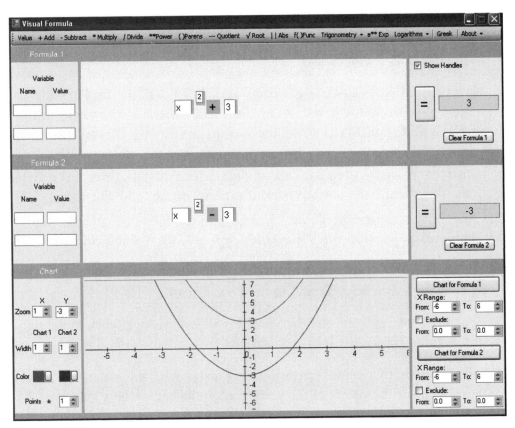

Figure 10.25
Different y-intercept values shift the parabolas up and down the y axis.

The generalization then arises that if the value of the y-intercept exceeds 0, then the graph shifts upward. On the other hand, if the value of the y-intercept is less than 0, then the graph shifts downward. When the value of the y-intercept equals 0, then the vertex of the graph rests on the x axis.

To employ Visual Formula to implement a set of non-linear equations that are shifted along the y axis, use these steps (refer to Figure 10.25):

1. Click the menu item for Value. To position the Value field, click in the upper equation composition area. Type x in the Value field.

2. Click the Power menu item. Click to place the field for the exponent to the upper right of the Value field. Type 2 in the Exponent field.

3. Click the Add menu item. Then click to the right of the Value field to position the plus sign.

4. Select Value from the menu, and then click to place the Value field after the plus sign. This is the y-intercept of the equation. To raise the vertex of the parabola 3 units above the x axis, type 3.

5. Now proceed to the lower-right panel and click the Chart for Formula 1 button to generate the graph. As Figure 10.25 illustrates, the vertex of the parabola that results rests above the x axis.

The y-intercept forced the top parabola in Figure 10.25 to shift three units above the x axis. To generate the bottom parabola, perform the following steps:

1. Click the menu item for Value. Then click in the lower equation composition area to position the Value field. Type x in the Value field.

2. Click the Power menu item. Position the field for the exponent to the upper right of the Value field. Type 2 in the Power field.

3. Click the Subtract menu item. To position the minus sign, click to the right of the Value field.

4. Click Value in the menu. To position the Value field, click after the minus sign. To lower the vertex of the parabola 3 units below the x axis, type 3.

5. In the Chart panel, set the x axis and y axis Zoom fields to 1 and -3, respectively.

6. In the lower-right panel, click the Chart for Formula 2 button to generate the graph. As Figure 10.25 illustrates, the vertex of the graph that appears rests three units below the x axis.

Parallel Lines

The general form of the line's slope-intercept equation is $y = mx + b$. In this equation, m describes the slope of the equation, and b provides the value of the y-intercept. Given that a set of equations possesses the same slope, if you vary only the value of b, you end up with a set of parallel lines.

Figure 10.26 illustrates the graphs of three lines. The middle line crosses the origin of the Cartesian plane. You could rewrite it as $y = x + 0$. The other two lines include positive and negative values for the y-intercept. The top line provides a y-intercept of 3. The lower line provides a y-intercept value of -3.

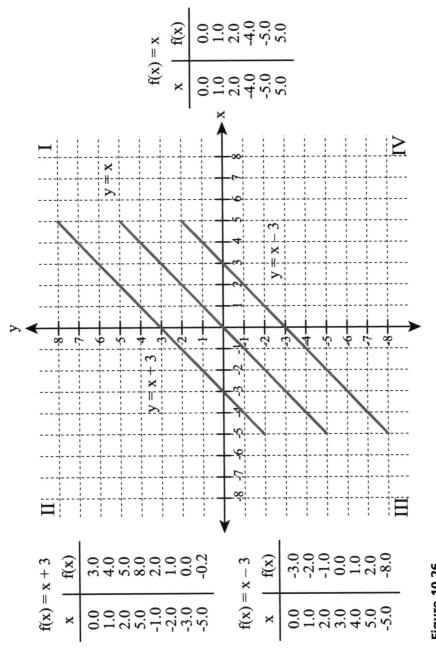

f(x) = x + 3

x	f(x)
0.0	3.0
1.0	4.0
2.0	5.0
5.0	8.0
-1.0	2.0
-2.0	1.0
-3.0	0.0
-5.0	-0.2

f(x) = x − 3

x	f(x)
0.0	-3.0
1.0	-2.0
2.0	-1.0
3.0	0.0
4.0	1.0
5.0	2.0
-5.0	-8.0

f(x) = x

x	f(x)
0.0	0.0
1.0	1.0
2.0	2.0
-4.0	-4.0
-5.0	-5.0
5.0	5.0

Figure 10.26
The value of the y-intercept raises or lowers the line on the *y* axis.

221

A generalization emerges from the work of these intercepts. If the intercept value is 0, then the line crosses the origin. If it is greater than zero, then the line crosses the y axis above the origin. If it is less than 0, then the line crosses the y axis below the origin. Whatever the y-intercept value, as long as the slopes remain the same, the lines remain parallel.

You can create parallel lines if you set the slope of the line to 1. In this instance, the equation assumes the form $y = x + b$, for the slope, m, equals 1. To use Visual Formula to generate a set of lines' slopes set to 1 but y-intercept definitions set at distinct values, follow these steps (refer to Figure 10.27):

1. Click the menu item for Value. Then click in the upper equation composition area to position the Value field. Type x in the Value field.

2. Click the Add menu item. Then click to the right of the Value field to position the plus sign.

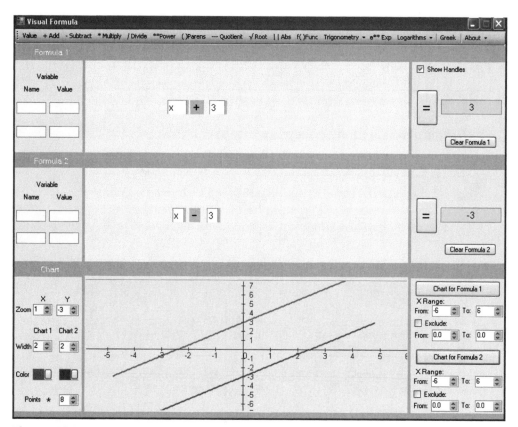

Figure 10.27
Use y-intercept settings to generate parallel lines.

3. Click the Value menu item. To position the Value field, click to the right of the plus sign. This is the y-intercept of the equation. To raise the y-intercept 3 units above the x axis, type 3 in the field.

4. Now proceed to the lower-right panel, and click the Chart for Formula 1 button to generate the graph. As Figure 10.27 illustrates, the line that results intersects the y axis above the x axis.

In Figure 10.26, you created a line that intercepts the y axis 3 units above the x axis. To create a line that intercepts the y axis 3 units below the x axis, use the following steps:

1. Click the menu item for Value. Then click in the lower equation composition area to position Value field. Type x in the Value field.

2. Click the Subtract menu item. Then click to the right of the Value field to position the minus sign.

3. Click the Value menu item. To position the Value field, click after the minus sign. To set the y-intercept 3 units below the x axis, type 3 in this field.

4. To generate the graph of the line, in the lower-right panel click the Chart for Formula 2 button. As Figure 10.27 illustrates, the resulting graph crosses the y axis below the x axis.

Odd Exponents and Translations

When you work with odd-numbered exponents and do not translate them up or down the y axis, the graphs you generate are symmetrical with respect to the origin of the Cartesian plane. When you change the position of the y-intercept for such equations, the shape of the graph remains the same, but it is no longer symmetrical with respect to the origin. Figure 10.28 illustrates the graphs of equations containing cubed variables. Both equations take the form $y = x^3 + b$. On the right side, the value of b is negative. On the left side, the value of b is positive.

To use Visual Formula to create graphs of lines generated by equations that contain variables with odd-numbered exponents, follow these steps (refer to Figure 10.29):

1. For the first equation ($y = x^3 + b$), click the menu item for Value. Then click in the upper equation composition area to position the Value field. Type x in the Value field.

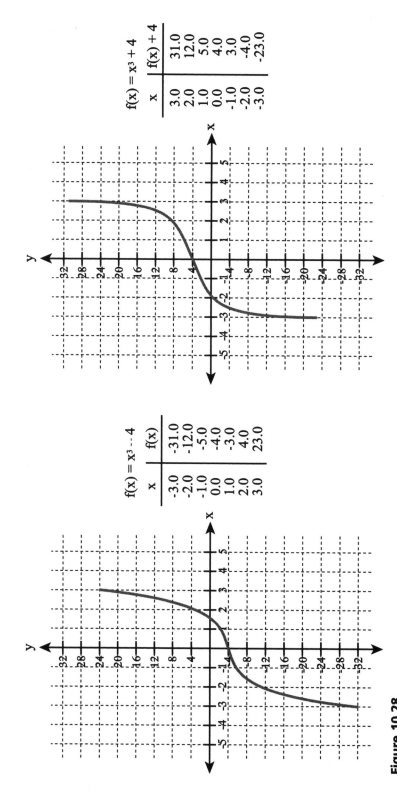

Figure 10.28
The value of the y-intercept moves the graph up or down without distorting it.

$f(x) = x^3 - 4$

x	f(x)
-3.0	-31.0
-2.0	-12.0
-1.0	-5.0
0.0	-4.0
1.0	-3.0
2.0	4.0
3.0	23.0

$f(x) = x^3 + 4$

x	f(x) + 4
3.0	31.0
2.0	12.0
1.0	5.0
0.0	4.0
-1.0	3.0
-2.0	-4.0
-3.0	-23.0

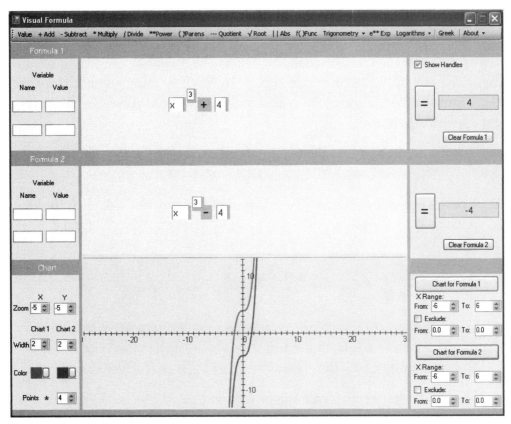

Figure 10.29
The translated results of a function that contains a cube creates a graph that is symmetrical to a line.

2. Click the Power menu item. Then click to the upper right of the Value field to position the Exponent field. After you position the Exponent field, type 3 in it.

3. Now click the Add menu item and in the equation composition area, click to the right of the Value field to position the plus sign the Add menu item provides.

4. Click the Value menu item. To position the Value field, click after the plus sign. This is the y-intercept of the equation. Type 4 in the field.

5. Set the Zoom values to −5.

6. To generate the graph, locate the lower-right panel and click the Chart for Formula 1 button. As Figure 10.29 reveals, the cubic exponent, combined

with the positive value of the y-intercept, causes the graph to cross the y axis above the x axis.

You see the second, lower graph in Figure 10.29. The lower graph crosses the y axis 4 units below the x axis. To create the equation that generates this graph, use the following steps:

1. Click the menu item for Value. Then click in the lower equation composition area to position Value field. Type x in the Value field.

2. Click the Power menu item. To position the Exponent field, click to the upper right of the value. After you position the Exponent field, type 3 in it.

3. Click the Subtract menu item. Then click to the right of the Value field to position the minus sign.

4. Now click Value in the menu. To position the Value field, click after the minus sign. Type 4 four in the field. This value lowers the vertex of the parabola 4 units below the x axis.

5. To generate the graph, locate the lower-right panel of Visual Formula and click the Chart for Formula 2 button. As Figure 10.29 illustrates, a second graph appears, lower than the first.

Translating Absolute Values

As previous exercises emphasized, when you plot the solutions to an equation that contains an absolute value, the graph that results is symmetrical with respect to the y axis, and you can shift equations containing absolute values along the y axis. Shifting involves changing the value of the y-intercept. Figure 10.30 illustrates shifting using positive and negative y-intercept values. One graph moves the y-intercept up to 6. The other moves it down to -6.

To use Visual Formula to graph the solutions of equations that shift the graphs of absolute values, follow these steps (refer to Figure 10.31):

1. For an equation that reads $y = |x| + b$, work in the top equation composition area. First, click the Abs menu item. Then click in the equation composition area to position the absolute value bars.

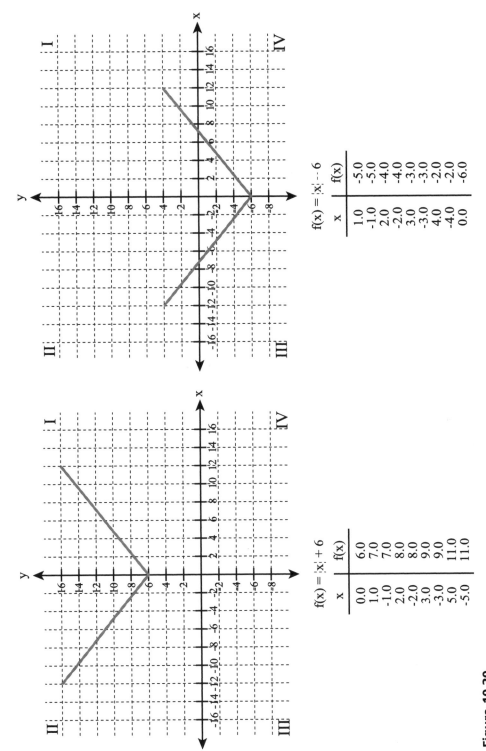

Figure 10.30
Equations involving absolute values generate graphs that are symmetrical to the *y* axis.

227

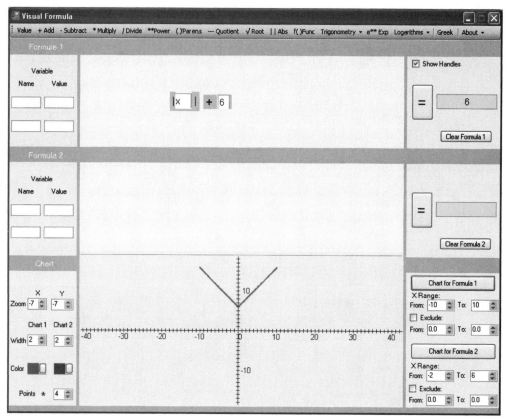

Figure 10.31
Absolute values combined with a y-intercept value allow you to shift a symmetrical figure upward or downward along the *y* axis.

2. Click the menu item for Value. To position the Value field, click between the absolute value bars. Type *x* in the Value field.

3. Click the Add menu item. To position the plus sign, click to the right of the second absolute value bar.

4. Select Value from the menu, and then click to place the Value field after the plus sign. This is the y-intercept of the equation. Type 6 in this field.

5. Now proceed to the lower-right panel of Visual Formula. Locate the X Range fields under the Chart for Formula 1 button. Click the From control and set the value of the field to −10. Click the To control and set the value of the field to 10.

6. In the Chart panel, locate the Zoom field. Click the x axis control and set the field value to -7. Click the y axis control and again set the field value to -7.

7. Now click the Chart for Formula 1 button to generate the graph.

To experiment with the graph of the absolute value figure you see in Figure 10.31, return to the upper equation composition area and change the value of the y-intercept to 4, 5, -4, and -6. The changes you make to the y-intercept value move the graph along the y axis without distorting it.

Flipping Across the Axis

Whether you are working with a linear or a non-linear equation, a negative coefficient has the effect of reversing the slope of the graph. A typical scenario with a linear equation involves seeing the line change so that instead of going from quadrant III to quadrant I, the line goes from quadrant II to quadrant IV. With a parabola, you see the vertex of the parabola flipped so that it opens downward.

Linear Flips

To use Visual Formula to show how changing the coefficient of a variable alters the slope or orientation of a graph, you can start out by working with a linear equation and generating a graph of a line with a positive slope. Then you can create a line with a negative slope. The following sections review the necessary steps. Refer to Figure 10.32 as you go.

The Positive Slope

Assume you are working with an equation that takes the form $y = m(x) + b$. To implement this equation, work in the top equation composition area. Use the following steps:

1. Click the menu item for Value. Then click in the equation composition area to position the Value field. Type 2 in the Value field. This is the field that corresponds to the coefficient m.

2. Click the Multiply menu item. Then click to the right of the Coefficient field to position the multiplication sign.

3. Click the Value field again and position the field to the right of the multiplication sign in the equation composition area. Type x in this field.

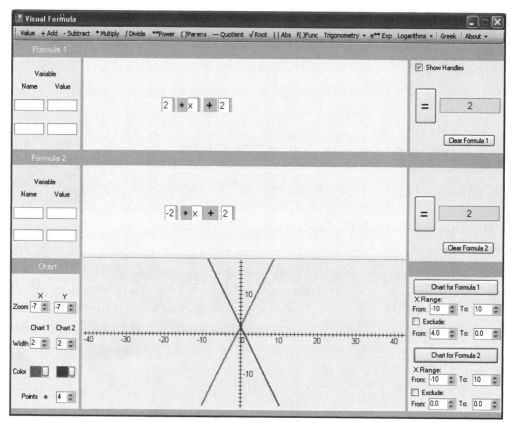

Figure 10.32
A line with a positive slope crosses a line with a negative slope.

4. Click the Add menu item and position the plus sign to the right of the x field.

5. Click to activate the Value menu item. Click after the plus sign to position the field. This is the field for the y-intercept value. Type 2 in the field.

6. Now go to the lower-right panel and find the To and From fields for the X Range setting. Click the To control and set the value of the field to −10. Click the From control and set the value of the field to 10.

7. On the Chart panel, find the Zoom fields. Click the x axis control and set the value of −7. Likewise, click the y axis control and set the value to −7.

8. Also, for the Width values, use the controls to set the Chart 1 and Chart 2 values to 2.

9. Now click the Chart for Formula 1 button. As Figure 10.32 illustrates, a graph of a linear equation with a positive slope of 2 and a y-intercept of 2 appears in the Cartesian plane.

The Negative Slope

In the previous section, you generated a line with a positive slope. Now complement this work by generating a line with a negative slope. The equation you work with in this instance assumes the form $y = -m(x) + b$. To implement this equation, work in the lower equation composition area. Use the following steps:

1. Click the menu item for Value. Then click in the lower equation composition area to position the Value field. Type -2 in the Value field. This is the field that corresponds to the coefficient m. The minus sign establishes a slope opposite of the one you implemented previously.

2. Click the Multiply menu item. Then click to the right of the Coefficient field to position the multiplication sign.

3. Click the Value field again, and position the field to the right of the multiplication sign in the lower equation composition area. Type x in this field.

4. Click the Add menu item, and position the plus sign to the right of the x field.

5. Click the Value menu item, and then position the Value field after the plus sign. This is the field for the y-intercept value. As before, type 2 in the field.

6. Now go to the lower-right panel and find the To and From fields for the X Range setting beneath the Chart for Formula 2 button. These values should already be set to correspond with those of the Chart for Formula 1 button, but to verify that this is so, click the To control and set the value of the field to -10. Click the From control and set the value of the field to 10.

7. Now click the Chart for Formula 2 button on the right. You can also click the Chart for Formula 1 button to refresh the previous graph. Graphs of the equations with slopes -2 and 2 and y-intercept 2 appear in the Cartesian plane. As Figure 10.32 illustrates, the negative slope slants down to the right.

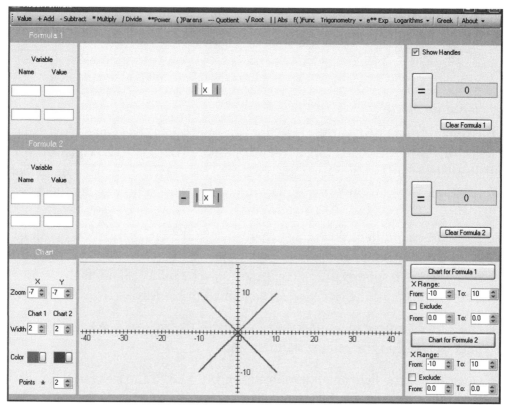

Figure 10.33
You can flip the graphs of equations containing absolute values if you multiply by a negative value.

Absolute Value Flips

An equation for an absolute value takes the form $y = |x|$. Such an equation generates a graph in a V shape. The vertex of the V opens upward. To flip this graph so that its vertex opens downward, you introduce a negative slope. The form of the equation becomes $y = -m|x|$. Figure 10.33 illustrates two graphs of equations that possess absolute values. The V above the x axis represents a positive slope. The V below the x axis represents a negative slope.

To use Visual Formula to implement these two equations, use the following approach:

1. Click the Abs (absolute value) menu item. Then click in the upper equation composition area to position the absolute value bars. Pull the bars apart so that they can accommodate a variable.

2. Click the Value menu item. Then click between the absolute value bars to place the Value field. In this field type x.

3. To generate the graph of this absolute value equation, locate the Chart for Formula 1 button in the lower-right panel and click on it. You see the graph that appears above the x axis in Figure 10.33.

To implement an absolute value function that generates the inverted graph shown in Figure 10.33, follow these steps:

1. Click the Subtract menu item. To position the minus sign the Subtract menu generates, click in the lower equation composition area.

2. Click the Abs (absolute value) menu item. Then click in the lower equation composition area to the right of the minus sign to position the absolute value bars. Pull the bars apart far enough to accommodate a variable.

3. Click the Value menu item. To position the Value field, click between the absolute value bars.

4. Now click the Chart for Formula 2 buttons to see the graph. This graph appears below the x axis.

To give your graphs the appearance of those illustrated in Figure 10.33, use the following approach:

1. Locate the X Range fields below both of the Chart for Formula 1 and Chart for Formula 2 buttons. These are in the lower-right panel.

2. Click the arrow controls for the From fields and set them to -10.

3. Click the arrow controls for the To fields and set them to 10.

4. On the Chart panel, set the x and y Zoom values to -7. Set the Width fields for both charts to 2.

5. Finally, set the Points field to 2.

Flipping Parabolas

To flip a parabola, you provide a negative value as the coefficient of x. Consider, for example, the equation $y = x^2$. You can rewrite this equation as $y = ax^2$. In this instance, the constant a equals 1, so if you make the equation explicit, then it reads $y = (1)x^2$. The value of the coefficient is 1, and the coefficient defines how the vertex of the parabola the equation generates opens. A positive value makes it open upward.

If you change the equation so that the value of the coefficient becomes negative, then the equation takes on this form: $y = (-1)x^2$. When you make the coefficient negative, you change the way the parabola opens. It now opens downward.

To put Visual Formula to work to implement an equation that generates a parabola that opens upward, you implement the equation that reads $y = (1)x^2$. To accomplish this task, use the following steps:

1. Click the menu item for Value. To position the Value field, click in the upper equation composition area. Type x in the Value field.

2. Then, to create an exponent, click the Power menu item. To position this field, click to the upper right of the Value field. After you position the Exponent field, type 2 in it.

3. To generate the graph of the equation, proceed to the lower-right panel and click the Chart for Formula 1 button. As illustrated in Figure 10.34, you see a parabola that opens upward from the x axis.

Figure 10.34 illustrates a second parabola, one that opens downward. You can express the equation that generates this parabola as $y = (-1)a^2$. Use these steps in Visual Formula to implement the equation:

1. Click the menu item for Subtract. Then click in the lower equation composition area to position the minus sign that corresponds to the Subtract menu item.

2. Next, click the Parens menu item. Click after the minus sign to position the parentheses, and then pull them far enough apart to accommodate a Value field.

3. Click the Value menu item. Click inside the parentheses to place the corresponding field. Type x in the Value field.

4. Click the Power menu item. To position the Exponent field, click to the upper right of the closing parenthesis. After you position the Exponent field, type 2 in it.

5. To generate the graph, in the lower-right panel of Visual Formula, click the Chart for Formula 2 button.

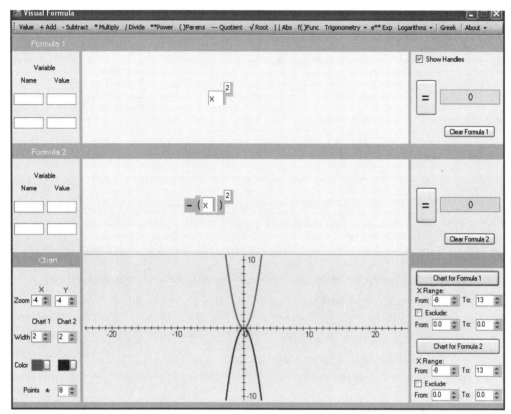

Figure 10.34
Multiplication by a negative value inverts a parabola.

Inverting and Shifting Parabolas

In addition to inverting parabolas, you can shift them along the x axis. To shift a parabola, you set up an equation that involves using the square of the difference of two values. The equation with which you shift a parabola assumes the following form:

$$y = (x - b)^2$$

In this form of the equation, the value of b designates the distance along the x axis you want to shift the vertex of the parabola. If b is a positive number, then you shift the parabola to the right on the x axis. If b is a negative number, then you shift the parabola to the left. Here is how you can rewrite the equation when b consists of a negative value.

$$y = (x - (-b))^2$$

$$y = (x + b)^2$$

This equation shifts the parabola to the left on the x axis. Following the path explored in the previous section, in addition to altering its position on the x axis, you can invert the parabola. To invert the parabola, you multiply the square of the difference or sum that characterizes the position of the parabola on the x axis by negative 1. Here is how you can write this equation so that you both invert the parabola and shift it to the left:

$$y = -1(x + b)^2$$

Multiplication by -1 flips the parabola. The vertex opens downward. The addition of the value associated with b shifts it to the left. In the sections that follow, you use Visual Formula to explore these and a few other activities.

To the Right

An equation that features the square of the differences of two values allows you to shift a parabola. As mentioned previously, if the value of b is positive, the expression $(x - b)^2$ shifts the vertex of the parabola to the right. The top equation composition area in Figure 10.35 illustrates the implementation of an equation of this type. The result is the parabola in the Cartesian plane with its vertex facing upward. On the other hand, the bottom equation composition area illustrates the implementation of an inverted parabola, which appears below the x axis in the Cartesian plane. Here are the procedures in Visual Formula for implementing these equations (refer to Figure 10.35):

1. To implement the equation that reads $y = (x - 4)^2$, click the Parens menu item. Then click in the upper equation composition area to position the parentheses. Pull the parentheses far enough apart to accommodate two fields and a minus sign.

2. Then click the menu item for Value. To position the field the Value menu item generates, click just after the opening parenthesis. Type x in the field.

3. Next, click the Subtract menu item. Click after the field inside the parentheses to position it.

4. Click the Value menu item again. Click inside the parentheses after the minus sign to position the field the Value menu generates. Type 4 in this field.

5. To create an exponent, click the Power menu item. To position the Exponent field the Power menu item provides, click to the upper right of the closing parentheses. In the Exponent field, type 2.

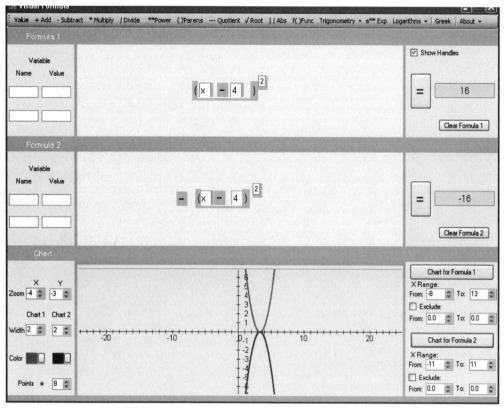

Figure 10.35
Defining an x-intercept and setting the value for the x axis allows you to shift and invert a parabola.

6. In the lower-right panel, set the X Range From field to −8 and the To field to 13.

7. To generate the graph, proceed to the lower-right panel and click the button for Chart for Formula 1. You see a parabola that opens upward from the x axis.

In Figure 10.35, the Cartesian plane shows the graphs of two equations. One opens upward; the other opens downward. The equation that opens downward reads $y = -(x-4)^2$. It is the same as the previous equation, except the value that orients whether the parabola opens up or down is −1. To implement this equation, use these steps:

1. Click the menu item for Subtract. To position the minus sign, click in the lower equation composition area.

2. Click the Parens menu item. To position the parentheses, click to the right of the minus sign. Pull the parentheses apart to allow for two fields and a minus sign.

3. Click the Value menu item. Inside the parentheses in the lower equation composition area, click to position the Value field. Type x in this field.

4. Now click the menu item for Subtract. To position the minus sign, click to the right of the Value field.

5. Then click the Value menu item again, and place the corresponding field to the right of the minus sign. Type 4 in the field.

6. Click the Power menu item. To position the Exponent field, click to the upper right of the closing parenthesis. After you position the Exponent field, type 2 in it.

7. Set the Zoom x axis value to -4 and the y axis value to -3.

8. To generate the graph, in the lower-right panel of Visual Formula, click the Chart for Formula 2 button.

To the Left

As Figure 10.36 shows, the square of the sum of two values generates parabolas that are shifted to the left of the y axis. Multiplying the sums by negative numbers inverts the parabolas. The equations you employ to shift and generate parabolas of this type work in the same fashion as the equations discussed in the previous section. The difference is only that the parabolas are shifted to the left.

When you shift the parabolas to the left, you in essence subtract a negative value. You can write the equation as $y = (x - (-b))^2$, but it is just as easy to write it in the form you see depicted in Figure 10.36. When you multiply the sum by -1, you invert the parabola.

To implement these two parabolas as shown in Figure 10.36, follow the steps in the previous section. At Step 3 in the upper equation and at Step 4 in the lower equation, instead of using a minus sign between the two fields within the parentheses, click the Add menu item and position the plus sign after the first Value field.

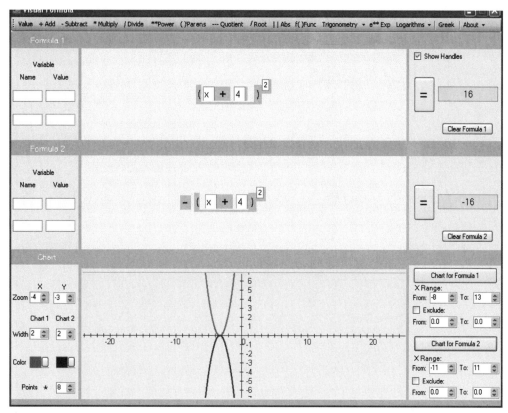

Figure 10.36
You shift the parabola to the right by squaring the sum of two numbers.

Absolute Values

In Figure 10.37, equations that feature the differences and sums of absolute values generate shifts to the right and the left of the y axis. You shift the V that is on the right of the y axis by subtracting 4 from the variable x. The equation that accomplishes this is $y = |x - b|$.

The equation that features the sum of two values generates the shift to the left. The V on the left of the y axis has been shifted by adding 4 to the value of the variable. The equation that accomplishes this is $y = |x + b|$.

To implement the top equation, refer to Figure 10.37 and use the following steps:

1. Click the Abs menu item. To position the bars for the absolute value, click in the upper equation composition area. Pull the bars far enough apart to accommodate two fields and a minus sign.

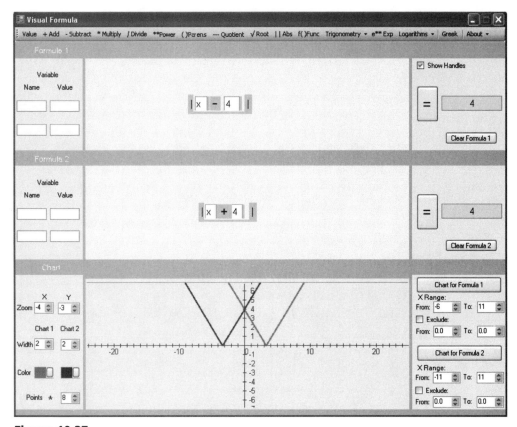

Figure 10.37
You shift an absolute value to the right by subtracting a constant from the variable.

2. Click the Value menu item. Click inside the absolute bars to position the Value field. Type x in this field.

3. To create the minus sign, click on the Subtract menu item. To position the minus sign, click inside the absolute value bars after the x Value field.

4. To create the field for the (?) shift constant (b), click the Value menu item. Then click within the absolute value bars after the minus sign. Type a 4 in this field.

5. To generate the graph of the absolute value equation, in the lower-right panel click the Chart for Formula 1 button. The V you see on the right of the y axis in Figure 10.37 appears.

A V also appears on the left side of the y axis in Figure 10.37. To generate this figure, work within the lower of the two equation composition areas and use the following steps:

1. Click the Abs menu item. To position the bars for the absolute value, click in the lower equation composition area. Pull the bars far enough apart to accommodate two fields and a plus sign.

2. Click the Value menu item. Click inside the absolute bars to position the Value field. Type x in this field.

3. To create the plus sign, click on the Add menu item. To position the plus sign, click inside the absolute value bars after the x Value field.

4. To create the field for the (?) shift constant (b), click the Value menu item. Then click within the absolute value bars after the plus sign. Type a 4 in this field.

5. To generate the graph of the absolute value equation, in the lower-right panel click the Chart for Formula 2 button. The V you see on the left of the y axis in Figure 10.37 appears.

Conclusion

In this chapter, you have used Visual Formula to explore the equations and relations discussed in other chapters. Having at hand a software application like Visual Formula that allows you to easily manipulate graphical representations of solutions of equations enables you to gain an understanding of how predictable patterns characterize the solutions of equations. For example, if a linear equation possesses a positive slope, then it slants upward into quadrant I. If a parabola possesses a negative coefficient, then its vertices open downward. Such basic observations of the patterns that characterize graphs allow you to work more confidently with the solutions of equations because, as you work with an equation, you can anticipate the solutions your work results in.

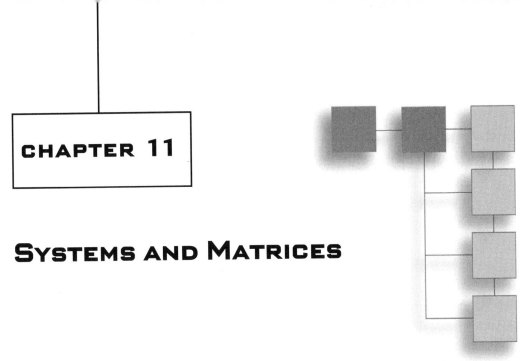

CHAPTER 11

SYSTEMS AND MATRICES

In this chapter, you explore how to find the solutions to equations that possess two variables. One of the most ready ways of solving such equations involves substitution. Given this groundwork, you then explore how to work with systems of equations that involve two or more variables. When you work with systems of equations, you can solve them by employing addition and subtraction to eliminate variables from the equations on a selective basis. This approach to solving systems of equations allows you to investigate how to view systems of equations as matrices. This chapter includes the following topics:

- Solving for two variables using substitution

- Using addition and multiplication

- Recognizing no solution and infinite solution scenarios

- Solving using different approaches to elimination

- Basic matrices

- Extended matrices

Shared Solutions

As Figure 11.1 illustrates, when two or more equations can generate the same sets of ordered pairs, they form a system of equations. When you solve a system of equations, you find sets of values that both equations generate. You can approach

Systems of Equations

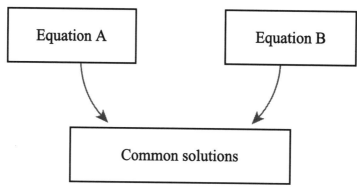

Figure 11.1
One ordered pair can be a solution to two or more equations.

solving systems of equations in various ways. One way is to generate ordered pairs, and then compare the ordered pairs to determine if any are the same for both equations. Another approach involves generating graphs for the equations that you plot on one Cartesian coordinate plane and then compare. If you are working with linear equations, the point at which the lines intersect constitutes a solution for the system of equations.

Any given equation is likely to generate an indefinite number of ordered pairs. The ordered pair that a given equation generates is a solution set. As with any two sets, if the sets share common elements, then the shared elements are known as the intersection of the two sets. Consider this set of equations:

$$y - x = 1$$
$$y + x = 2$$

Given this set of equations, you can then ask whether a coordinate pair exists that satisfies both equations. To apply the graphical approach to answering this question, you can use Visual Formula to implement the equations and generate graphs of them. To implement the equations in Visual Formula, you must rewrite them in this way:

$$y = x + 1$$
$$y = 2 - x$$

Figure 11.2 illustrates these equations as implemented in Visual Formula. For both equations, you create two Value fields. In the top equation, you use the Add menu item to position a plus sign between the fields. For the lower equation, you

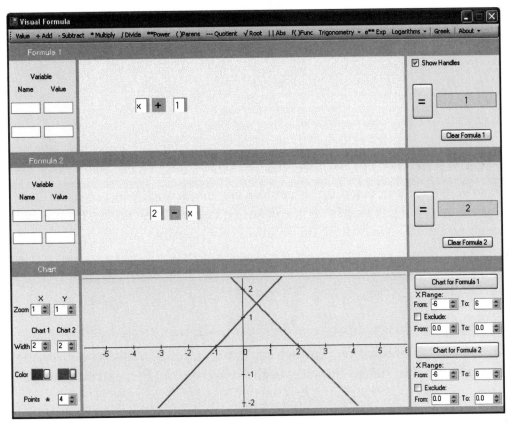

Figure 11.2
The intersection of the two lines constitutes the intersection of the solution sets of the two equations.

use the Subtract menu item to position a minus sign between the fields. You type the variable *x* and the constant values as shown. You can then click on the Chart Formula 1 and Chart Formula 2 buttons to generate the graph. In the left panel, you change the Color and Width fields for the lines to achieve the effects shown.

When you inspect the point of intersection between the two lines in Figure 11.2, you can assess that the solution pair is likely to be (0.5, 1.5). To test these values, you insert them into the equations. The test for the first equation shows the pair to be valid:

$$y - x = 1$$

$$1.5 - 0.5 = 1$$

$$1 = 1$$

The test for the second equation also shows the pair to be valid:

$$y + x = 2$$

$$1.5 + 0.5 = 2$$

$$2 = 2$$

Substitution

To solve a system of equations in a more systematic way, you use substitution. Toward this end, you first solve one of the equations in the system for one of its variables. You then substitute the solution into the other equation.

Here is a system of equations that you can solve in this way:

$$x + y = 12$$

$$3x + y = 4$$

To solve this set of equations through substitution, you can solve either equation for either variable. In this instance, begin by solving the first equation for y:

$$x + y = 12$$

$$y = 12 - x$$

You can then proceed to substitute the expression $12 - x$ into the second of the equations. To do so, you proceed as follows:

$$3x + y = 4$$

$$3x + (12 - x) = 4$$

$$2x + 12 = 4$$

$$2x = 4 - 12$$

$$x = \frac{-8}{2}$$

$$x = -4$$

Having arrived at this solution for x, you can then return to either of the equations in the system and solve for y. Accordingly, if you use the first equation, you proceed as follows:

$$-4 + y = 12$$

$$y = 12 + 4$$

$$y = 16$$

Given the solution to y, you then have at hand the ordered pair $(-4, 16)$. You can test the validity of this ordered pair by substituting its two values into the equations:

$$-4 + 16 = 12$$

$$12 = 12$$

Likewise, with the second equation,

$$16 = 12 - (-4)$$

$$16 = 16$$

Exercise Set 11.1

Use substitution to solve these systems of equations for the value of x and y. Check your answers.

a. $6x - 2y = -4$
   $3x + 4y = 1$

b. $4x + 6y = -6$
   $-4x + 4y = 16$

c. $x - 6y = 4$
   $2x - 2y = 7$

d. $3x - 2y = 7$
   $x + y = \dfrac{1}{2}$

e. $2x + y = 6$
   $3x + 4y = 4$

Systems Solved by Adding and Multiplying

In addition to graphing the results of equations and using the substitution method, you can also solve equations with a method that involves using multiplication and addition processes to eliminate variables from the equations. To use this approach, you first assess the system of equations to determine a value by which you can multiply one of the equations so that you can make one or another of its coefficients the additive inverse of the corresponding coefficient in the other equation. You then multiply by this value and carry out an addition operation to arrive at a new equation in which you have eliminated one of the variables. You repeat this process until you arrive at values for each of the variables in the system.

To see how this works, consider this system of equations:

$$4x - 4y = -1$$

$$-4x + 2y = 0$$

When you assess this system of equations, you can see that the coefficients of x are additive inverses. Since your goal is to arrive at a new equation in which you eliminate one of the two variables, adding these two equations immediately provides you with a desired result. When you carry out the addition, your activity takes the following form:

$$
\begin{array}{r}
4x - 4y = -1 \\
-4x + 2y = 0 \\
\hline
-2y = -1
\end{array}
$$

The addition eliminates x as a variable and leaves you with the equation $-2y = -1$. To find the value of y, you need to eliminate the coefficient of y, and to accomplish this, you multiply the equation by $\frac{1}{2}$:

$$-2y = -1\left(\frac{1}{2}\right)$$

The result of this activity is the value of y:

$$y = \frac{1}{2}$$

This, then, provides you with half of your goal. Now that you have the value of y, you can proceed with discovering the value of x. To discover the value of x, you bring forward the first equation from the system of equations:

$$4x - 4y = -1$$

Your goal this time around is to eliminate the coefficient of y. To accomplish this, you make use of the fact that you know the value of y. The coefficient of y in the equation is -4. You must multiply the equation that establishes the value of y by a number that generates the additive inverse of -4. To reach this goal, you multiply $y = \frac{1}{2}$ by 4. Your activity in this respect takes the following form:

$$y(4) = \frac{1}{2}(4)$$

$$4y = \frac{4}{2}$$

$$4y = 2$$

The result is an equation that eliminates the y variable if you add it to the first equation in the system of equations. Here is the operation that accomplishes this task:

$$\begin{array}{r} 4x - 4y = -1 \\ 4y = 2 \\ \hline 4x = 1 \end{array}$$

The result of the operation is an equation that isolates x. You can then multiply this equation by $\frac{1}{4}$ to arrive at the value of x. Here is the multiplication and the result:

$$\frac{1}{4}(4x) = 1\left(\frac{1}{4}\right)$$

$$x = \frac{1}{4}$$

Now you know the values of both x and y. The value of x is $\frac{1}{4}$, and the value of y is $\frac{1}{2}$.

To test the correctness of your calculations, you can substitute the values of x and y into the equations of the original system. Here is the substitution for the first equation:

$$(4)\frac{1}{4} - (4)\frac{1}{2} = -1$$

$$1 - 2 = -1$$

$$-1 = -1$$

Here is the substitution for the second equation:

$$-4\frac{1}{4}+2\frac{1}{2}=0$$

$$-1+1=0$$

$$0=0$$

Exercise Set 11.2

Solve the following systems of equations using the elimination method. Check your answers.

a. $3a+2b=5$
   $a+4b=10$

b. $a-2b=6$
   $2a-3b=4$

c. $6a-12b=16$
   $3a-4b=8$

d. $5a+4b=5$
   $2a-4b=8$

e. $2a+3b=17$
   $5a+7b=29$

Variations on Themes

While it is best to conform to the basic addition and multiplication routines for solving systems of equations, in a few instances, you benefit if you perform a few preliminary activities to make your work easier. The actions you take involve practical measures that you often take when working with fractions.

Change the Order

One measure involves examining the system of equations to discover whether it might be best to switch the order of the equations to make addition and multiplication activities easier. Here is an example involving the system of equations that resembles the one you explored in the previous section:

$$-4x+2y=0$$

$$x-4y=-1$$

You can make it easier to work with this system of equations if you leave the coefficient of x in the second equation unchanged and instead manipulate the first equation. To make it possible to preserve the coefficient of x in the second equation, you reverse the order of the equations. The second equation becomes the first:

$$x - 4y = -1$$

$$-4x + 2y = 0$$

The changed order does not alter the value the equations generate. It only makes it so you can work with them more readily. Given this reordering, then, you can proceed with the elimination of the x variable.

Preliminary Multiplications

In some instances, you work with systems of equations that contain decimal values. In such situations, if you inspect the decimal values, you might find that if you multiply them by a power of 10 (10, 100, and so on), you can eliminate the decimal values. Elimination of the decimal values makes it much easier to proceed as you work with multiplications you require to eliminate the x or y variables. Here is an example of a system of equations that contains decimal values:

$$-0.4x + 0.6y = 0.04$$

$$0.02x - 0.4y = 1.4$$

For both of these equations, if you multiply by 100, you can eliminate the decimal points and so arrive at terms that consist of integers. Your actions take the following form:

$$-0.4x + 0.6y = 0.04 \quad \text{(multiply by 100)}$$
$$0.02x - 0.4y = 1.4 \quad \text{(multiply by 100)}$$

This multiplication results in a new version of the system that preserves the value relationship of the first:

$$-40x + 60y = 4$$

$$2x - 40y = 140$$

Given this adjusted view of the system of equations, you can now proceed much more readily toward a solution for the system.

Exercise Set 11.3

Solve each system of equations. Check your answers.

a. $6a + 4b = 15$
   $a + 2b = 12$

b. $a - 4b = 12$
   $7a - 6b = 8$

c. $6x - 12y = 16$
   $3x - 4y = 8$

Systems with No Solutions

Figure 11.3 illustrates two lines with the same slope. They are parallel to each other, so they never intersect. The equations as given read this way:

$$y = x + 3$$
$$y = x - 3$$

$f(x) = x + 3$

x	f(x)
0.0	3.0
1.0	4.0
2.0	5.0
5.0	8.0
-1.0	2.0
-2.0	1.0
-3.0	0.0
-5.0	-0.2

$f(x) = x - 3$

x	f(x)
0.0	-3.0
1.0	-2.0
2.0	-1.0
3.0	0.0
4.0	1.0
5.0	2.0
-5.0	-8.0

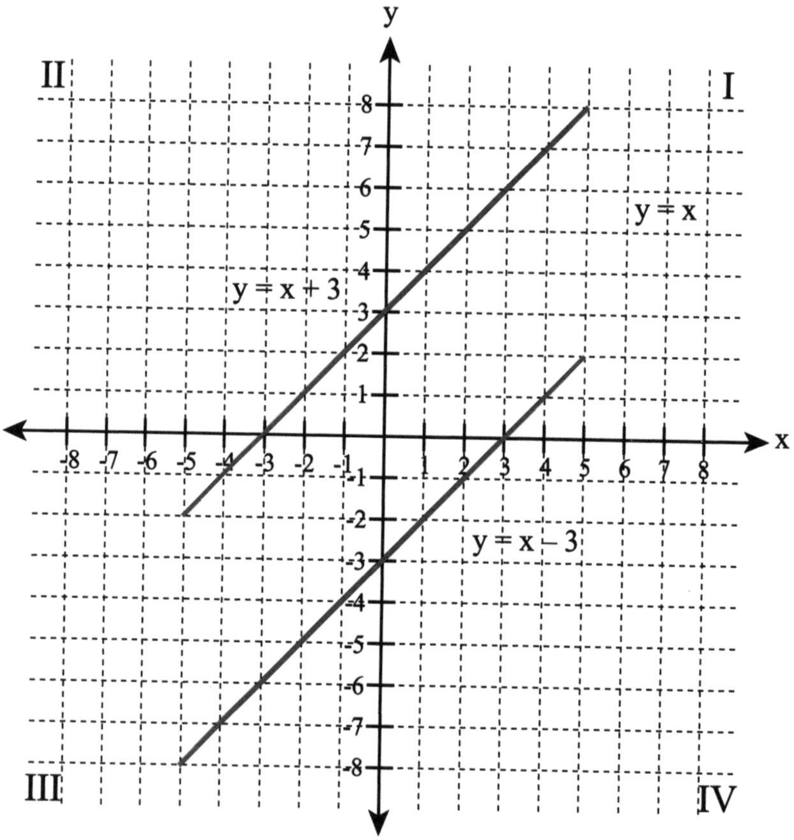

Figure 11.3
Lines that do not intersect have no solution.

If you consider the two equations that generate these lines, you end up with a system that has this appearance:

$$x - y = -3$$
$$x - y = 3$$

If you try to arrive at a solution for this system of equations, you might proceed by multiplying by -1 so that you can eliminate the x variable. Your work proceeds along the following lines:

$$x - y = -3$$
$$-x + y = 3$$

Given this result, you can then add $-x + y = 3$ to the first equation:

$$x - y = 3$$
$$\underline{-x + y = 3}$$
$$0 + 0 = 6$$

The addition operation produces an equation that is inconsistent because 0 is not equal to 6. As it is, when you attempt to find values that allow you to create a consistent addition product, your efforts fail. The system does not allow the lines to intersect, so no solution exists.

Exercise Set 11.4

Determine which of these equations creates parallel lines.

a. $6a + 4b = 15$
   $a + 2b = 12$

b. $a - 3b = 1$
   $-2a + 6b = 5$

c. $6x - 12y = 16$
   $3x - 4y = 8$

d. $y = -3x + 5$
   $y = -3x - 2$

e. $3y - 2x = 6$
   $-12y + 8x = -24$

An Infinite Number of Solutions

If an inconsistent system has no solutions, another type of system, known as a dependent system, possesses an infinite number of solutions. The reason this occurs is that when you evaluate such systems, you find that you can express one variable in terms of the other. You have at hand such a system when you can multiply one of the equations in the system by some value that produces an equation that is the same as the other equation in the system. Equations that possess such a relationship with each other are known as dependent equations. To see how this can happen, consider this system of equations:

$$4x + 6y = 2$$

$$8x + 12y = 4$$

To make it easier to work with the two equations, reverse them:

$$8x + 12y = 4$$

$$4x + 6y = 2$$

Then to make it so that you can eliminate one of the variables, multiply the second equation by -2 to create an equivalent equation:

$$4x + 6y = 2 \quad \text{(multiply by } -2\text{)}$$

The outcome of this activity is this equation:

$$-8x - 12y = -4$$

If you then add this equation to the first of the equations in the system, your activity proceeds along the following lines:

$$8x + 12y = 4$$
$$\underline{-8x - 12y = -4}$$
$$0 + 0 \ = 0$$

The system you are dealing with, then, consists of one equation expressed in two different ways, so to reach a solution for the system, you can solve $8x + 12y = 4$ for x and y. One approach to this involves substitution and finding the solution for *x*. Accordingly, you might proceed in this way:

$$4x + 6y = 2$$

$$\frac{4x}{4} + \frac{6y}{4} = \frac{2}{4}$$

$$x + \frac{3y}{2} = \frac{1}{2}$$

$$x = \frac{1}{2} - \frac{3y}{2}$$

$$x = \frac{1 - 3y}{2}$$

Given this finding, you can identify an ordered pair by using the value you possess for the *y* variable. This takes the following form:

$$\left(\frac{1 - 3y}{2}, y\right)$$

Working from this basis, you can proceed to furnish any value you choose for *y* to arrive at the value of *x*. In this way, you can potentially generate an infinite number of ordered pairs. Among these are the following:

$$(-4, 3) \qquad \left(-\frac{5}{2}, 2\right) \qquad (-13, 9)$$

Exercise Set 11.5

Explore these systems of equations and determine if they are dependent.

a. $\frac{1}{3} + \frac{1}{4} = \frac{1}{16}$

   $\frac{1}{6} + \frac{1}{2} = \frac{12}{16}$

b. $6x + 5y = 22$

   $18x + 15y = 32$

c. $4x + 2y = 20$

   $24x + 12y = 8$

d. $3y - 2x = 6$

   $-12y + 8x = -24$

e. $y = -3x + 5$

   $y = -3x - 2$

Systems with Three Variables

When you deal with systems of three equations with three variables, you extend the addition and multiplication activities you perform when you work with systems of two equations with two variables. The goals and procedures remain the same. Your task is to move through the equations, multiplying and adding so that you can express the equations so that they identify the values of the constituent variables.

To examine how to work with a system of three equations with three variables, consider this system:

$$2x - 4y + 6z = 22 \qquad A$$

$$4x + 2y - 3z = 4 \qquad B$$

$$3x + 3y - z = 4 \qquad C$$

To make it easier to identify the equations, you can associate them with letters of the alphabet. As you go, the letters allow you to continue to identify the equations as you rewrite after performing operations involving addition and subtraction on them.

STEP 1

For starters, the first goal involves examining the system to see if there is a convenient way to isolate the x variable. Toward this end, you multiply equation A by $\frac{1}{2}$, eliminating the coefficient of x.

$2x - 4y + 6z = 22$	A	Original version of A.
$\frac{1}{2}(2x) - \frac{1}{2}(4y) + \frac{1}{2}(6z) = \frac{1}{2}(22)$	A	Multiply A by $\frac{1}{2}$.
$x - 2y + 3z = 11$	A	Simplify A.
$4x + 2y - 3z = 4$	B	Not changed.
$3x + 3y - z = 4$	C	Not changed.

If you examine equation B, you see that you can multiply the new form of equation A by -4 to obtain an equation that eliminates the x variable from equation B. Along the same lines, if you multiply the new form of equation A by −3, you obtain an equation you can use to eliminate the *x* variable from equation C. Here is the form your work assumes:

$x - 2y + 3z = 11$	A	From the previous rewriting.
$4x + 2y - 3z = 4$	B	Original version of B.
$-4x + 8y - 12z = -44$	A	Multiply A by −4.
$10y - 15z = -40$	B	Add A(−4) to B.

Then you attend to equation C:

$3x + 3y - z = 4$	C	Original version of C.
$-3x + 6y - 9z = -33$	A	Multiply A by −3.
$9y - 10z = -29$	C	Add A(−3) to C.

STEP 2

You now have a system of equations in which you have eliminated the *x* variable from two of the equations. You now need to isolate the *y* and *z* variables in the same way. Here is the system of equations as you have rewritten them thus far:

$x - 2y + 3z = 11$	A	Coefficient of x is 1.
$10y - 15z = -40$	B	Added A to remove x.
$9y - 10z = -29$	C	Added A to remove x.

To proceed with the isolation of *y* in equation B, you multiply equation B by $\frac{1}{10}$. In this way, you reduce the coefficient of *y* in equation B to 1. Here is the form your work assumes:

$10y - 15z = -40$	B	Start with B from STEP 2.
$y - \dfrac{15}{10}z = -\dfrac{40}{10}$	B	Multiply B by $\dfrac{1}{10}$.
$y - \dfrac{3}{2}z = -4$	B	Rewrite to simplify.

You can now put this rewritten version of B to work to eliminate the y variable from equation C. To accomplish this, you multiply B by -9 because 9 is the value of the coefficient of y in equation C. Here is how your work proceeds:

$$9y - 10z = -29 \qquad\qquad \text{C} \qquad \text{Start with C from STEP 2.}$$

$$(-9)y - (-9)\frac{3}{2}z = (-9)(-4) \qquad \text{B} \qquad \text{Multiply B by } -9.$$

$$-9y + \frac{27}{2}z = 36 \qquad\qquad \text{B} \qquad \text{Simplify B}(-9).$$

$$\frac{7}{2}z = 7 \qquad\qquad\qquad \text{C} \qquad \text{Add B}(-9) \text{ to C.}$$

To solve equation C for z at this point, you use these steps:

$$\left(\frac{2}{7}\right)\frac{7}{2}z = 7\left(\frac{2}{7}\right) \qquad \text{C} \qquad \text{Remove the coefficient.}$$

$$z = \frac{14}{7} \qquad\qquad\qquad \text{C} \qquad \text{The coefficient of } z \text{ is 1.}$$

$$z = 2 \qquad\qquad\qquad\quad \text{C} \qquad z \text{ is known.}$$

STEP 3

The system now takes this form:

$$x - 2y + 3z = 11 \qquad \text{A} \qquad \text{Need to isolate } x.$$

$$y - \frac{3}{2}z = -4 \qquad \text{B} \qquad \text{Need to isolate } y.$$

$$z = 2 \qquad\qquad\quad \text{C} \qquad z \text{ is known.}$$

Given that you have identified the value of z, you can now use your knowledge to eliminate the z variable from equations A and B. To accomplish this, you first work with equation B. Then you work from there to equation A.

Beginning with equation B, then, given that the coefficient of z is $-\frac{3}{2}$, you multiply equation C by $\frac{3}{2}$ to arrive at an equation you can add to B to eliminate z.

Here is how your work proceeds:

$$y - \frac{3}{2}z = -4 \qquad \text{B} \qquad \text{Start with B from STEP 3.}$$

$$z = 2 \qquad \text{C} \qquad \text{Start with C from STEP 3.}$$

$$\left(\frac{3}{2}\right)z = \frac{3}{2}(2) \qquad \text{C} \qquad \text{Multiply C by } \frac{3}{2}.$$

$$\frac{3}{2}z = 3 \qquad \text{C} \qquad \text{Simplify C } \left(\frac{3}{2}\right).$$

$$y = -1 \qquad \text{B} \qquad \text{Add C } \left(\frac{3}{2}\right) \text{ to B; } y \text{ known.}$$

This then provides you with the value of y. At the same time, it remains for you to eliminate the z variable from equation A. To eliminate the z variable from equation A, you repeat much of the activity you just performed. This time around, you consider that the coefficient of z in equation A is 3. Given this value, you multiply equation C by -3 to arrive at an equation you can subtract from equation A to remove the z variable from equation A. Here is how your work proceeds:

$$x - 2y + 3z = 11 \qquad \text{A} \qquad \text{Start with A from STEP 3.}$$

$$(-3)z = -3(2) \qquad \text{C} \qquad \text{Multiply C by } -3.$$

$$-3z = -6 \qquad \text{C} \qquad \text{Simplify C.}$$

$$x - 2y = 5 \qquad \text{A} \qquad \text{Add C to A.}$$

STEP 4

Now that you have eliminated the z variable from equation A, your system of equations takes the following form:

$$x - 2y = 5 \qquad \text{A} \qquad x \text{ not yet isolated.}$$

$$y = -1 \qquad \text{B} \qquad y \text{ is known.}$$

$$z = 2 \qquad \text{C} \qquad z \text{ is known.}$$

You have yet to isolate x. When you accomplish that task, you then have all the values for the three variables. From your work so far on equation B, you know that $y = -1$, so you can use this knowledge to eliminate the y variable from equation A in a ready fashion. Accordingly, the coefficient of y in equation A is

-2, so you can multiply equation B by 2 to arrive at an equation you can add to equation A to eliminate the y variable. Here is how you proceed:

$x - 2y = 5$	A	Start with A from STEP 4.
$2y = (2) - 1$	B	Multiply B by 2.
$2y = -2$	B	Simplify B.
$x = 3$	A	Add B to A.

STEP 5

With the isolation of x, you now have values for all three of the variables in the equation. You can show them as follows:

$x = 3$	A	x is known.
$y = -1$	B	y is known.
$z = 2$	C	z is known.

To write the solutions for the original set of equations, you can employ parentheses in which you list the solutions in the order x, y, and z:

$$(3, -1, 2)$$

Exercise Set 11.6

Solve the systems of equations.

a. $2x + y + z = -2$
   $2x - y + 3z = 6$
   $3x - 5y + 4z = 7$

b. $2x - 3y + z = 5$
   $x + 3y + 8z = 22$
   $3x - y + 2z = 12$

c. $x + 2y + c = 1$
   $7x + 3b - z = -2$
   $x + 5y + 3z = 2$

d. $a + b + 0c = 0$
   $a + 0b + c = 1$
   $2a + b + c = 2$

e. $a + b + c = 6$
   $2a - b + 3c = 9$
   $-a + 2b + 2c = 9$

Matrices

If your work is a system of equations, you work primarily with the coefficients of the terms of the equations. If you organize the terms of an equation so that their variables are in a standard order, then you arrive at the representation of systems of equations you have worked with so far in this chapter. Consider, for example, a system along the lines of the following:

$$3x - 4y = 1$$
$$5x + 2y = 19$$

You can proceed to solve the system of equations for the x and y values by using the approach given in the previous section. At the same time, you can use an approach that involves using matrices. A matrix consists of an array or collection of numbers. In a matrix, you organize the numbers in a rectangular fashion, in rows and columns. Matrices are always identified according to their rows and columns. If a matrix contains 2 rows and 3 columns, then it is said to be a 2×3 matrix. If a matrix contains 2 rows and 2 columns, then it is said to be a 2×2 matrix.

Mathematicians usually identify matrices by enclosing them in square brackets. They identify the elements within by using letters with subscripts or by providing the numbers themselves. A 3×3 matrix might be represented this way:

$$\begin{bmatrix} a_1 b_1 c_1 \\ a_2 b_2 c_2 \\ a_3 b_3 c_3 \end{bmatrix}$$

A 2×2 matrix might be represented this way:

$$\begin{bmatrix} a_1 b_1 \\ a_2 b_2 \end{bmatrix}$$

A vast and interesting field of study investigates the behavior of matrices, and the use of matrices in programming related to the graphics for computer game development and the logic of games involves matrices extensively. In this context, matrices provide an alternative approach to solving the system of equations.

If you examine the coefficients of the system of equations given above, you see that you can create a 2×3 matrix. In other words, the matrix consists of 2 rows and 3 columns. You can write it as follows:

$$\begin{bmatrix} 3 & 4 & 1 \\ 5 & 2 & 19 \end{bmatrix}$$

If you work with a set of three equations with three variables for which you want to find values, you might start with this set of equations:

$$x - y + 5z = -6$$

$$3x + 3y - z = 10$$

$$x + 3y + 2z = 5$$

This becomes the basis of a 3×4 matrix, which you present in this way:

$$\begin{bmatrix} 1 & -1 & 5 & -6 \\ 3 & 3 & -1 & 10 \\ 1 & 3 & 2 & 5 \end{bmatrix}$$

When a variable has no visible coefficient, implicitly its coefficient is 1. You use this fact when you create a matrix to represent a system of equations. Implicit coefficients appear as 1. Along the same lines, negative coefficients remain negative.

One further point is that you can combine equations with different numbers of variables. For example, a system similar to the one just shown might take the following form:

$$x - 5z = -6$$

$$3x + 3y - z = 10$$

$$3y + 2z = 5$$

When you translate such a system of equations into a matrix, to preserve the orders of the variables, you insert zeros. Here is how you represent such a system:

$$\begin{matrix} 1 & 0 & -5 & -6 \\ 3 & 3 & -1 & 10 \\ 0 & 3 & 2 & 5 \end{matrix}$$

In this system of equations, you account for the missing y and x variables in the first and third equations by inserting zeros.

Note

In the discussion in this chapter, the enclosing square braces that often characterize matrices do not appear. This is a measure taken to make the presentation of the matrices easier. For general purposes, enclosing braces is often regarded as a matter of personal preference.

Working with a 2-by-3 Matrix

A matrix provides a convenient way to systematically solve for the values of a system. Your activity in this respect proceeds in the same way that it did when you worked with systems of equations and left the variables visible. When you work with matrices, however, you work with a system that consists of rows and columns, and the goal of your activity is to arrive at matrices that take the following form:

$$\begin{bmatrix} 1 & 0 & 0 & | & a \\ 0 & 1 & 0 & | & b \\ 0 & 0 & 1 & | & c \end{bmatrix} \quad \text{or} \quad \begin{bmatrix} 1 & 0 & | & x \\ 0 & 1 & | & y \end{bmatrix}$$

Accordingly, for each row in the matrix, you proceed with multiplication and addition activities, as you did in the previous section, and your goal is to eliminate all values save those that correspond to one of the columns and the final column. The final column provides you with a variable value.

The system of equations presented in the previous section appears as follows:

$$3x - 4y = 1$$
$$5x + 2y = 19$$

The matrix you create using its coefficients assumes this form:

$$\begin{bmatrix} 3 & -4 & 1 \\ 5 & 2 & 19 \end{bmatrix}$$

To solve for the values of this matrix, you begin by examining the first row and determining a value that allows you to transform the 3 into 1. This value is the multiplicative inverse of 3, which is $\frac{1}{3}$. Accordingly, when you carry out this multiplication, you arrive at this matrix:

$$\begin{matrix} 1 & -\dfrac{4}{3} & \dfrac{1}{3} \\ 5 & 2 & 19 \end{matrix}$$

You can then proceed to evaluate the second row. Your goal is to discover the number by which you can multiply the first row in order to eliminate a column. You seek a number that allows you to transform the first row so that you can add it to the second and eliminate the value (5) in the first column. This number is -5. Accordingly, your work proceeds in this way:

$$1 \quad -\frac{4}{3} \quad \frac{1}{3} \qquad \text{First row.}$$

$$-5 \quad \frac{20}{3} \quad -\frac{5}{3} \qquad \text{First row multiplied by } -5.$$

You then add the first row as transformed to the second row:

$$5 \quad 2 \quad 19 \qquad \text{Second row.}$$

$$-5 \quad \frac{20}{3} \quad -\frac{5}{3} \qquad \text{Add the new first row.}$$

$$0 \quad \frac{26}{3} \quad \frac{52}{3} \qquad \text{Result of the addition.}$$

Your matrix now assumes this form:

$$1 \quad -\frac{4}{3} \quad \frac{1}{3}$$

$$0 \quad \frac{26}{3} \quad \frac{52}{3}$$

At this point, you evaluate the second row to discover a way to reduce the value in the second column to 1. To accomplish this, you can multiply the elements in the row by $\frac{3}{26}$, the multiplicative inverse of $\frac{26}{3}$. Here is the form this activity assumes:

$$0 \quad \frac{26}{3} \quad \frac{52}{3} \qquad \text{The original row.}$$

$$0 \quad 1 \quad \frac{156}{78} \qquad \text{Multiply by } \frac{3}{26}.$$

$$0 \quad 1 \quad \frac{2(78)}{(78)} \qquad \text{Factor.}$$

$$0 \quad 1 \quad 2 \qquad \text{Eliminate the fractions.}$$

You now have a new matrix, which appears this way:

$$1 \quad -\frac{4}{3} \quad \frac{1}{3}$$

$$0 \quad 1 \quad 2$$

Your target now becomes finding a way to eliminate the second column value from the first row. To accomplish this, you multiply the second row by a number that transforms it so that when you add it to the second row you eliminate the target value. This number is $\frac{4}{3}$. To carry out these activities, you proceed in this way:

$$0 \quad 1 \quad 2 \qquad \text{The original row.}$$

$$0 \quad \frac{4}{3} \quad \frac{8}{3} \qquad \text{Multiplied by } \frac{4}{3}.$$

Given this transformation of the second row, you add it to the first:

$$1 \quad -\frac{4}{3} \quad \frac{1}{3} \qquad \text{First row.}$$

$$0 \quad \frac{4}{3} \quad \frac{8}{3} \qquad \text{Transformed second row.}$$

$$1 \quad 0 \quad \frac{9}{3} \qquad \text{The result of the addition.}$$

$$1 \quad 0 \quad 3 \qquad \text{Simplify the first row.}$$

Your matrix now assumes its final form:

$$1 \quad 0 \quad 3$$
$$0 \quad 1 \quad 2$$

Given this matrix, you can identify the solutions of the system as $x = 3$ and $y = 2$.

Exercise Set 11.7

Here are some systems of equations to transform into matrices and solve for two values.

a. $3x + 2y = -4$
   $5x - y = 2$

b. $5x + 2y = 7$
   $6x + y = 8$

c. $3x + 2y = -4$
   $2x - y = -5$

d. $a + 4b = 8$
   $3a + 5b = 3$

e. $6a - 2b = 4$
   $7a + b = 13$

Working with a 3-by-4 Matrix

To work with 3×4 matrices, you follow the same path you follow with 2×3 matrices. The only difference is that a few more steps are involved. Consider, for example, this system of equations:

$$x - y + 5z = -6$$

$$3x + 3y - z = 10$$

$$x + 3y + 2z = 5$$

If you transform this into a 3×4 matrix, you assign values of 1 to the appropriate coefficients and drop the variables:

$$
\begin{array}{rrrr}
1 & -1 & 5 & -6 \\
3 & 3 & -1 & 10 \\
1 & 3 & 2 & 5
\end{array}
$$

To develop a solution set for this matrix, your goal involves arriving at a matrix that possesses this form:

$$
\begin{bmatrix}
1 & 0 & 0 & | & a \\
0 & 1 & 0 & | & b \\
0 & 0 & 1 & | & c
\end{bmatrix}
$$

For each row, then, you seek to transform the values so that you see a 1 and a corresponding value.

For the current matrix, the first column of the first row is already set to 1, so you can shift your attention to the second row. You find a value by which you can multiply the first row that allows you to eliminate the first element from the second row. This value is -3. To multiply the first row by this value, your actions take the following course:

$$
\begin{array}{rrrr}
1 & -1 & 5 & -6 \\
-3 & 3 & -15 & 18
\end{array}
\qquad \text{Multiply first row by } -3.
$$

You then add the transformed version of the first row to the second row:

$$
\begin{array}{rrrr}
3 & 3 & -1 & 10 \\
-3 & 3 & -15 & 18 \\
\hline
0 & 6 & -16 & 28
\end{array}
\qquad \text{Result of the addition.}
$$

This gives you the following matrix:

$$\begin{matrix} 1 & -1 & 5 & -6 \\ 0 & 6 & -16 & 28 \\ 1 & 3 & 2 & 5 \end{matrix}$$

The next step involves determining the value by which you can multiply the first row to make it possible to eliminate the first element from the third row. It ends up that you can achieve this goal if you multiply by -1. Accordingly, you carry out the multiplication:

$$\begin{matrix} 1 & -1 & 5 & -6 \\ -1 & 1 & -5 & 6 \end{matrix} \quad \text{Multiply first row by } -1.$$

You then add the transformed version of the first row to the third row:

$$\begin{matrix} 1 & 3 & 2 & 5 \\ -1 & 1 & -5 & 6 \\ 0 & 4 & -3 & 11 \end{matrix} \quad \text{Result of the addition.}$$

Your rewritten matrix takes this form:

$$\begin{matrix} 1 & -1 & 5 & -6 \\ 0 & 6 & -16 & 28 \\ 0 & 4 & -3 & 11 \end{matrix}$$

You now have the first column of the matrix in good form, so you can proceed to work with the second column. Toward this end, you inspect the second row. To transform the second element of this row so that it becomes a 1, you multiply by $\frac{1}{6}$. The result of the multiplication is this row:

$$0 \quad 1 \quad -\frac{16}{6} \quad \frac{28}{6}$$

After you factor the fractions, your matrix assumes this form:

$$\begin{matrix} 1 & -1 & 5 & -6 \\ 0 & 1 & -\dfrac{8}{3} & \dfrac{14}{3} \\ 0 & 4 & -3 & 11 \end{matrix}$$

To eliminate the second element from the first row, you can make use of the transformed version of the second row. The value of the second element in the second row is 1, so you do not have to make any changes to reach your objective. You simply add the second row to the first. When you do so, your work takes on this form:

$$1 \quad -1 \quad \frac{15}{3} \quad -\frac{18}{3}$$ Previous first row set up for the addition.

$$0 \quad 1 \quad -\frac{8}{3} \quad \frac{14}{3}$$ The transformed second row.

$$1 \quad 0 \quad \frac{7}{3} \quad -\frac{4}{3}$$ New first row.

Here is the new matrix:

$$
\begin{array}{cccc}
1 & 0 & \dfrac{7}{3} & -\dfrac{4}{3} \\[2ex]
0 & 1 & -\dfrac{8}{3} & \dfrac{14}{3} \\[2ex]
0 & 4 & -3 & 11
\end{array}
$$

You now proceed to multiply the second row by -4 to create values that you can add to the third row to eliminate the second element. Here are the activities you perform:

$$0 \quad 4 \quad -\frac{9}{3} \quad \frac{33}{3}$$ Change third row to fractions.

$$0 \quad -4 \quad \frac{33}{3} \quad -\frac{56}{3}$$ Second row multiplied by -4.

$$0 \quad 0 \quad \frac{23}{3} \quad -\frac{23}{3}$$ New third row (second row + first row).

Here is the new matrix:

$$
\begin{array}{cccc}
1 & 0 & \dfrac{7}{3} & -\dfrac{4}{3} \\[2ex]
0 & 1 & -\dfrac{8}{3} & \dfrac{14}{3} \\[2ex]
0 & 0 & \dfrac{23}{3} & -\dfrac{23}{3}
\end{array}
$$

You can now reach the first of the major goals of your operation, which is to discover the value that corresponds to the third row. Toward this end, you multiply the third row by the multiplicative inverse of $\frac{23}{3}$. Here is the matrix that results from this operation:

$$
\begin{array}{cccc}
1 & 0 & \dfrac{7}{3} & -\dfrac{4}{3} \\[3ex]
0 & 1 & -\dfrac{8}{3} & \dfrac{14}{3} \\[3ex]
0 & 0 & 1 & -1
\end{array}
$$

Given that you know the value of the third element in the third row, you can multiply this row by $-\frac{7}{3}$ to create a set of values you can add to the first row to eliminate the third element from that row. The result of the multiplication is as follows:

$$
\begin{array}{cccc}
0 & 0 & -\dfrac{7}{3} & \dfrac{7}{3}
\end{array}
$$

When you add this row to the first, your matrix that results takes this form:

$$
\begin{array}{cccc}
1 & 0 & 0 & 1 \\[3ex]
0 & 1 & -\dfrac{8}{3} & \dfrac{14}{3} \\[3ex]
0 & 0 & 1 & -1
\end{array}
$$

To eliminate the third element from the second row, you multiply the third row by $\frac{8}{3}$. The result of the multiplication takes this form:

$$
\begin{array}{cccc}
0 & 0 & \dfrac{8}{3} & -\dfrac{8}{3}
\end{array}
$$

When you add this to the second row, your matrix then assumes its final form:

$$
\begin{array}{cccc}
1 & 0 & 0 & 1 \\[2ex]
0 & 1 & 0 & 2 \\[2ex]
0 & 0 & 1 & -1
\end{array}
$$

You can write the solution values for this matrix as $x = 1$, $y = 2$, and $z = -1$.

Exercise Set 11.8

Here are some systems of equations with three values that you can solve using matrices.

a. $4x - y + 3z = -3$
$3x + y + z = 0$
$2x - y + 4z = 0$

b. $x - 2y + 3z = 4$
$5x + 7y - z = 2$
$2x + 2y - 5z = 3$

c. $x + y + z = 4$
$2x - y - 3z = 4$
$4x + 2y - z = 1$

d. $x - 2y - 3z = 3$
$2x - y - 2z = 4$
$4x + 5y + 6z = 4$

e. $3x + 2y + 2z = 3$
$x + 2y - z = 5$
$2x - 4y + z = 0$

Conclusion

In this chapter, you have investigated how to solve equations that contain two variables. A central approach in this respect involves substitution. Accordingly, you solve an equation for one of its values, and then substitute the solution back into the equation to solve for the remaining value. Working with substitution provided a starting point for examining systems of equations. Systems of equations can involve any number of different variables. They can also involve any number of equations.

In this chapter, you started out by examining how to work with systems of two equations. You then moved to three. You first used multiplication and addition to approach equations as sets of variables with coefficients. From this you proceeded to examine systems of equations on a different basis. This basis involved matrices. By considering only the coefficient values of systems of equations, you could generate the elements of matrices. In this chapter, you concentrated on working with 2×3 and 3×4 matrices. While matrices of much larger dimensions exist, working with these has introduced you to the skills that prove most primary in working with systems of equations.

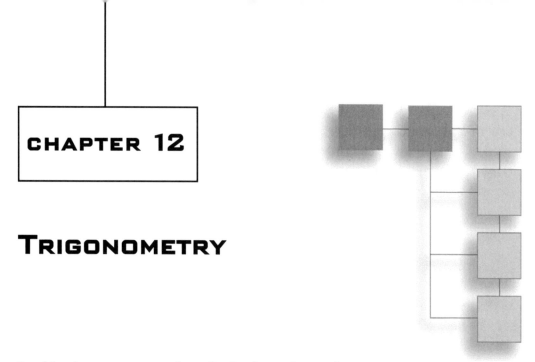

CHAPTER 12

TRIGONOMETRY

In this chapter, you explore the basic notions of trigonometry. You begin by reviewing the Pythagorean theorem. Exploring the standard triangle in this way puts you in a position to begin a preliminary inquiry into the notion of how you can arrive at a ratio between the lengths of the sides of a triangle from which you can know the sine of an angle. A further step involves exploring ways to measure angles. You can measure angles in degrees or radians. A radian can be viewed as an arc of a circle equal in length to the radius of the circle. Radians allow you to begin to explore trigonometric ratios and extend the sine ratio. These ratios consist of those involving the cosine, tangent, cotangent, secant, and cosecant. Toward familiarizing you with such notions, this chapter addresses the following topics, among others:

- How the slope of a linear graph relates to the side of a triangle

- Recognizing the standard form of a right triangle

- Transferring knowledge of a right triangle to a coordinate plane

- Interpreting a coordinate plane as a circle

- Explaining an angle using a unit circle

- Using a unit circle to explore the trigonometric ratios

The Ratios of Trigonometry

A set of functions, known as the trigonometric functions, allow you to extend the work of algebra and geometry in several directions. To understand the trigonometric functions, you can start by examining the ratios that exist between the angles and sides of a right triangle. To explore how these ratios are related to the activities previous chapters discussed, you can begin with an examination of the right triangle and how it relates to a line you generate using a linear equation.

Angles and Sides

Two of the angles of a right triangle are acute angles. In other words, they are angles of less than 90°. One is usually labeled as angle A. The other is labeled as angle B. A third angle is equal to 90°. According to the standard way of depicting a right triangle, the 90° angle is labeled as C. Likewise, a small square tucked into the angle identifies angle C as a right angle (see Figure 12.1).

The line opposite angle A is line BC. It is called the opposite side. You can designate the length of this line using the letter *a*. The line opposite to angle B is called the adjacent side. It is adjacent to angle A. You can designate its length with the letter *b*.

Opposite the right angle is the hypotenuse of the triangle. This side of the right triangle is always the longest side of the triangle. You can refer to it geometrically as line AB. You can also designate the length of this side using the letter *c*.

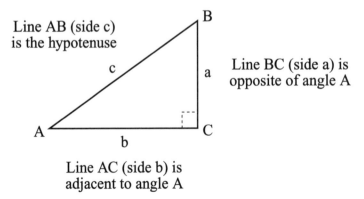

Line AB (side c)
is the hypotenuse

Line BC (side a) is
opposite of angle A

Line AC (side b) is
adjacent to angle A

Figure 12.1
Identify angles and lines of a right triangle in a standard way.

The Pythagorean Theorem

Given the standard way of identifying a right triangle, you can then introduce the Pythagorean theorem as a way to relate the three sides of a right triangle. Here's the standard equation for the Pythagorean theorem:

$$c^2 = a^2 + b^2$$

You rewrite this equation to eliminate the exponent of c:

$$c = \sqrt{a^2 + b^2}$$

When you put the Pythagorean theorem to work in a Cartesian plane, you can see that the lines you create using linear equations can be mapped in a fairly direct way to a right triangle. As Figure 12.2 illustrates, if you regard the origin of the coordinate system as corresponding to angle A, then you can establish the rise and the run of the triangle as the opposite and adjacent sides. The adjacent side follows the x axis. The rise of the opposite side follows the y axis. You can regard the line itself as the hypotenuse. You use the Pythagorean theorem to determine the length of the line.

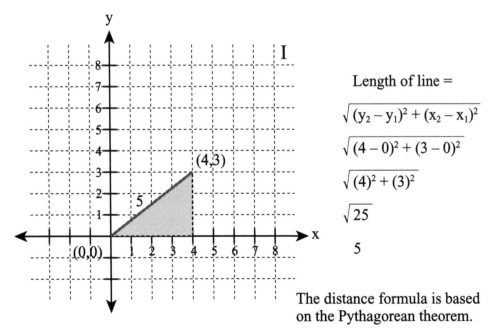

Length of line =

$$\sqrt{(y_2 - y_1)^2 + (x_2 - x_1)^2}$$

$$\sqrt{(4 - 0)^2 + (3 - 0)^2}$$

$$\sqrt{(4)^2 + (3)^2}$$

$$\sqrt{25}$$

5

The distance formula is based on the Pythagorean theorem.

Figure 12.2
The length of the line is 5.

The position of the right triangle you create when you generate a figure using linear equations gives you a point of reference that centers on the origin of the Cartesian plane. For a triangle you depict the angle according to the standard model discussed in the previous section; this is angle A. A convenient way to label an angle is to use the Greek letter theta, θ. Accordingly, the angle of θ is always relative to the run and rise of the triangle.

As Figure 12.3 illustrates, if you work within the first coordinate of the Cartesian plane, as the angle of θ increases, the slope of the line becomes more pronounced. The length of the opposite side increases. The length of the adjacent side decreases. As you saw when you investigated slopes, the ratio of the adjacent to the opposite side allows you to determine a value for θ.

Circles and the Sine of 2

You can transfer a right triangle you construct in a Cartesian coordinate system to a circle. When you translate the triangle to a circle, the center of focus remains on the angle that characterizes the origin (θ). As Figure 12.4 illustrates, the hypotenuse of the triangle provides a way to establish the radius of the circle. Along with the hypotenuse of the circle, you can also establish a chord on the circle. The chord in this instance is one that is twice the length of the opposite side. To create such a chord, you can flip the right triangle downward, from quadrant I into quadrant IV. You identify the chord by using the term 2θ.

If you take half the distance of the cord, you have a line that you define using θ alone. This line is known as the sine of θ. The sine of theta, then, corresponds to the ratio that you establish between the distance of the hypotenuse and the distance of the opposite side.

$$\sin \theta = \frac{y}{r}$$

If you want to determine the sine of θ as shown in Figure 12.4, you can put to work the information the graph provides. Accordingly, if you work within quadrant I of the Cartesian plane, you can see that the coordinate pair that describes the point on the circumference of the circle for the line is (4,3).

To calculate the length of the line that extends from the center of the circle (or the origin of the Cartesian plane), you use the Pythagorean theorem. Following

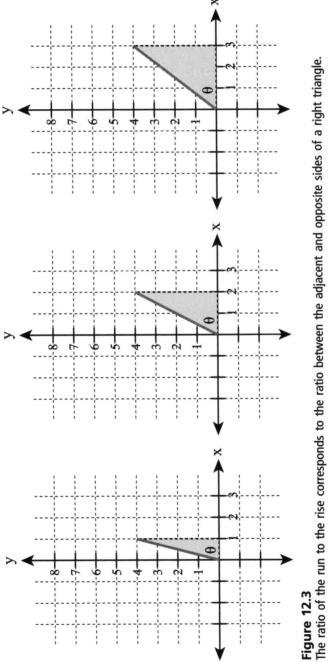

Figure 12.3
The ratio of the run to the rise corresponds to the ratio between the adjacent and opposite sides of a right triangle.

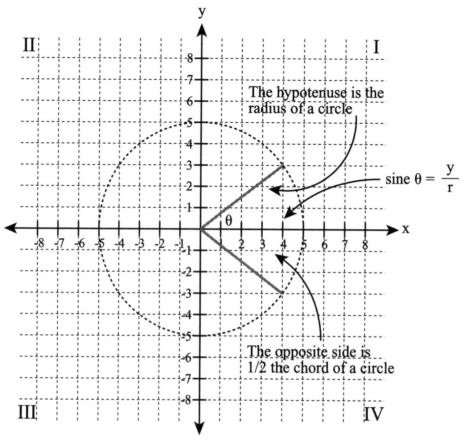

Figure 12.4
Trigonometric notions arise from explorations of circles and coordinates.

the generalization of the situation Figure 12.5 provides, you can see you can calculate the sine of θ using the data you possess with the point (4,3). First you calculate r, the hypotenuse. Then you find the ratio of y to r.

Degrees and Radians

When you first learn to relate an angle to a circle, your activity often begins with an orientation toward the circle that begins with the Cartesian plane. As Figure 12.6 illustrates, you extend a line (r) from the center of a circle to its perimeter. Using the standard form of an angle, you identify the x axis extending to the right from the origin as the initial side of the angle. The line that creates the angle constitutes the terminal side. You measure the angle (θ) created by the initial side and the terminal sides in degrees that describe the perimeter of the circle.

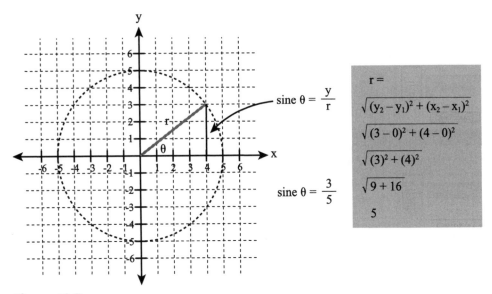

Figure 12.5
The ratio of the rise to the hypotenuse gives you the sine of the angle.

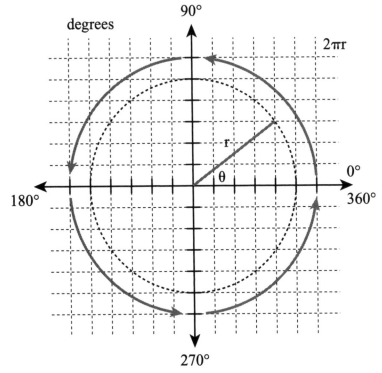

Figure 12.6
Degrees of a circle allow you to measure angles.

The measure of an angle θ has no maximum value in degrees. If it extends upward from the origin, following the path of the y axis of the Cartesian plane, its measure is 90°. Since the line is perpendicular to the initial side, you call it a right angle. If the line extends to the left of the origin, its measure is 180°, and you call it a straight angle. An angle of 270° follows the y axis downward and is also perpendicular to the initial side. You can call it a right angle, also.

If an angle measures 450°, it is the same as one revolution of the circle plus 90°, so it is a right angle. If an angle measures 540°, it is the same as one revolution of the circle plus 180°, and it is a straight angle. In this respect, if someone tells you to turn a screw 1440° degrees to the right, then, you determine the number of terms by dividing the degrees by the circumference of a circle: $\frac{1440°}{360°} = 4$. The measure of the angle from the initial size to the terminal side is 0. No remainder is left after the division.

Circumference and Radians

The radius of a circle consists of a line extending from the center of the circle to any point on its perimeter. The circumference of a circle is a measure of the arc of a complete circle. To calculate the circumference of a circle, you multiply 2 times π by the radius of the circle. Here is the equation:

$$C = 2\pi r$$

The variable C signifies the circle's circumference, while r represents the radius, and π is an irrational number with an approximate value of 3.14. Given this representation of a circle, you can describe a circle in terms of radians.

A radian is an arc on the perimeter of a circle that is equal in length to the radius of the circle. Given the equation $C = 2\pi r$, then, there are 2π radians in a complete circle. In other words, if you travel around the circle a distance equal in length to the radius multiplied by 2π, you end up where you started.

A radian is an arc equal in length to the radius of a circle. If you use an approximate value for π of 3.14 and multiply by 2, then you can say that 6.28 radians can be placed head to tail to complete one revolution of a circle.

As Figure 12.7 illustrates, you can relate the size of an angle using radians. The procedure involves using π alone or making π part of a quotient. To accomplish this task, consider how to designate the four directions of the compass using

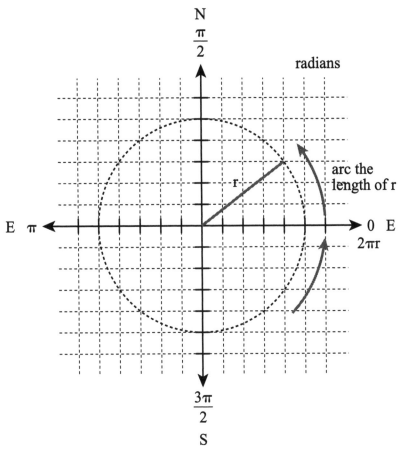

Figure 12.7
Radians allow you to readily measure angles.

radians. You start to the east. This direction corresponds to the positive direction of the *x* axis.

East is usually considered the initial side of angles, so this is at degree 0. The radian value of east is also 0. To now set the compass values for north, west, and south, consider that if a complete revolution of a circle involves 2π radians, then half a revolution (180°—west) involves π radians. If half a revolution involves π radians, then a quarter of a revolution (90°—north) involves $\frac{\pi}{2}$ radians. When you add $\frac{\pi}{2}$ radians to π radians, you arrive at $3\frac{\pi}{2}$ radians. This is three-quarters of a revolution or an angle of 270°—or south.

Table 12.1 provides you with radian and degree measurements for the angles that represent the cardinal directions of the compass.

Table 12.1 Compass Direction Measurements		
Degrees	**Radians**	**Compass Direction**
0	0	East
45°	$\frac{\pi}{4}$	Northeast
90°	$\frac{\pi}{2}$	North
135°	$3\frac{\pi}{4}$	Northwest
180°	π	West
225°	$5\frac{\pi}{4}$	Southwest
270°	$3\frac{\pi}{2}$	South
315°	$7\frac{\pi}{4}$	Southeast

Degrees to Radians

To convert degrees to radians, you use this formula:

$$\frac{\text{Angle in degrees}}{180} = \text{Angle in radians}$$

Here are a few examples of use of this conversion:

$$180 \text{ degrees} = \frac{180}{180} = (1)\pi \text{ radians}$$

$$120 \text{ degrees} = \frac{120}{180} = \frac{2\pi}{3} \text{ radians}$$

$$25 \text{ degrees} = \frac{20}{180} = \frac{\pi}{9} \text{ radians}$$

Exercise Set 12.1

For each of the following degree measurements, identify the measurement in radians.

a. 30°

b. 60°

c. 180°

d. 90°

e. 315°

f. 45°

g. 360°

h. 135°

i. 270°

j. 210°

Radians to Degrees

To convert radians to degrees, you multiply by $\frac{180}{\pi}$. Here are a few examples:

$$\frac{\pi}{4}\text{radians} = \frac{\pi}{4} \cdot \frac{180}{\pi} = \frac{180}{4} = 45°$$

$$7\frac{\pi}{4}\text{radians} = \frac{7\pi}{4} \cdot \frac{180}{\pi} = \frac{1260}{4} = 315°$$

$$\frac{2\pi}{3}\text{radians} = \frac{2\pi}{3} \cdot \frac{180}{\pi} = \frac{360}{3} = 120°$$

Exercise Set 12.2

For each of the following radian values, name the corresponding degree value.

a. $\frac{\pi}{4}$

b. $\frac{\pi}{6}$

c. $\frac{\pi}{2}$

d. $\frac{\pi}{3}$

e. $\frac{3\pi}{2}$

f. $\frac{5\pi}{4}$

g. 2π

h. $\frac{\pi}{9}$

i. $\frac{7\pi}{4}$

j. π

Trigonometric Ratios

You measure angles using degrees and radians. You usually measure the lengths of sides using real numbers. You relate the measurements of angles to the measurements of sides using ratios. A set of six such ratios constitute the primary trigonometric ratios. You have already examined the ratio that generates the sine of the angle (theta) θ.

If you extend the discussion that began with the sine of the angle θ, you can then work forward to explore the ratios defined for the cosine and tangent of θ. You then move on from there to explore the ratios defined for cotangent, secant, and cosecant. Figure 12.8 illustrates the standard form of the right triangle with the sides explicitly identified.

Each of the trigonometric ratios provides information on the angle θ. In this respect, then, you refer to "the sine of theta," "the cosine of theta," and so on, and in each instance, the ratio that you explore involves a relation between two of the three sides of a right triangle. Table 12.2 details the ratios.

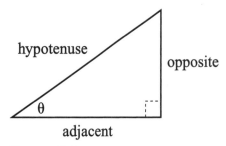

Figure 12.8
The opposite and adjacent sides and the hypotenuse of the right triangle generate the trigonometric ratios.

Table 12.2 Trigonometric Ratios

Item	Ratio	Mnemonic
Sine	$\sin \theta = \frac{opposite}{hypotenuse}$	$\frac{O}{H}$
Cosine	$\cos \theta = \frac{adjacent}{hypotenuse}$	$\frac{A}{H}$
Tangent	$\tan \theta = \frac{opposite}{adjacent}$	$\frac{O}{A}$
Cotangent	$\cot \theta = \frac{adjacent}{opposite}$	$\frac{A}{O}$
Secant	$\sec \theta = \frac{hypotenuse}{adjacent}$	$\frac{H}{A}$
Cosecant	$\csc \theta = \frac{hypotenuse}{opposite}$	$\frac{H}{O}$

Note

Figure 12.9 features a mnemonic diagram that might prove useful as you memorize the trigo-nometric ratios. The letter O designates the opposite side, the letter A designates the adjacent side, and the letter H designates the hypotenuse. Start with STS to remember sine, tangent, and secant. For the names of the other ratios, you prefix "co." Then proceed from the notion that the sine of theta is the ratio of O/H.

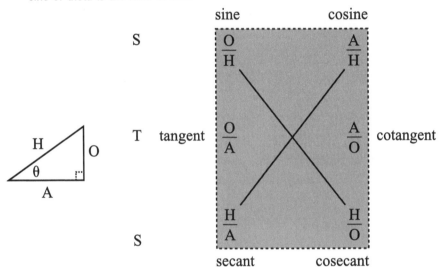

Figure 12.9
Recall STS, begin with sine and O/H.

Exercise Set 12.3

Show all six trigonometric ratios for right triangles with the designated values. Where the value of the hypotenuse is not given, calculate it and proceed from there.

a. Opposite – 3, Adjacent – 4

b. Opposite – 5, Adjacent – 4, Hypotenuse – 6

c. Opposite – 5, Adjacent 4, Hypotenuse – $\sqrt{41}$

Ratios and Degrees

Generating values for the geometric ratios usually involves either knowing the lengths of three sides of a right triangle or calculating this information using the information available to you. As discussed previously, the most common starting position for using the ratios involves employing the Pythagorean theorem to

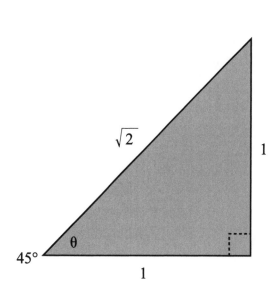

$$\sin45° = \frac{opposite}{hypotenuse} = \frac{1}{\sqrt{2}}$$

$$\cos45° = \frac{adjacent}{hypotenuse} = \frac{1}{\sqrt{2}}$$

$$\tan45° = \frac{opposite}{adjacent} = \frac{1}{1}$$

$$\cot45° = \frac{adjacent}{opposite} = \frac{1}{1}$$

$$\sec45° = \frac{hypotenuse}{adjacent} = \frac{\sqrt{2}}{1}$$

$$\csc45° = \frac{hypotenuse}{opposite} = \frac{\sqrt{2}}{1}$$

Figure 12.10
Set the sides to 1 to calculate basic values.

calculate the length of the hypotenuse. If you know the length of the hypotenuse and the lengths of the two sides, then you can proceed to calculate any of the values made available to you through the trigonometric ratios.

To extend this notion, consider a right triangle that possesses adjacent and opposite sides that are 1 unit in length. Figure 12.10 illustrates such a triangle. Given this version of a right triangle, you can then readily substitute the values the triangle provides. For the sine and cosine values, the approximate value of $\frac{1}{\sqrt{2}}$ is 0.707. For the secant and cosecant values, the approximate value of $\frac{\sqrt{2}}{1}$ is 1.414.

The important feature of such calculations is that they enable to you familiarize yourself with a basic way to generate values for different types of angles. Some angles appear often in trigonometric operations. Among these are 30 and 60 degrees.

Figure 12.11 illustrates an equilateral triangle. The significance of an equilateral triangle, among other things, rests in the fact that you can create such a triangle by joining the adjacent sides of two right triangles, as Figure 12.11 shows. If the length of the opposite side of the right triangles is 1 and the hypotenuse is 2, then

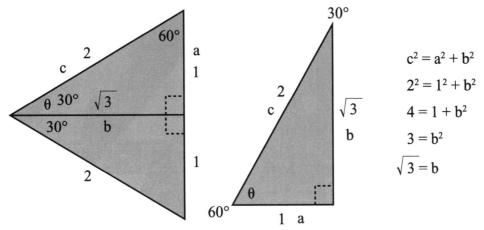

Figure 12.11
Calculate the value of the adjacent side.

Table 12.3 Ratios Applied to Other Angles

Values for 30°	Values for 60°
$\sin 30° = \frac{opposite}{hypotenuse} = \frac{1}{2}$	$\sin 60° = \frac{opposite}{hypotenuse} = \frac{\sqrt{3}}{2}$
$\cos 30° = \frac{adjacent}{hypotenuse} = \frac{\sqrt{3}}{2}$	$\cos 60° = \frac{adjacent}{hypotenuse} = \frac{1}{2}$
$\tan 30° = \frac{opposite}{adjacent} = \frac{1}{\sqrt{3}}$	$\tan 60° = \frac{opposite}{adjacent} = \frac{\sqrt{3}}{1}$
$\cot 30° = \frac{adjacent}{opposite} = \frac{\sqrt{3}}{1}$	$\cot 60° = \frac{adjacent}{opposite} = \frac{1}{\sqrt{3}}$
$\sec 30° = \frac{hypotenuse}{adjacent} = \frac{2}{\sqrt{3}}$	$\sec 60° = \frac{hypotenuse}{adjacent} = \frac{2}{1}$
$\csc 30° = \frac{hypotenuse}{opposite} = \frac{2}{1}$	$\csc 60° = \frac{hypotenuse}{opposite} = \frac{2}{\sqrt{3}}$

you can employ the Pythagorean theorem to calculate values to use in the trigonometric ratios.

If you apply the Pythagorean theorem to slightly modified versions of the triangle Figure 12.10 illustrates, you can readily arrive at the trigonometric ratios for two other angles that prove important. These are the values that correspond to 30° and 60°. Table 12.3 lists the calculations that result when you the apply the trigonometric ratios to the information Figure 12.11 provides using an equilateral triangle.

Note

When working with the values shown in Table 12.3, it is common to manipulate the resulting quotients so that radicals do not appear in the denominators. To eliminate the radical, you multiply by 1 using the value given by the square root. Here are a few examples:

$$\sec 30° = \frac{hypotenuse}{adjacent} = \frac{2}{\sqrt{3}} \cdot \frac{\sqrt{3}}{\sqrt{3}} = \frac{2\sqrt{3}}{3}$$

$$\cot 60° = \frac{adjacent}{opposite} = \frac{1}{\sqrt{3}} \cdot \frac{\sqrt{3}}{\sqrt{3}} = \frac{\sqrt{3}}{3}$$

Rotation

The trigonometric ratios all translate into functions that can generate distinct patterns when applied to a Cartesian plane. As you increase the values you introduce to the functions, the patterns change in restricted, predictable ways. The most ready way to generate such patterns involves translating the three sides of the standard triangle (opposite, adjacent, and hypotenuse) so that you can understand them in relation to the coordinates you plot on the Cartesian plane (x, y). Work earlier in this chapter anticipates this activity. Table 12.4 shows you how the sides of a triangle relate to the values you generated using values typical of your work with the Cartesian plane. In each instance, you work with a standard triangle.

As Figure 12.12 illustrates, if you use combinations of negative and positive values for x and y, you rotate the triangle around the origin of the plane through all four quadrants. The values x and y correspond to the values of x and y on the axes of the plane if the vertex of angle θ resides at $(0,0)$.

Table 12.4 Trigonometric Ratios

Item	Ratio	Mnemonic
Sine	$\sin \theta = \frac{opposite}{hypotenuse}$	$\sin \theta = \frac{y}{r}$
Cosine	$\cos \theta = \frac{adjacent}{hypotenuse}$	$\cos \theta = \frac{x}{r}$
Tangent	$\tan \theta = \frac{opposite}{adjacent}$	$\tan \theta = \frac{y}{x}$
Cotangent	$\cot \theta = \frac{adjacent}{opposite}$	$\cot \theta = \frac{x}{y}$
Secant	$\sec \theta = \frac{hypotenuse}{adjacent}$	$\sec \theta = \frac{r}{x}$
Cosecant	$\csc \theta = \frac{hypotenuse}{opposite}$	$\csc \theta = \frac{r}{y}$

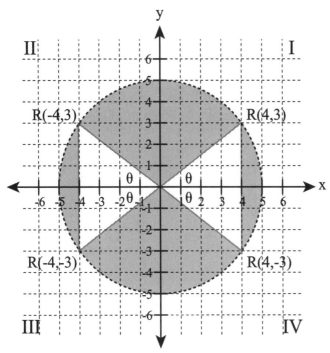

Figure 12.12
As you rotate a standard triangle around a circle centered on the origin of the Cartesian plane, the values that describe the perimeter of the circle change from positive to negative depending on the quadrant.

Rotation and the Unit Circle

The unit circle is a convenient vehicle for working with rotation and other trigonometric activities. A unit circle is a circle that you graph with its center on the origin of a Cartesian plane and its radius set to 1. Figure 12.13 illustrates a unit circle. Such a representation of a circle proves useful when you seek a convenient way to relate measurements of angles to measurements of rotation. When you set the diameter of a circle to 1, if an angle measures, for example, $\frac{\pi}{2}$ (90°), then the radian measure of the angle also tells you the length of the arc that the angle designates on the perimeter of the circle. At the same time, as emphasized previously, even though you work with radians, you can always convert back to degrees if you have a need to do so.

If you employ a unit circle to map the cardinal and a few other coordinates and their related sine values, you see a pattern unfold. With each revolution, you move a distance of 2π radians. Regardless of how large the angle of rotation, it is

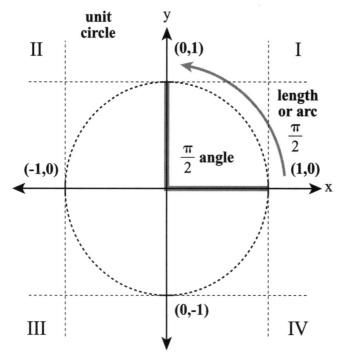

Figure 12.13
A unit circle allows you to relate angles and arcs.

still the case that the same set of values can be used to map the arc. When you factor 4π radians, you find that the terminal side of the angle rests on the *x* axis, as does the terminal angle of 6π or 8π radians. The same holds true for all the other angles that are multiples of 2π as well. As the arc rotates around the circle, it visits the same points over and over. While the length of the arc grows, factoring allows you to understand the arc in terms of a stable set of radian and degree values.

Figure 12.14 illustrates inner and outer rings surrounding a unit circle. The inner ring shows you the coordinate values of the points on the perimeter of the unit circle. The outer ring displays radian values associated with the plotted points.

Plotting Sine Values

Figure 12.15 illustrates what happens if you calculate the sine values of the angles depicted in Figure 12.14. To make it so that the graph provides a fuller representation of the way that the values fluctuate from positive to negative, the range has been extended beyond that of a single rotation of a circle. The extension of the range does not affect the overall pattern.

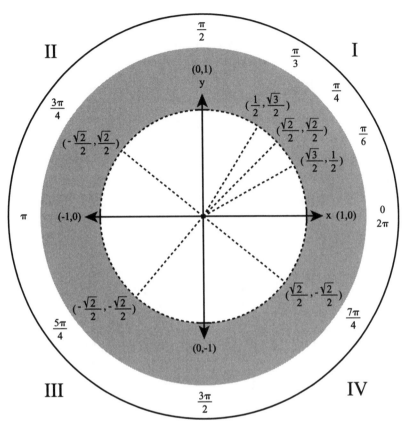

Figure 12.14
The inner shaded ring provides coordinate values while the outer ring shows radians.

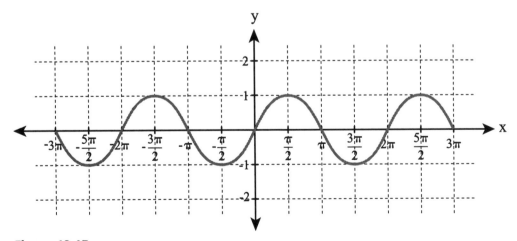

Figure 12.15
When you plot sine values, you create a periodic pattern that fluctuates evenly from 1 to −1 on the
y axis.

The overall pattern assumes a value of 0 at the origin—which represents an angle of 0. If you move to the right, allowing the x axis to map the increase of the value of the angles, the resulting sine values using the y coordinate increase to 1. This occurs when you reach the x value of $\frac{\pi}{2}$. As you move past $\frac{\pi}{2}$, the value of the sine decreases, reaching 0 when you are at π on the x axis. As you move past π, the value of the sine drops into the negative range. When you reach $\frac{3\pi}{2}$, the value on the y axis is -1. This represents the lowest point. After that, the value begins to rise, and at 2π you are back at 0. The name usually applied to this pattern is sinusoidal. It is a periodic pattern that evenly fluctuates from 1 to -1 for each distance of 2π represented by the x axis.

Negative Values

Figure 12.15 involves negative values on the x axis. The negative values reflect the fact that angles can be negative. When an angle is negative, the direction you move on the perimeter of the circle is in a counterclockwise direction. In this situation, you measure angles and radians just as you would if you moved in a clockwise direction, except that the value of $-\frac{\pi}{2}(-90°)$ is found on the lower part of the y axis, while $-\frac{3\pi}{2}(-180°)$ is found on the upper part. Figure 12.16 illustrates a few negative angles you encounter as you move along a negative arc of a unit circle.

Plotting Cosine Values

As Figure 12.17 illustrates, when you plot cosine values using a Cartesian plane, plot angle values on the x axis, and move to the right to show increasing values of angles, the resulting y coordinate value is 1 when the angle of your circle is 0. When you reach $\frac{\pi}{2}$ (90°), the value of the y coordinate value drops to 0. From there, as you move past $\frac{\pi}{2}$, the value of the cosine decreases, reaching -1 when you are at π. As you move past π, the value of the cosine begins to increase, reaching 0 again at $\frac{3\pi}{2}$. After that, the value begins to rise, and at 2π you are back at 1.

The same pattern characterizes movement in the negative direction along the x axis. As Figure 12.17 illustrates, at $-\frac{\pi}{2}$, the value of the cosine falls to 0. From there, it proceeds further downward to -1 at $-\pi$. As you move to $-\frac{3\pi}{2}$, the values of the cosine increase, and at -2π you are back to 1.

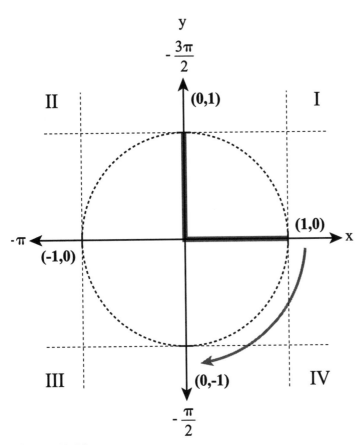

Figure 12.16
When you move in a negative direction, the values progress in a predictable way, and you move in a counterclockwise direction.

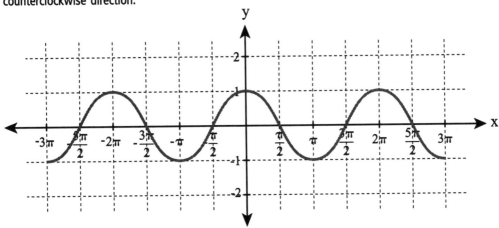

Figure 12.17
At 0 on the x axis, the value of the cosine is 1.

Table 12.5 Generating Tangent and Cotangent Values

Item	Discussion
$\tan \theta = \frac{\sin \theta}{\cos \theta}$	If the value of the of $\cos \theta$ in this function is 0, then the value of the tangent is undefined. When you plot tangent values on a Cartesian plane, the resulting curve rises indefinitely as it approaches a line extending vertically from any point on the x coordinate at which $\cos \theta$ is 0. To formally state this, you can say that tanu is not defined at any value of $\frac{\pi}{2} + k\pi$. In this case, k is any integer value. As you see in Figure 12.18, such values are $\frac{\pi}{2}$, $-\frac{\pi}{2}$, $\frac{3\pi}{2}$, and $-\frac{5\pi}{2}$. Given this situation, the period of the tangent values is π.
$\cot \theta = \frac{\cos \theta}{\sin \theta}$	If the value of the of $\sin \theta$ is 0, then the value of the cosecant is undefined. When you plot cotangent values on a Cartesian plane, the resulting curve rises indefinitely as it approaches a line extending vertically from any point on the x coordinate at which $\sin \theta$ is 0. A formal way to say this is that $\csc \theta$ is not defined at any value of $\pi + k\pi$. The value of k is any integer. As you see in Figure 12.19, such values are π, 2π, $-\pi$, -2π, 3π, and 0. Given this situation, the period of the tangent values is π.
$\sec \theta = \frac{1}{\cos \theta}$	The cosine and secant functions are reciprocals of each other. The value of the cosecant is undefined when it falls on a vertical line passing through a point on the x axis at which the cosine value is 0. Given this situation, the period of the secant values is 2π.
$\csc \theta = \frac{1}{\sin \theta}$	The sine and cosecant functions are reciprocals of each other. The value of the cosecant is undefined when it falls on a vertical line passing through a point on the x axis at which the sine value is 0. Given this situation, the period of the cosecant values is 2π.

Defining Tangents and Cotangents

Table 12.5 provides you with a summary of how to generate tangent and cotangent values. To generate a tangent value, you divide $\sin \theta$ by $\cos \theta$. To generate a secant value, you use the reciprocal of $\cos \theta$. A variety of approaches to arriving at the different values of the trigonometric functions exist. The approach given in Table 12.5 proves one of the easiest to follow.

Plotting Tangent Values

When you plot tangent values on the Cartesian plane, you cannot define them at certain points. These points are those that occur as 0 when you plot cosine values. Such values are $\frac{\pi}{2}$, $-\frac{\pi}{2}$, $-\frac{3\pi}{2}$, $\frac{3\pi}{2}$. You can see why this occurs if you consider the shapes of the periodic waves that characterize the plotting of the cosine of θ (see Figure 12.17 earlier in this chapter). Whenever the value of the cosine reaches 0, then the value of the tangent is undefined.

It is undefined because, as you plot tangent values on a Cartesian plane, the resulting curve rises or falls indefinitely as it approaches lines extending vertically

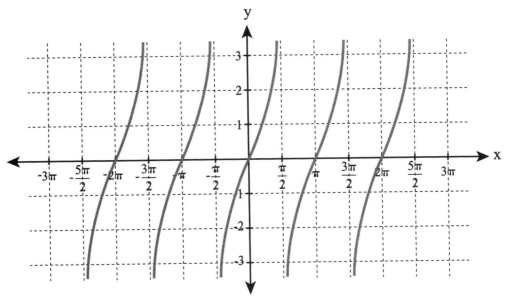

Figure 12.18
As you approach values at which the cosine reaches 0, the tangent values become undefined.

from points on the x coordinate at which cos θ is 0. Such a curve occurs when the value of the denominator becomes increasingly smaller. The tangent values in turn become increasingly larger. The values increase indefinitely. This is known as an asymptotic curve.

As Table 12.5 explains, you can formally state that certain values are undefined if you say that tan θ lacks definition at any value of $\frac{\pi}{2} + k\pi$. The value of k is any integer. In Figure 12.18, among the values of x defined in this way are $\frac{\pi}{2}$, $-\frac{\pi}{2}$, $\frac{5\pi}{2}$, and $-\frac{5\pi}{2}$.

Plotting Cotangent Values

When you plot cotangent values on the Cartesian plane, as with tangent values, at certain points you cannot define them. As the discussion in Table 12.5 indicates, if the value of the sin θ is 0, then the value of the cotangent is undefined. When you plot cotangent values, the resulting curve rises indefinitely as it approaches a line extending vertically from any point on the x coordinate at which sin θ is 0.

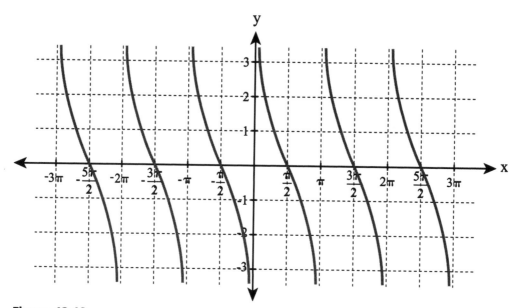

Figure 12.19
As you approach point values at which the sine reaches 0, the cotangent values become undefined.

A formal way to say this is that cot θ is not defined at any value of $\pi + k\pi$. The value of k can be any integer. Given this situation, as Figure 12.19 illustrates, such values are 0, π, 2π, 3π, $-\pi$, -2π.

Plotting Secant Values

The value of the secant is undefined when it falls on a vertical line passing through a point on the x axis at which the cosine value is 0. The cosine and secant functions are reciprocals of each other.

When you plot a secant value, if you begin on the x axis at 0, the value of the secant is 1. As you move toward $\frac{\pi}{2}$ from 0, the value of the secant rises on an asymptotic basis. In other words, it approaches $\frac{\pi}{2}$ but never reaches it, and its value becomes infinitely large.

After passing $\frac{\pi}{2}$, you are in the next phase of the secant. At this point, the secant values shift to below the x axis. They start at an infinitely negative value, and then increase in the range that is greater than $\frac{\pi}{2}$. The increase continues until you reach π. At π the value of the secant is -1. Then values begin to infinitely decrease as they near $\frac{3\pi}{2}$. To complete the period, the secant values shift to above the x axis.

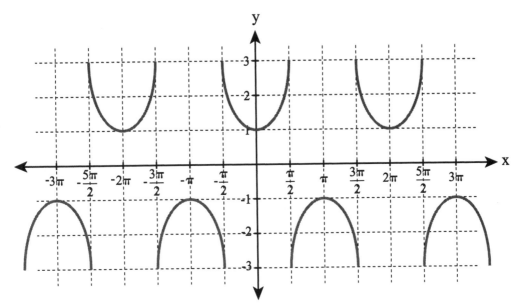

Figure 12.20
The secant is undefined where the cosine value is 0.

They begin infinitely large at $\frac{3\pi}{2}$ and then decrease as they near 2π. At 2π the secant value is 1.

The secant values create a periodic pattern that alternates above and below the x axis, and the period of the secant graph is 2π. In Figure 12.20, for example, you can identify a period as beginning at 0 and extending to 2π.

Plotting Cosecant Values

The value of the cosecant is undefined when it falls on a vertical line passing through a point on the x axis at which the sine value is 0. The sine and cosecant functions are reciprocals of each other.

To plot a cosecant value, you can begin on the x axis at $\frac{\pi}{2}$. The value of the cosecant at this point is 1. As you move to the left, toward 0 from $\frac{\pi}{2}$, the value of the secant rises infinitely as it approaches 0. It is undefined at 0. Moving in a positive direction along the x axis from $\frac{\pi}{2}$, the value of the cosecant increases. As they approach π, they become infinitely large. At π the value for the secant is not defined. After passing beyond π, the cosecant values, shift to below the x axis. They begin at an infinitely large negative value, and then increase as they move toward $\frac{3\pi}{2}$. At $\frac{3\pi}{2}$ the value of the cosecant is -1.

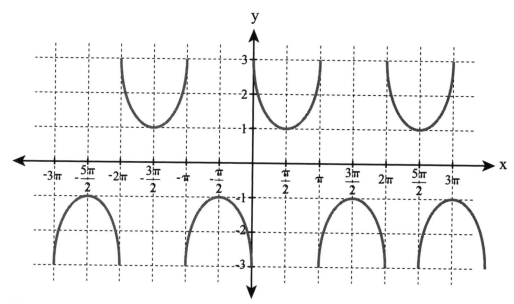

Figure 12.21
The cosecant is undefined where the sine value is 0.

The cosecant values create a periodic pattern that alternates above and below the x axis, and the period of the secant graph is 2π. As Figure 12.21 illustrates, a period begins at 0 and extends to 2π.

Using Visual Formula

You can use Visual Formula to explore a variety of trigonometric relationships. To view the trigonometric functions Visual Formula provides, click the Trigonometry menu item. You see a selection that includes the six basic trigonometric functions. To explore but one possibility, consider the notion that the value of the cosecant is the reciprocal of the value of the sine:

$$\csc \theta = \frac{1}{\sin \theta}$$

You can superimpose one graph on another using Visual Formula to see how this is so. You know, for example, that at any point at which the value of the sine equals 0, the value of the cosecant is undefined. In other words, it

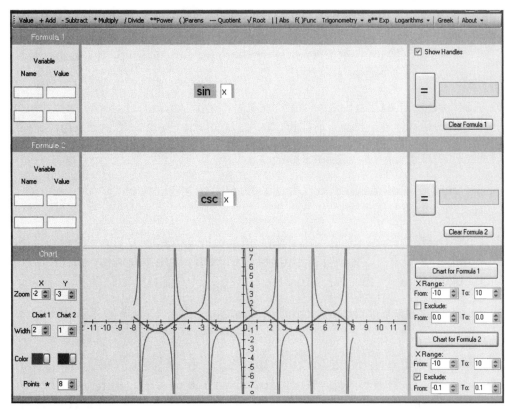

Figure 12.22
The cosecant and sine are reciprocals, and where the value of the sine is 0, the value of the cosecant is undefined.

constitutes an infinitely large or infinitely small value that you cannot represent on a graph.

To employ Visual Formula to examine this relationship between the two trigonometric functions, refer to Figure 12.22 and follow these steps:

1. Click the Trigonometry menu item. You see a selection of six trigonometric functions. Select the sin (sine) item. Then click in the upper equation composition area to position the function.

2. Click the Value menu item. Then immediately to the right of the sin function box, click to position the Value field. Click in the box and type *x*.

3. Now move to the lower-right panel and locate the X Range fields. Click the control for the From field and set the value to −10. Click the control for the To field and set the value to 10. (You can also type the values −10 and 10.)

4. Now locate the Chart panel and set the Zoom values. Click the control for the X field and set it to −2. Click the control for the Y field and set it to −3.

5. Set the Width field to 2 for Chart 1.

6. Set the two Color fields to red and purple (or darker colors that you can readily distinguish).

7. Click the picker for the Points field and set the value to 8. The picker sets the number of points Visual Formula uses to plot graphs. For this operation, it is essential to set this value to 8.

8. Then click the Chart for Formula 1 button. You see the graph of the sine function.

Now you proceed to chart the function that is the reciprocal of the sine function. This is the cosecant function. When you chart the cosecant function, the two graphs show you that when the value of the sine is 0, the value of the cosecant is undefined. Refer to Figure 12.22 and follow these steps:

1. Now move to the Visual Formula top menu and click the Trigonometry menu item. You see the six trigonometric functions. Click the csc item.

2. Click in the lower of the two equation composition areas to position the csc function.

3. Click the Value menu item. Then click immediately to the right of the csc function to position the Value field. Type an x in this field.

4. Now find the X Range fields that lie beneath the Chart for Formula 2 button. Set the From field to −10. Set the To field to 10.

5. Click the Exclude check box. In the From field, type −0.1. In the To field, type 0.1.

6. Click the Chart for Formula 2 button to generate the graph for the cosecant. The arms of the graph extend infinitely upward at points at which the sine values are 0.

After generating the graphs shown in Figure 12.22, generate other graphs using the same approach. Here are some primary relationships to explore:

$$\cot \theta = \frac{1}{\tan \theta}$$
$$\sec \theta = \frac{1}{\cos \theta}$$

Conclusion

This chapter brings to an end your exploration of pre-calculus as presented in this book. Accordingly, you first reviewed the Pythagorean theorem and examined the standard right triangle. When you examined this triangle, you took a close look at the ratio between the lengths of the sides of the triangle and how they allow you to see how one of the most fundamental of the trigonometric ratios, the sine, comes to life.

Having explored these beginnings, you then examined ways to measure angles. While degrees provide a reliable approach to such measurements, radians often prove easier to work with. A radian is the arc of a circle equal in length to the radius of the circle. Using radian measures, you are able to express angles of a circle and translate them to a Cartesian coordinate system that allows you to plot different trigonometric values. Toward this end, you explored standard graphs depicting cosine, tangent, cotangent, secant, and cosecant values. Such values generate periodic graphs that can be understood if you consider a few key points.

As is explained in the opening chapters of this book, the intent has not been to provide you with a comprehensive context in which to explore all the topics you might explore in an examination of pre-calculus mathematics. Instead, the intention is to provide you with points of contact that you can use to reacquaint or familiarize yourself with some aspects of pre-calculus mathematics that might benefit from an alternative type of presentation.

While successfully meeting the challenges a calculus course presents depends to a great extent on systematically studying algebra and trigonometry, it remains that viewing such studies in the context of a game leading to a bigger game puts you in a position to gain much more satisfaction than you would otherwise from your endeavors. To learn anything is a victory.

Memorizing rules and applying them in silent ways is a traditional approach to mathematics. Engaging in a gradually expanding discussion in which you continuously broaden your ability to voice what you know provides an alternative approach to the study of math. It is an approach often spoken about in classes involving students and others interested in developing games. It is the approach that forms the starting and ending points of this book. If such an approach enables you to have a greater sense that you can learn mathematics, then this book has served its purpose.

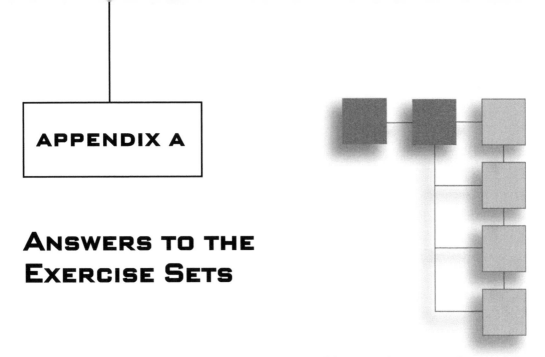

APPENDIX A

ANSWERS TO THE EXERCISE SETS

You'll find the solutions to almost all of the problems in this text in the PDF file on the CD.

As mentioned at the front of the book, most math books do not provide worked out problems, so the appendix that contains these is presented electronically. The electronic presentation makes it possible to provide step-by-step solutions to the problems rather than just the answers. Also, solutions to almost all of the problems are provided rather than those for just the even or odd ones.

To access the solutions place the CD in you disc drive and follow the instructions. Copying the pdf file to your drive is a good idea.

You can print pages from the PDF file to have solutions ready at hand when you work the problems. Use this approach to start with. It provides you with a comfort zone as you work. As you become more confident, you might then simply view the solutions electronically.

INDEX

License Agreement/Notice of Limited Warranty

By opening the sealed disc container in this book, you agree to the following terms and conditions. If, upon reading the following license agreement and notice of limited warranty, you cannot agree to the terms and conditions set forth, return the unused book with unopened disc to the place where you purchased it for a refund.

License

The enclosed software is copyrighted by the copyright holder(s) indicated on the software disc. You are licensed to copy the software onto a single computer for use by a single user and to a backup disc. You may not reproduce, make copies, or distribute copies. or rent or lease the software in whole or in part, except with written permission of the copyright holder(s). You may transfer the enclosed disc only together with this license, and only if you destroy all other copies of the software and the transferee agrees to the terms of the license. You may not decompile, reverse assemble, or reverse engineer the software.

Notice of Limited Warranty

The enclosed disc is warranted by Thomson Course Technology PTR to be free of physical defects in materials and workmanship for a period of sixty (60) days from end user's purchase of the book/disc combination. During the sixty-day term of the limited warranty, Thomson Course Technology PTR will provide a replacement disc upon the return of a defective disc.

Limited Liability

THE SOLE REMEDY FOR BREACH OF THIS LIMITED WARRANTY SHALL CONSIST ENTIRELY OF REPLACEMENT OF THE DEFECTIVE DISC. IN NO EVENT SHALL THOMSON COURSE TECHNOLOGY PTR OR THE AUTHOR BE LIABLE FOR ANY OTHER DAMAGES, INCLUDING LOSS OR CORRUPTION OF DATA, CHANGES IN THE FUNCTIONAL CHARACTERISTICS OF THE HARDWARE OR OPERATING SYSTEM, DELETERIOUS INTERACTION WITH OTHER SOFTWARE, OR ANY OTHER SPECIAL, INCIDENTAL, OR CONSEQUENTIAL DAMAGES THAT MAY ARISE, EVEN IF THOMSON COURSE TECHNOLOGY PTR AND/OR THE AUTHOR HAS PREVIOUSLY BEEN NOTIFIED THAT THE POSSIBILITY OF SUCH DAMAGES EXISTS.

Disclaimer of Warranties

THOMSON COURSE TECHNOLOGY PTR AND THE AUTHOR SPECIFICALLY DISCLAIM ANY AND ALL OTHER WARRANTIES, EITHER EXPRESS OR IMPLIED, INCLUDING WARRANTIES OF MERCHANTABILITY, SUITABILITY TO A PARTICULAR TASK OR PURPOSE, OR FREEDOM FROM ERRORS. SOME STATES DO NOT ALLOW FOR EXCLUSION OF IMPLIED WARRANTIES OR LIMITATION OF INCIDENTAL OR CONSEQUENTIAL DAMAGES, SO THESE LIMITATIONS MIGHT NOT APPLY TO YOU.

Other

This Agreement is governed by the laws of the State of Massachusetts without regard to choice of law principles. The United Convention of Contracts for the International Sale of Goods is specifically disclaimed. This Agreement constitutes the entire agreement between you and Thomson Course Technology PTR regarding use of the software.